Billy "the Hill" and the Jump Hook

Billy
"the Hill"

and the Jump Hook:

The Autobiography of
a Forgotten Basketball Legend

Billy McGill and Eric Brach

University of Nebraska Press | Lincoln and London

Library of Congress Cataloging-in-Publication Data
McGill, Billy.
Billy "the Hill" and the jump hook: the autobiography of a forgotten
basketball legend / Billy McGill and Eric Brach.
pages cm.
ISBN 978-0-8032-4687-4 (hardback: alk. paper)
1. McGill, Billy. 2. Basketball players—United States—Biography.
I. Brach, Eric. II. Title.
GV884.M385 2013
796.323092—dc23 [B]   2013008894

Set in Adobe Garamond Pro by Hannah Baker.
Designed by J. Vadnais.

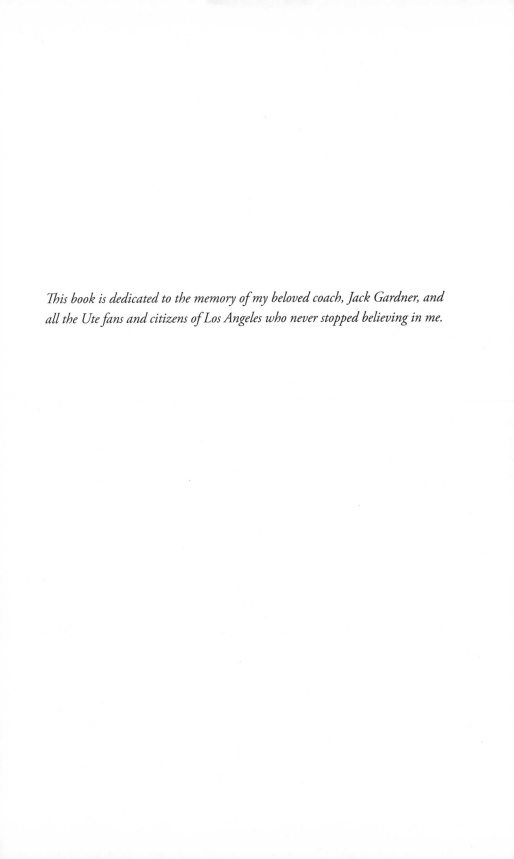

This book is dedicated to the memory of my beloved coach, Jack Gardner, and all the Ute fans and citizens of Los Angeles who never stopped believing in me.

Contents

Preface

Without a doubt Billy McGill is one of the most interesting people I've ever had the pleasure to meet. Of any person of I've ever grown close to, he's certainly the most different from me; between us stands forty-plus years of age difference, a foot of height, and wide disparities in our upbringings. I was not raised under the sad shadow of pre–Civil Rights Act American segregation, nor affected by the chilling ripple effects thereof. If I had the power to go back in time and remove these obstacles from a younger Billy's path, I would.

This work is the fruit of research and over two years of conversations and interviews, not only with Billy but also with his teammates, contemporaries, and fans. That's the first question everyone asks when they hear about this project: how did we do it? How did Billy use me to help find his voice? The answer is simple: we talked. I asked questions, and Billy unearthed dusty memories not regarded for fifty or sixty years in order to provide the material for this book. I recorded our meetings and crafted his story in the best way I could.

The second question is always about what Billy is like. People want to know: is Billy sad or angry that he didn't make it big in the NBA after such a great youth and college career? The answer is: well, of course. I've watched hours of game footage, and it's clear to me that Billy was one of the cleanest, purest scorers the game of basketball has ever seen. That he didn't make it in the NBA is attributable to a combination of factors, surely: the fact that the league was tiny and struggling during his time is certainly one of them. In Billy's day the league boasted only nine teams and drew an average of only six thousand to seven thousand fans to each game. There were no endorsements; there were no TV contracts. In those days teams had to keep their payrolls as small as possible to stave off bankruptcy. He had the bad luck to enter the league when seven out of the nine teams had future Hall-of-Famer centers (Bill Russell, Wilt Chamberlain, Walt Bellamy, Bob Pettit, Willis Reed, Nate Thurmond, and Jerry Lucas)—literally, there was just nowhere for him to play. And, of course, there was always the issue of the knee.

One of Billy's near-constant refrains since I've known him is, "Man, if it weren't for this knee, I'd be living up on the hill. I'd be in the Hall and I'd be famous, instead of where I am." And maybe that's true. In fact, it almost definitely is. If times had been different, Billy could have reached the highest heights. If Billy's family had stayed together and his father could have looked out for him, or if medical technology was then where it is today, or even if there weren't such stigmas at the time against black players suffering injuries, inducing Billy to hide his trouble rather than get the healing care he needed—if any of these corrective factors had been in place, Billy wouldn't be only an LA blacktop legend or a Utah favorite son. He'd be a household name.

Let's be clear: this is no Cinderella story. Though Billy was unstoppable, a machine, the first and still the only Los Angeles player ever to be taken with the number one pick of the NBA draft, his name has never been sung from the rooftops—and sadly, it may never be. Even though he invented a shot that's now a staple of every big man from Kareem Abdul-Jabbar to Yao Ming, even though the University of Utah dissolved its own color line to allow Billy to integrate the team, even though he smashed every NCAA scoring record for centers ever established . . . when he dies a piece of an amazing story may forever die with him.

And that's not right.

Every year tens of thousands of kids just like Billy flood into high school gyms with one goal on their minds: the NBA. And yet of these kids, just a few hundred get major college scholarships. Only a few dozen of those ever make it to the pros. And far fewer of them ever truly reach their dreams.

Even for the ones who do—even after all the groundwork laid by guys like George Mikan and Billy McGill, guys who got paid pennies playing through the '50s, '60s, and '70s before the NBA got rich with TV money—there are still great hardships. Even with the enormous contracts of today, players are still going broke, unprepared for the lives that lie in wait for them after their days playing the game wind down. Quick: what do Derrick Coleman, Latrell Sprewell, Allen Iverson, and Scottie Pippen have in common? The answer? Even though they made twenty-three All-Star Game appearances and made 450 million dollars in NBA salary money between them—that's *half a billion* dollars between four guys—they all still ended up broke just a few years after they retired. Just like Billy.

The more things change, the more they stay the same.

Stories of champions are time and again retold. But what happens to those players—even right at the pinnacle, just inches from that brass ring—who get winnowed out along the way? What happens to the guys who fight their way to the tops of the peaks only to fall, and fall hard? Stories like that are more often than not forgotten. And that's a real disservice, not only because this is a hard truth, one that all high school athletes and sports phenoms should understand and accept before they force themselves through that wringer, but because this story, both as an archetype and as the life that Billy actually lived, is—as much as it hurts—a damned good one.

And it deserves to be remembered.

Eric Brach

Prologue

The Shot.

I've already picked up my dribble. I've got nowhere else to go. The only choice is to go straight up with the ball and shoot. But between me and the basket stands seven feet and two inches of perhaps the greatest basketball player who's ever lived: Wilt Chamberlain.

I leap, preparing to unleash my shot, and as I do, my first thought is, "I'm in trouble." This man has built his legend smacking lesser men's jumpers into the stands, and who am I? A sixteen-year-old playing pickup against the greatest of all time. But it's too late to go back now. I've left the ground, and with just a half second until my feet return to the hardwood, I have to get rid of the ball.

Chamberlain's growling, snarling at me, and his fangs are bared. He looks like he's chasing after raw meat, and his eyes make it clear: my shot is the steak.

Like a ballerina I twist in the air, getting my body between Wilt and the ball as my free arm curls away from the basket. Chamberlain launches heavenward as I release.

At the crest of its trajectory, the ball hangs aloft in midair as if held by angels. Chamberlain's outstretched arm reaches toward it as it soars, rotating slowly, gently, toward the hoop and going up, up, up . . .

The Beginning

It's September 1939 when I'm born on a ranch in San Angelo, Texas. "Ranch" isn't quite right; it's a big old house with a shed out back and a little creek running down by its edge. Mama Sadie keeps vegetables in the yard—collard greens and turnip greens and that—and in the shed, Mr. John Henry keeps a couple of animals. All our neighbors keep animals, too. We have to. If we didn't we'd starve.

The ranch belongs to my grandmother, Mama Sadie. When my mother leaves me to make her life in California, I'm left in her care. I'm too young to feel abandoned; this is just how it is. Mother goes, and Mama Sadie raises me with help from my aunt, Gloris Jean.

Besides the animals and the neighbors who live down the street, it's just the three of us and Mama Sadie's husband, Mr. John Henry. Mr. John Henry's not my biological grandfather—what happened to him, I can't say; I just know that by the time I come around, Mama Sadie's living with him. My father, whom I don't know, is in California with my mother.

Without a real dad around, I look up to Mr. John Henry. But he isn't much of a talker, or much of a warm man, either. He does have arms like a pair of sledgehammers, and those arms go to work when he slaughters pigs, which he does like this: he slams them twice in the forehead with the flat part of the head of an ax. The first shot sends the pig sprawling to the ground, stunned and drooling, and the second one finishes the animal off. Mr. John Henry grew up in the country, and he can wring chickens' necks off with one hard twist of his wrist, too. But these acts are too gruesome for a little kid to aspire to, so I spend most of my time not with Mr. John Henry but with Aunt Gloris Jean.

Gloris Jean is a good bit older than I; she was already in her teens when I was born. She's beautiful—the prettiest person I've ever seen—and so sweet that I take to her instantly, following her everywhere she goes. When she walks into town, I'm at her heels; when she has chores to do, I cling to her ankles and listen to her sing. Gloris Jean fixes my plates at meals. At night, when I'm scared, it's Gloris Jean I run to.

After Mr. John Henry kills a fattened pig, he carries it into the shed and trusses it. Freshly slaughtered pigs are pink and also brown, dirty from having thrashed in the mud and caked with matted blood and hair. Once the pigs are dead, he slits their throats and, hanging them from a hook, bleeds them out into a bucket. The red liquid heat pools and congeals, and as the pigs stare out at the world with ice-dead eyes the hue of skimmed milk, Mr. John Henry slits their bellies and guts them, pulling out their innards onto a low table to sort.

One time I sneak in to watch him working the carcass. I'm so amazed at what I see that I tell a few of the neighbor kids, and when they don't believe me, the next time I bring a few of them along to peek. But Mama Sadie catches me, and she yells for Gloris Jean—Gloris Jean, whose job it is dole out the punishment along with the love; Gloris Jean, who'll catch me and spank me on my bottom with a wooden spoon.

I sprint away from the shed door and Gloris Jean comes running after me, cajoling and yelling. I know what's coming, and I duck and dodge, all the while expecting her to catch up and pay me out the debt I've earned. Only thing is, she doesn't. Somehow she can't catch me; yesterday she could, and now she can't. This is unusual and I know it. I'm a little kid, a child just barely old enough to go to the bathroom alone, but this teenage girl—this nascent woman already mostly grown—can't snag me. I'm too quick for her.

"Athletes in the blood," intones Mr. John Henry when he's told the news. "He must have got it from his father." My ears perk up, and when I'm sent off without any supper, I don't care. No one has ever mentioned my father to me, and I'm desperate to learn more about him. Who is he? What did Mr. John Henry mean? All night I lie in bed thinking about what kind of man my father must be.

Come the next day I've made up my mind to ask Gloris Jean about my dad. Unfortunately I never get the chance. Early that morning she says she feels sick and she needs to go lie down. Soon after she gets to lying down quite a bit. Whenever I ask her to come outside—to play, to walk with me into town—she says she can't, she's tired. Soon she's so tired that she stops joining us at the table altogether, and one night, with just three plates at dinner, Mama Sadie leans over and says to Mr. John Henry as though I'm not there, "I think it's time for Dorothy to come get Billy Junior."

Dorothy: my real mother. To me my mother is a concept more than a person. Visions of her in my life are mere shadows: a passing smell, a pair of legs under the table during a holiday visit to the ranch. She finally does come when Gloris Jean leaves us, and I'm too young to be told why—why my mother is now, suddenly, ready for me, and why, just as quickly, Gloris Jean is gone. When they take Gloris Jean away, she's lying down looking peaceful, and I'm glad to see that she's resting comfortably with her eyes closed. I'd hate to see them wide open, staring cloudy and milky blue. I understand that she's dead, but I don't like the thought of Gloris Jean's body trussed and bled, caked with mud as her innards spill out into a bucket.

I'm five years old.

My real mother arrives vibrant and beautiful and like a statue of my aunt expanded to a grander size. She has shiny hair and soft skin, and I quickly find I like to nestle into her.

"You love me, right, Billy?" she asks one day not long after her arrival, and I nod yes.

"Good," she says, "because you're going to come with me."

"Where?" I ask. "To the store?"

"To California," says my mother. "To Los Angeles."

"Why?"

"Why? Why, to live!"

When it dawns on me that my mother is leaving again and will be taking me with her, I don't know if I'm more excited or scared. San Angelo is all I know, and I don't know what moving means. Can I take my pillow? Will I need to bring a change of socks?

Without fuss Mr. John Henry piles the four of us into his used Model A Ford, and we drive together to the San Angelo bus station. Maybe I should be sad to be leaving, but I'm not; this is the first time I've ever ridden in a car, and I marvel at how fast the world seems to speed along. I'd seen it driven—it looked big and ominous—and I'd always longed to ride in it. But finally being inside, feeling stationary while the broad Texas night sky passes above me, is surreal. The hot wind rushes by faster than I've ever felt it, even in the fiercest windstorm, and as I stare up into the needlepoint quilt of light above, I can't fathom how, if we're moving so fast, those heavenly bodies shining down upon us remain so still. This moment—gazing into the night sky as we hurtle away from the ranch, watching the stars wink down on us in our west Texas valley—fixes itself into my mind. I am now headed irreversibly into the world beyond.

When I lower my gaze for only a moment, I see that Mama Sadie's face is wet.

In short order we reach the bus depot, and as deeply and quickly as I'd fallen in love with the car, the target of my affections shifts when I spot the gleaming coach.

I leap out of the Model A to sprint toward the bus and Mama Sadie has to pull me back to wrap me in her embrace. She, like Mr. John Henry, has strong, country arms like whole hams, and she hugs me so tightly I can hardly breathe. I hug her back, or at least try to, then start again inching myself toward the idling beast in the dirt parking lot.

Mama Sadie gives my mother a deep hug of her own, then passes her a bag filled with fried chicken for the long ride ahead. At last, with our tickets in her hand, my mom steers me gently, hand between my shoulder blades, toward the hulking, lumbering bus.

As we board the driver takes one look at us and points toward the very back. We traipse past old, weathered ranchers with skin the color of their straw hats, and then among folks who look like me and my mother, until at last we find a pair of seats in the next-to-last row. As the bus pulls away, my mother and I wave good-bye to San Angelo. Mr. John Henry stands firm, arms crossed, and I can see tears now in my mother's eyes. I rifle through her bag for a flour-dredged drumstick, and she catches my hand and puts my head into her lap.

"Don't eat up all the chicken now, Bilbo; it's for later." Those are the last words I hear as I softly drift off to sleep, unaware in my simple youth that I'll never be back to San Angelo again.

When I awaken the next morning, all of my senses are firing. The rumbling of the bus's diesel engine drums deep within my ears. The thick, acrid smell of the chemical toilet just behind us coats my throat. Every five minutes, it seems, another person comes back to use it, and I start to hate the men in their hats who shuffle quickly past only to return, minutes later, trailing malodorous clouds.

But all that unpleasantness is successfully pushed out of my head as I watch the American landscape fly by. Texas was flat land and bunchgrasses as far as the eye could see, but now everything is littered with red rocks and rubble-rabble, little cactuses that poke up out of the ground like a kid's head from a tussle of sheets. I press my face to the glass, pulling it away only to nibble now and again on more fried chicken, transfixed by the sight of the world beyond the window.

While I pass the time with my attentions on life outside the bus, my mother draws the attention of other passengers in it. My mother is beautiful and knows it; she loves to be watched, talked to, paid compliments. She loves—I think the word is—to flirt. We are barely under way on our second day and haven't even pulled over for a rest break before she draws the eye of the man sitting across the aisle.

To me he is a wonder; he's like no man I've ever seen. He isn't black like we are, and he's not white either. He's the color of tobacco or sun tea. Not that white men wouldn't have found my mother attractive, but white men don't look like him, and white men don't sit at the rear of the bus near the toilet.

"What are you?" I ask, interrupting his conversation with my mother, and she shushes me as he grins. They go back to talking, not answering my question, and for the next six hours, I'm left sitting there to wonder: if he's not white and he's not black, then what is he? And which water fountain does he drink out of?

I never get the chance to find out. He and my mother talk to each other in grown-up voices for a long time, and he gets up to leave somewhere before we do, somewhere before the driver rears his head back and calls out, "Next stop, end of the line: Los Angeles's Union Station."

Groggy from the journey, I stumble off the bus, grasping my mother's hem as porters pull bags from the coach. There are more people here than I've ever seen in my entire life.

Amid them all stands one who looks intently in our direction. He's enormous. I wrap my arms around my mother's leg—it's all I can do not to run back on the bus and hide at the sight of this giant. But my mom leans down to me and puts her hand on the small of my back. She points in his direction. "Go on to him," she says.

"Who?"

She points again. "Your father! Malone McGill." Malone. My father. I've never seen him before. "Go on, give your father a hug!" She gives me a little push.

I let go timidly, then, in a rush of confidence, trot forward to inspect him. He is strong, stout, wide. His hair's cropped short and his skin is dark, glistening in the light of the bus station like a film of residue on the surface of a lake. Finally, I extend my hand to shake as I've been taught. "Pleased to meet you; I'm Billy," I say.

He laughs. "Billy!" His eyes twinkle. And then he lifts me into the air.

My father Malone's biceps are huge, pushing through his shirt. Mama Sadie and Mr. John Henry had strong, powerful arms, too, but my father is no country ranch hand. His iron embrace as he kneels down to catch me feels like being pressed in a woodworking vise. He ensnares me, lifting me up and swinging me through the air like I'm some kind of special prize and kissing me on the cheek as he holds me aloft above the rest of the bus station crowd.

I don't know it, but this hug and kiss will be the only ones I receive from my father in my whole life.

Of course, I *don't* know that, not yet, so when my dad stuffs our suitcases into his Model A Ford—the same kind of car I'd ridden in with Mr. John Henry just days before—I'm bubbling over with excitement. We cruise through the streets of Los Angeles, and I'm beside myself in astonishment at all of these people and all of these houses. It's not like flat old Texas; there's such height here. I've never seen so many humans all at once, and it amazes me.

Still, more than anything, I'm amazed by my parents. My mother is stunning: light skinned, with a creamy complexion, she has a beauty mark right on her chin. (I'd seen back in San Angelo some women who drew one in with eyebrow pencil, but I'm proud to say my mother's isn't painted on.) My father, my mom tells me, is a boxer, and he has the perfect pretty boy image to match his huge arms: hair glossed up and combed back into a conk, a style common to both singers and fighters.

A beauty and a pugilist: my mother and father are the picture-perfect couple. A few days earlier I couldn't break my gaze away from the speeding landscape around me; now I'm reunited with and completely entranced by the seamless sight of my mom and my dad.

Welcome to LA

Back in Texas there were only so many neighborhood kids. We all played together; we didn't worry ourselves over things like age—if you lived close enough to play and you wanted to come out and run around, you did. My first summer in LA is the same way.

My mom, dad, and I have an apartment in a big white house—a boardinghouse, it's called—and all the youth who live in it play in the streets together. Nobody worries about being five or three or eight; if you're there, you play, and that's that. So it isn't until autumn rolls around and my mother enrolls me in kindergarten that I realize just how much bigger I am than all the other six-year-olds.

We live just down San Pedro Avenue from my grade school, 28th Street Elementary. I walk in that first day and my teacher thinks I'm in the wrong classroom; I tower over everybody. During recess it becomes evident that my gift entails more than just height; it's athleticism too. I can run faster, jump higher, throw a football and hit a baseball farther than anyone else in my class. Even my teachers begin to talk.

When a new kid comes to town, one of two things happens: either the other kids get curious and try to make friends, or they get angry and torment the new arrival. In my case, everyone tries to befriend me . . . everyone, that is, except one boy.

He's older than me. A third grader, maybe. He's used to being the big man on campus, and he doesn't appreciate all the attention that I'm lapping up. So even though I'm barely old enough to leave the house alone, he makes up his mind to take a piece out of my hide.

One day this bully lies in wait outside the schoolhouse after the last bell. When I leave to walk home—and I do walk home; even as young as we are, little kids don't get buses in poor, black LA neighborhoods—he follows me.

After a block or two I quicken my pace. He speeds up to match me. I cross another block before looking over my shoulder again; he's still back there, stalking. I begin to run-walk, and he does, too; at last I'm sprinting at full speed toward my front door. As I reach it I see him lagging just behind. He's chased me all the while, and when I step inside he glowers at me.

It starts to happen again and again. The bully follows me to my block. He follows me to my yard. One day he runs me all the way to the steps of our boardinghouse. It just so happens that on that day my mother and father are there, fanning themselves on the porch. I want to hide in the arms of my father; I want to get to him and turn him on the boy. He's my father; surely he'll watch out for me. He'll make everything right. He will be my protection. But before I can open my mouth, before I can plead for his aid, he looks down at me with disdain in his eyes and already he's shaking his head.

"Billy," he says, "what are you letting that boy run you home for?"

I'm stunned. He gets up and storms inside, and I'm left on the porch, next to my mother but totally alone.

After that it gets worse. The bully waits for me every day after school. I can't pay attention in classes; eventually I come to hate school itself. I zone out, staring at the clock, nervously waiting for the bell. When it rings I leave in a dead run. For weeks I wallow in fetid shame, sprinting home every day. One day, though, a realization strikes me: I run as fast as I can every day, and he does, too. Yet he never catches me.

I'm faster than that boy.

The realization sweeps over me. Of course I am faster than that bully; I've always been. He's been running me home for weeks and he's never once caught up. Gloris Jean couldn't catch me, and he can't either.

The next day I stare at the clock, watching the hands loop around the face. This time, though, I'm filled not with dread but with anticipation. And when the bully begins his inevitable chase, I twist the situation to my advantage. I stop running and instead, laughing, I turn around. I begin shuffling along backward on my heels, facing him all the while. And still he can't catch up.

"Come on, fat boy!" I begin to taunt. I see the boy's face twist and turn red as he tries to speed up, but still I make it home easily. This gives me a feeling of control and confidence. Over the next few days I toy with the boy, running backward more and more, until at last I just go ahead and run backward the whole way home, goading him all the while. "Come on!" I yell, skipping heels first along San Pedro. "Come get me!"

He can't, but every day he persists in chasing me, growing angrier and angrier. Every day my confidence swells until finally I surprise him: I let him catch me.

And then I smack him.

It's not a hard punch—I'm still only six, after all. And this bully is far bigger than I am. But my willingness to face my fear catches the bully off guard, and after I land a shot on him, he, bewildered, scampers off. Now that he knows I'm willing to stand up and fight for myself, he gives up and lets me alone.

Of course, it doesn't hurt that my father is a boxer.

Part of my toughness—and all of my fighting ability, I should think—comes directly from my dad. My father is a man not given to any aspect of softness in word or deed. Like a movie legend he dreams of rising from the trenches to become the world champion, but he passes his days toiling in a massive meatpacking plant called Cudahy's to pay the bills.

My dad is gone by the time I wake up in the morning, and he usually just makes it back in time for supper at night. Though I don't see him much, I'm proud that on Fridays he comes home with both his pay and a piece or two of meat along with it. He must get along well with his supervisor to be allowed to sneak home cuts of beef like that, I think. Come to think of it, his supervisor probably has a closer relationship with him than I do.

As with Mr. John Henry, my dad and I are not very close. He's always in training or at work. In fact, the one thing my dad is passionate about— the only thing, it seems—is boxing. He may not ask me about my school-work or my friends, he may not tuck me in or kiss me good-night, but if I ask him about boxing he'll talk. And no matter how little else we inter-act, my father makes time on Saturday afternoons for the two of us to spar. It's the one thing I can count on: every weekend he outfits me with a spare pair of his boxing gloves, and the two of us go at it—a grown man and a tall child, circling each other in the front yard.

The gloves are comically large on me, and I can't do any actual damage, but my father doesn't kid around; he wears his headgear and a waist belt, like he's fighting an actual opponent. He doesn't hit me his hardest, of course, but I do—he makes me. My father teaches me how to stand, how to hold my hands—wrists at an angle, like I am gripping a hamburger, and thumbs over the knuckles on my index fingers—and how to throw jabs, combos, flurries. He tutors me in footwork, blocking, and the means to cultivate quick reflexes. Basically, he shows me how to fight, and as the months slip by, though he never takes much interest in any other aspects of my life, when it comes to punching my father is there.

Of course, my father's easy way with his fists is a double-edged sword. Whenever I do something bad—no matter how small an infraction—my father is waiting. He doesn't chase after me like Gloris Jean used to; instead he calls me back to the house and waits for me with his arm resting across the open doorway. He beckons me in, and I have no choice but to com-ply—after all, he's the man of the house. And it's not when I return, but when I step just past him that he strikes.

A rabbit rap to the back of the head or sometimes a hard slap at the back. Sometimes it's an open palm to the face. And his smacks aren't like Gloris Jean's, either. He's a man, a fighter, and they hurt.

He isn't a drunk, my father. He's very calm and measured. That almost makes it even worse when he takes me inside and lays into me, as he does on occasion—not with his belt, as other fathers do, but with his fists. And when things go badly—and they get worse as I grow older and his boxing career begins to falter—he finds more and more excuses to take it out on my poor body.

My father does well on the amateur circuit, and after winning a few exhibitions, he's finally booked into a major prize fight: Monday night in the Ocean Park Arena. It's March of my fifth grade year, and all day at school I brag to my friends about how he's going to win.

He doesn't. A 193-pounder named Hank Thurman TKO's him in the third round.

Still, my dad is undeterred, and right as my school year ends he gets booked into another big match: a late-June fight at the Grand Olympic Auditorium. It's just down from the LA Coliseum, practically in our neighborhood, and there are placards all over. "Malone McGill!" they read in big, black, block letters. The fight is broadcast on the radio and on TV; he's so proud, and I settle into a neighbor's living room to watch it. I'm so excited; I've never experienced him fight before—except in our house, of course. He's never brought me to his gym, though I've wanted to go, and I'm on the edge of my seat, ready to go wild when I see my daddy win.

But again, he doesn't. This time he only makes it two rounds before he's knocked out, and this time it's for good. An 0-2 professional fighter is not much of a draw, and after that second loss the promoter stops calling. Most of the placards in the neighborhood come down, and that hurts him. The ones that remain become cruel reminders, and they hurt even worse. And that's when he really begins aiming his punches toward his own house.

Introduction to the Game

To a kid academics just don't matter much. The only way a kid learns to devote himself to studying is if his parents impress upon him its importance—and mine certainly do not. My dad, unable to resurrect his boxing career, as often as not ignores me. Besides, I wouldn't turn to him for help anyway—it's better to avoid him when things gets rough, knowing how he is. As for my mother, though she loves me dearly, she never received much schooling herself, so she doesn't push me either. The result is that I begin to struggle in school. A lot.

But despite it all, there is one good thing about going to school. Just down the road from 28th Street Elementary sits the 28th Street YMCA. It's only a few blocks' walk, and almost immediately after I learn about its existence I become a regular.

For me—for all of us inner-city kids—the YMCA is heaven. It's one of the few safe places I know to play in, and it's also one of the few places where I can escape from the pressures of home. Though I might cut up in school, neither I nor anyone I know ever even dreams of starting trouble at the Y. We wouldn't dare. Writing graffiti or anything like that, it would mean your ass—that much is understood. Plus, why would we wreck the only place that's really all our own? Kids don't even fight at the Y. There's fighting in the schoolyard and fighting in the street, and even students as young as us are willing to scrap now and again in an empty lot. But fighting in the Y? Forget about it. That building is much too holy.

When I first start going, I head straight to the games room every day like all the other kids. The pressures of home fade away in diversions like checkers, cards, and ping-pong. But one day, as I play Go Fish with some other boys, I'm interrupted.

"How old are you?" asks a voice, and I turn to find the YMCA director, Mr. Ward, staring down at me. I stand up.

"Seven," I say.

"Seven?" he repeats, scrutinizing me. My chin comes up to his belt buckle. "Wait here." Five minutes later he returns with a big, orange-brown ball, which he places into my outstretched palms.

You know how they say that sometimes one moment can change your life? This is my moment. That day Mr. Ward leads me into the small YMCA gymnasium and introduces me to the game. He shows me the court, the hoop, the basket, the foul line, the backboard, how to dribble. "It's ten feet from the floor to the rim," he says, "and that never changes." For once my height is an advantage, not something that sets me apart or makes me a target.

I don't spend much time in the games room after that.

Every day from then on Mr. Ward works with me, teaching me the nuances and tactics of basketball. Where he learned these things, I don't know; he is supposed to be an administrator, not a coach. All the same, he puts me through every drill he can devise: drills for shooting, dribbling, positioning, rebounding, footwork. Often he sequesters half of the gym just for the two of us, leaving the other eight or ten or twenty kids only half a court on which to play pickup games. This attention from Mr. Ward, the first real interest any male figure has ever shown to me, is like manna from heaven, and I eat it up. In an instant that little gym becomes my true home.

When you're young you don't question what your elders tell you to do; you just do it. All I want to do is play, but Mr. Ward is determined to keep working me, running me through tall-man skills like boxing out as well as small-guard skills like manning up and learning how to pass. The more he teaches me, the more comfortable I feel and the better I get. It reaches the point where when I do start finding myself in pickup games, I can't play with the other kids my age—none of them can come close to matching up against me. I'm tall, but I can shoot; I can crash the glass, but I can also move. While I don't start working any harder in school, basketball forces upon me two kinds of mental discipline: that needed to learn, and that needed to at least sit down and shut up so I don't have to stay after class and miss playing. I'm so driven that even if Mr. Ward gets called away from the gym, I just do on my own whatever workout plan he leaves me with.

Mr. Ward says he never saw any other player with the God-given ability to just play like I have, and his affection and appreciation just make me want to work even harder. I start spending even my Saturdays on the court, playing until I have to be kicked out so Mr. Ward can go home himself. He has kids of his own he wants to spend time with.

Of course, this leaves little time for my Saturday boxing matches, and my own father becomes even more of a mystery.

One Friday I go to the Y after school as usual to go work on my game. When I get there, though, something's different—I head to the gym, but Mr. Ward isn't inside.

I turn around and roam the halls, finally finding Mr. Ward in his office. He's sitting at his desk, surprised, as if he's forgotten about me, and I ask him what's going on. For a moment I'm nervous. For a moment I'm afraid that Mr. Ward has decided he's done spending time with me. But that's not it at all.

"Sorry, Billy," he says. "Got a lot to do. The Champ is coming."

"The Champ?"

He leans in, a big grin jumping off his face like popcorn out of a skillet. "Tomorrow," he says. "Joe Louis is coming to our Y."

I'm floored. The heavyweight champion of the world is coming to our 28th Street Y?

I'm so excited I skip my workout and run home so I can tell my father the minute he gets back from work. He's a boxer, and Joe Louis is the best. I can see it in my mind's eye: he'll come home and I'll run up to greet him; he'll put his little package down and sweep me up into his arms as I shout to him the news. He'll be so excited that he won't know what to say, and tomorrow he'll be first in line, right there next to me in his best clothes as he shakes the Champ's hand. He'll tell him how I'm learning the gloves myself, and he'll beam proudly and the Champ will, too.

I crash through the door and take my place on the couch, not moving for an hour, then two hours, then three as I await my father's return. Finally, after the sun has set, I hear the telltale whine of the door sliding on its hinges. I pop up and race to the entryway.

"Dad!" I yell, crashing into him.

"Jesus!" His arms are not open.

"Dad," I repeat. "Guess what! Joe Louis is coming to the YMCA."

"Yeah?" he says. That's all.

Undeterred, I press on. "Yes!" I say. "Tomorrow!"

He says nothing.

"Don't you want to come?" I venture. "With me?"

He doesn't.

The next day I meet Joe Louis at the Y. Mr. Ward makes it a point to have me at the front of the line, so I can be the first one to shake his hand.

"Champ," he begins, "this is Billy. Billy is our best basketball player here at the Y. He's really going to be something someday." I blush and nod, shaking a hand that's like a meaty, oversized paw, pleased and embarrassed that Mr. Ward would say something so nice about me to Joe Louis. It's not until I get home that I realize that the world champ, the Brown Bomber, managed to find time to come all the way down to my gym and say hello to me, but a far less busy boxer who lives much closer by has never once done the same.

The First Day of the Rest of My Life

As time goes on my relationship with my mother and father continues to sour. My disappointment over the Joe Louis episode spills over, and I throw myself into my own pursuits in order to put distance between us. Basketball is one escape for me; a second becomes music. By the time I reach the age of eleven, I'm already becoming known around the neighborhood as something of an accomplished conga drummer.

I'm introduced to the congas by a pair of older boys who live down the road. I've noticed them since I first moved from San Angelo—they get together on sunny days and play the congas in their front yard. As a kid myself, I'm enamored of anything that can make loud noise, and to me, with those birch-colored percussion instruments, those brothers are gods.

At first I just hang around the brothers' lawn whenever they're playing, but it doesn't take long until I'm able to start playing rhythms. After a while they come to take a bit of a shine to me, like I'm their mascot or something. They let me play with them eventually, and as with basketball, the more I play, the easier it seems to get.

I come to love playing percussion with these boys; I do it every chance I get. But the one aspect of it that bugs me is drumming's constrictive nature. I'm young; I want to break out and go wild, but I'm consigned to the rhythm role and a constant beat. With basketball, on the other hand, there's nothing to hold you back—you can do just about anything that you can imagine, and improvisation is a skill that's always prized. You just do what feels natural. As I grow, basketball begins to feel ever more natural to me, so I just take to it more and more. In fact, there's only one thing I can imagine doing on the court that I haven't done. Yet.

One Saturday morning just before I turn thirteen, I'm hard at work doing layup drills. Mr. Ward's shouting encouragement and feeding me bounce passes, and I'm driving to the hoop over and over again. Across the small gym a gaggle of kids huddles around the other basket playing a pickup game, and as I repeat my training sequence over and over—catch pass, step, layup; catch pass, step, layup—I imagine ditching the practice and going to play with the other kids instead. It would be so nice to just walk across the court and win a game—and I know I would win. No one my age can stop me; already I play almost exclusively with junior high school kids, and still I'm usually the best on the floor.

"Billy!"

Mr. Ward's voice snaps me back into focus. He bounces me another basketball. "Time to work."

I catch the ball and step toward the hoop, smoothly banking it off the backboard.

"Again!" he cries. Another one. Perfect. "Again!"

Once more I turn with longing to watch the kids scrimmaging. Mr. Ward bounces another pass at me. "Again!"

Just then something in me clicks. I'm sick of this drill! I hate shooting the same old layups over and over! All my anger—at not being able to just play, at not being able to control life at home, at everything—bubbles up within me, and I take the ball and drive hard to the basket. I go up to the rim as fiercely as I can, and as I rise I make up my mind that I'm going to shoot a "college layup"—a layup in which the shooter slaps the backboard as hard as he can as he banks in the basketball. The echo of the clap is thunderous and it stings the palm—I'm looking forward to that. But as I take off something odd happens: I go up much higher than I anticipated. I pass the rim and I don't stop going up. My arm is outstretched; my hand reaches past the bottom of the backboard and keeps rising. My fingertips soar above the rim and then curl over it to drop the ball through from above.

What I've done doesn't hit me until my feet have already come back down to the hardwood: I've dunked. I'm twelve years old, and I've just successfully dunked on a regulation basketball rim.

I turn and see Mr. Ward standing there, smiling and watching me with wide eyes. One of the kids from the pickup game comes running over, his tennies clomping on the parquet floor like the hooves of a clattering bull running over stone-paved streets.

"McGill just dunked!" he screams. "McGill just dunked!"

The other kids turn and watch as he runs over to me—he's jumping in the air with his fists extended like he's the one who just threw down. I don't even smile; my brain's still running through a replay in my mind, seeing the ball and remembering the kiss of metal on the ends of my fingers, the caress of the trailing rope of the nylon netting as it graced my inner forearm on the way back down.

This is what it's like, I think. This is what it's like to stuff a basketball.

"You dunked? How did it feel?" they all want to know.

It feels great.

After that first time there's no stopping me. I go dunk crazy. I go to the gym at school and dunk during lunch. I dunk in pickup games. I dunk with a crowd of little kids watching. I start throwing up jump shots and missing on purpose just so I can run in, grab the rebound, and dunk.

I've always been a good athlete, but being a slam-dunking sixth grader changes things. Now, not only does basketball serve as an outlet for me, it serves as my primary means of socialization—a funny thing, given how often I had to isolate myself at the Y to get to the level I'm at. People want to play ball with me all the time, and though I can put on a show with my dunking, thanks to all that time spent on Mr. Ward's dribbling drills and footwork and outside shooting, I'm more than just a sideshow. I'm good, really good. Basketball becomes something people admire me for, something that becomes a font of strength.

And it's a good thing, too. A very good thing. Because as I continue to develop as a player, my family life grows ever worse.

Things Come Together; Things Fall Apart

I've known since I was young that my mother is a very beautiful woman. The stresses in her life, though, start taking their toll on her body. For one, there is the trouble with my father. He's grown quicker and quicker to hit us as years roll by, and that leaves marks on my mother deeper than the skin. And on top of that there's her job. My mother works at a huge, dilapidated dry-cleaning plant full of chemicals. Day in, day out, she presses shirts, pants, uniforms, and overalls, working ten-hour shifts. Between the heat from the presses and the rancid fog from the solvents, her eyes and her health in general falter. Over time these stresses become too much to bear. The abuse at home and the trials of her employment lead her, at last, to break. She turns to the bottle for solace, and of course that just makes it worse.

My father can't understand her descent—he still harbors those boxing ambitions, as bitter as they've turned, and keeps his body a temple—so my mother's drinking he sees not as a cry for help but as a weakness. This enrages him, and it strains their relationship even further, fueling a vicious cycle in which he hits her and she drinks. At last the situation comes to a head.

Just days after I graduate from 28th Street Elementary, my mom walks into the living room after my father has left for work. "How long will it take you to pack your things?" she asks.

"Pack my things?" I don't understand. For school? Junior high won't begin for a few months yet.

"All your things," she says, corralling me into the corner of the apartment. "How long?"

The gravity of this moment strikes me as I look into my mother's eyes. We're leaving the house. We're leaving my father. Right now. Forever.

"I don't know," I venture. "An hour?"

My mother nods. "Good." She smooths her dress. "Go do it."

At around noon a truck pulls into the alley behind our house, where our peeping neighbors can't watch. No one will be able to see us slink away or call my father at Cudahy's to warn him. He will not come rumbling back home in a fury to stop us.

My mother and I carry our things through the hallway and out the back door. I'm lithe with my little shopping bags of clothes and underwear—it's easier for me to steal away from home now; leaving San Angelo was just practice for the real thing. I trundle through the doorframe; outside an old truck idles. After my mom and I finish loading the truck, the silent driver steers us out the alley and onto the street.

"Where are we going?" I ask, and I am met with a simple "Hush." We drive for just a mile or so, and then the driver pulls up in front of a small one-bedroom house. He deposits us and our things unceremoniously on the sidewalk, and as we're unloading the front door of the building opens.

A man approaches, one I've never seen before. He knows my mother, though—he reaches out for her and she dives into his arms; he holds her and kisses her on the cheek.

We're not just running away from my father, I suddenly realize. We're running to another man.

"Hello," this unknown figure says to me, and he extends his palm. "My name is Lonnie Griffin, but you can call me Daddy Lonnie."

I shake his hand. He does not hug me.

He grabs a valise like he already owns it—like he already owns us, I think—and leads my mother inside.

Dutifully, I follow.

That night I slip out of the house and under the cover of darkness run back to our old place at 33rd Street. I book it under streetlights and past jazz clubs, over the weed-cracked pavement and around the men loafing on the corners, sweating in white sleeveless undershirts. The rich, heavy smell of summer tinges the leaden night air.

When I reach our old home, I lift my head above the chipped paint of the windowsill to peer inside.

All the lights in the apartment are on. There's no noise—no radio; even the hum of the refrigerator seems to have silenced itself in deference—but inside I can see my father sitting frozen, staring at the walls. He looks like a department store mannequin, frozen in space and with even the ability to breathe stripped and gone. It swaddles me in sorrow to see my father as dejected as this. His hands—those giant hands—sit folded in his lap now, as if he's an old man waiting for Redemption. The skin of his hands, I notice, is cracked, like a walnut shell broken open for its meat. The sight of him is too much to bear, and I stumble away. There in the darkness, downtrodden and separated from all I've known, I resolve to face forward and never again return to our old place. Alone again, I creep back to what has become my new home.

From the next morning on, at my mother's insistence, I do start calling Mr. Griffin "Daddy Lonnie," though I don't think he much cares either way. His body language makes it clear that he's no more interested in me than my real father ever was, and it strikes me as funny that though to date I've had three men playing father in my life—Mr. John Henry, Malone McGill, and this—not one of them seems to have had much use for me. Mr. Ward is the closest thing I've ever had to a real dad. Too bad he's already got kids of his own.

With a summer ahead of me in a new hood with no friends, I naturally throw myself back into basketball. Every day I hitchhike to the courts at

South Park, at the intersection of 51st and Avalon. Maybe I should be nervous about hitching, but I'm not; maybe my folks should be concerned, too, but they aren't. Daddy Lonnie could take me or leave me; as far as I can tell I'm just part of the package to him. And as for my mother—well, now that she has the attentions of a new man, I'm starting to fade from her picture. But I don't mind. Whatever else is happening to me, at least basketball is there. And at South Park basketball is really there. Hoopsters from all over Los Angeles trek to South Park daily to play. The courts overflow with talent; all the best high schoolers in the city and some college kids, too, come out to South Park to hoop.

It's a little bit of a transition for me, moving from the indoor, parquet courts at the YMCA to the paint-lined blacktop of South Park. For one thing, it's not quite quiet out on 51st street. In the gym the only sounds came from the net, the floor, and the backboard, peppered by the occasional echoes of other children. But out here at South Park all kinds of people hang around. There're the greasers who gather with their girls, and burgeoning doo-wop quartets stand under the shade of trees to practice away their Saturdays. Barry White—still not yet a big star—comes out there with his little group, and they sing and practice by the oaks near the courts. But that's not for me, and even if it was, I quickly learn that you can't just go over and hang with one of the groups that's not your own. Only girls are allowed, by the unspoken codes of the neighborhood, to flit between the circles. But that's fine by me. I just want to play ball.

At South Park we play make-it, take-it, winner stays. That means if you score you keep possession, and if you win you keep the court. That also means that coughing up the ball might cause you to never get it back, and since there are only so many courts and always teams waiting to get in, one mistake can leave a guy sitting around with nothing else to do all the rest of the day. So from square one I'm forced to keep my game top-notch and tight. There's no room for mistakes.

We play three-on-three at South Park, and part of the fight is staying focused in front of all the waiting players and hangers-on, many of whom, unlike me, already have facial hair. When I first start heading over, nobody knows me and nobody wants to take me, a stringy preteen, on their squad.

But after a few weeks the older guys who act as de facto captains start fighting over who gets me for their team. Imagine that: a twelve-year-old kid getting fought over by guys with drivers' licenses.

Whenever I work the post and go up hard to the hoop, I take fists and elbows to the body over and over from guys who can probably bench-press me. It's rough, but all that physicality slowly builds me up; it makes me hard, gives me strength to match my height, and by the time the summer ends and the school year rolls around, I know I'm a force to be reckoned with.

By the time I enter Carver Junior High, I've grown so fast that I'm a six-foot-five preteen. And while none of the other seventh graders are as tall as I am, there are still a few jumbo-sized dudes in junior high—and just as at 28th Street Elementary, Carver hosts one big man on campus who doesn't like having a new arrival to compete with.

My first week of school he comes after me, an alpha-male ninth grader challenging me to a fight on the baseball field. It's kindergarten all over again.

The day of the fight the ball field is packed with students forming a makeshift ring around us in the dirt. I hardly know anybody at school, yet there's already a mass of students itching to find out whether or not I'm tough. No one is cheering for me.

As when I was younger, my opponent is much bigger than I am; he moves like Paul Bunyan's lumbering ox and tries to wrestle me to the ground where he can pin me and start whaling away. But I won't have it. He doesn't know me and doesn't know that my father was a boxer; he doesn't know that I spent years learning how to make sure that any after-school bully who tries to beat fear into me is going to find I know how to stand my ground.

And that's what I do. Blow by blow I parry, counter, and land a punch. The ogre of a boy—name of Waylon, I learn, as I hear his friends jeer—never even gets close. Time after time he tries to approach, and I just push him back with shots to the chin and step aside. Within a minute he gets cut; the blood dripping down his face tells him it's not going how he expected. He expected me to tussle furiously and lose. Instead I'm staying cool, keeping measured, and imagining myself in the Grand Olympic Auditorium. When Waylon at last tires and tries to step through my light flurries to wrap his arms around me in a bear hug, I dodge across and lay him out with a haymaker hook he hasn't a chance of seeing coming.

Waylon hits the ground. He doesn't get up. My dad isn't there to see me earn the right to walk tall in peace, but I think he would have been proud.

The fight teaches me I've got to find some friends, and fast. I soon find a kid in some of my classes with whom I hit it off: Willis Thomas. He's friendly, he doesn't live too far away, and most important, he's just as obsessed with basketball as I am. As we get to know each other, I learn that Willis's dad doesn't figure much in his life, either. And I find out once we hit the court that Willis has a great crossover dribble and an excellent southpaw jump shot. Within a week I start calling him "Lefty," and we become comrades-in-arms.

Lefty isn't quite so tall as I am, but he is meticulous to a fault. Every day he comes in with his hair combed just so, with his shirt and khaki slacks ironed to perfection. Just as he frets over his appearance, he works equally hard to make his basketball game sharp. We meet in the halls after school, head on over to the gym, and work each other like Mr. Ward used to work me, only this time it's a two-way street. He can't dunk—not yet, anyhow—but he's got ups and the purest jump shot I've ever seen. In one-on-one we match up well together despite my height advantage, and together we decide to start a little team of our own. Between his outside shooting and my inside game, we are unstoppable on the court.

Carver Junior High doesn't have a basketball club per se. Instead the school plays host to a few standing squads of loose teams that scrimmage each other semiregularly. A lot of guys laxly flow between squads, but Lefty and I make sure we always play together. And no matter who else joins us, our group is nearly always the team to beat.

Our PE coach starts scheduling regular matches among the school's squads, and mine and Lefty's win them all. Eventually word gets around that there's a top-tier team at Carver that can beat the pants off anyone, and other junior high schools become interested. They start sending their own teams to come to our school to play us.

These games are special. Other teams arrive on their official buses and file off wearing their crisp, matching uniforms and basketball shoes. When they walk into the gym to find Lefty, me, and a few other guys doing layup drills in our mismatched tennies and whatever gym clothes are clean, they nearly always point at us and laugh. A few of them even act like they're doing us a favor just by showing up. Before the games they strut around, arrogant, laughing at us instead of warming up, especially if they're from richer schools like those near the Hollywood area. Those teams are usually all white and come in with big chips on their shoulders.

And the victories over these teams are the sweetest of all.

When the games begin we show no mercy; what outside teams coming into our gym don't realize, even as our stands fill up—fill up with students, teachers, even local fans from the area—is that they are walking into a hornet's nest. Game after game we pound the ball down their necks and leave them to stagger home bewildered.

This goes on for months. We never do get to travel to other gyms to play—no matter how good we get, the heads of Carver never try to put together an official squad—but our musty and dusty gym, old and unloved, is good enough for us. It's got dirty white mats on the walls and not a single pennant hanging from the rafters, but it's where we reign over junior high LA, and it's home.

Of course, my real home—the place where I live—is nowhere near as inviting.

Daddy Lonnie and I still aren't getting along. As little affection as my father ever showed for me, Daddy Lonnie shows even less. It reaches the point where he gets mad at me even for little things, like when I mention that I'm hungry.

"You eat too much," he says, gruff as if the milkman had forgotten to come around. When I make the mistake of mentioning that my father used to bring home meat on Fridays, Daddy Lonnie—who works as a mechanic and cleaner on a car lot—just gets even madder.

One time he and my mother go to a friend's house on a weekend afternoon to drink and play cards. I'm more or less left to fend for myself, but my mother makes sure to tell me to turn off the oven sometime in the early afternoon because she has a roast in there.

Well, I do what she says and turn off the oven. But I am so hungry all the time that I cut myself a little piece from the roast. That one bite is so nice, and as dinnertime comes and goes and my folks don't show up, I help myself to another slice of meat. Then another. Then another.

By the time they return there's nothing left in the roasting pan but the string and a little bit of gravy. Needless to say, this does not improve my relationship with Daddy Lonnie.

Lefty, I learn, isn't much better off. His father abandoned him and his mom a long, long time ago. I've had three almost-dads, counting Mr. John Henry, and he has none. Which of us had it worse? Hard to say. The two of us show our pain in our own ways. I lose my confidence. I still can't stay focused in school—never could—but as I hit junior high I find I also can't talk to girls. Lefty, for his part, is smooth with the ladies, but he has a problem, too: he stutters. He grooms himself until he shines, but he still has to fight against slipping and stumbling whenever he opens his mouth.

My problem of never having enough to eat translates to school as well. I get fifty cents a day for food, which covers the cost of a small tray of whatever the public lunch is. But even when I'm a thirteen-year-old seventh grader it's never enough. I'm six feet five and still growing; I'm barely getting enough at home; Daddy Lonnie, who controls the purse strings, certainly isn't giving me any cash to buy extra lunch at school. And I have to eat. So I take to cutting classes to hustle for lunch money.

Every day I shoot dice in the smoke-filled bathrooms of our little junior high. I pad my rolls to make sure I win, so when lunchtime comes, I regularly have two or three dollars in my pocket. It may not be enough to pay for a pot roast, but at least I don't go hungry.

I'm worst at math, so I skip that the most. Besides, who can choose to sit through the squeal of chalk on a blackboard when just a few feet away you can be listening to the cracking echo of the bones as they leave your hand?

I love that sound. But it's that sound that gets me busted. One day, as some other guys and I are crouched on our knees in that smoke-smelling, pee-crusted room skipping class and shooting for sevens, the crack of the dice is trumped by the slam of a heavy, oaken door slapping open against the blue-painted wall.

And in walks Mr. Camrada.

Mr. Camrada is a big, bald bull of a man. He's our school principal, and he is the only man at Carver Junior High who intimidates me. When kids get caught doing bad, Mr. Camrada grabs them by the ear and drags them into his office in the recesses of the school. And when Mr. Camrada busts in on our craps game, my first thought is that I am in for it bad.

Wordlessly, Mr. Camrada brings us down to his office and calls us in one at a time. Sitting there on that bench outside his office as I watch one boy after another go into the dragon's den, I start sweating. By the time he calls me in all the other boys have already had their turn and walked out ashen.

He plants his hands firmly on the desk and growls at me. "I don't want to see you shooting craps in my school ever again. Do you understand?" He cracks his knuckles.

"Yes, sir," I gulp.

He stares at me, a piercing gaze that could deflate a balloon. I don't even realize it, but I'm holding my breath. Here comes something bad. I tense.

"Get out of here," he says, and that's it. He lets me go. He doesn't even confiscate my ill-gotten money. I'm flabbergasted.

I'd never met Mr. Camrada before that bathroom incident, but during my first week of school, right around the same time I got caught up by the bully, I saw him one morning at the playground. I was shooting hook shots from the top of the key, just as Mr. Ward had shown me—feet firmly planted, body perpendicular to the basket—and nailed ten out of ten in a row. Hook shots are harder than set shots because you're not facing the basket and the angle of release can be tricky to get the hang of.

I don't think Mr. Camrada had ever seen a display like that. As I walk back down the halls toward my class, amazed that I've somehow skirted serious punishment, I try to figure how it is I've gotten off so easy. My best guess—my only guess—is that maybe it's due to my basketball talents that he decided to take it easy on me.

I've got to be careful, I tell myself. I've got to get on the straight and narrow or next time I'll be in real trouble.

Of course, I don't actually stop playing craps at school. I just become way more careful about it.

The Hill

As strong as my shooting hand is on the tiles, it's nothing compared to my hand on the court. Word spreads into the community at large about the near-unbeatable ragged team from Carver Junior High, and eventually we begin to catch attention from the press. Not the *Los Angeles Times*, of course. The *Times* is for bankers and office workers. The *Times* is for white LA. In my neighborhood people read the *Sentinel*, the black-owned daily that focuses on information and issues relevant to LA's Afro-American community.

The number one sportswriter at the *Sentinel* is a man named Brad Pye Jr. He writes about legends and has met all of the greats, but while Lefty and I are still fresh-faced teenagers, Mr. Pye begins joining the throngs at Carver Junior High to watch us play eighth grade basketball. And sometimes he files reports about us.

With our names in the paper, Lefty and I become minor celebrities. Pye says I'm strong and I'm tall as a hill; next thing I know, nobody's calling me Billy anymore. Everyone's calling me Hill. But once again, as well as days go on the court, nights grow ever darker off.

Cracks begin to arise in the foundation of our already shaky home life. Mom still loves me, of course, but I've long since ceased to be the focus of her attentions. Daddy Lonnie, for his part, only ever really tolerated my presence so he could be with her. But when their ardor starts to cool, that makes things bad for my mom and me.

She can't very well up and leave him, of course—if she does there'll be no one else. Leave one husband with another man waiting in the wings, okay, but leave a second and you'll get a reputation as a woman who can't be satisfied. My mother is trapped; she has no choice but to stay with Daddy Lonnie, even as life grows dark in our home. And from this prison of desperation, she begins to throw herself back into the drink.

When summer comes, we move from our little eastside home to a house closer to south central LA. The move feels to me like an ominous reflection of the pain that has taken root in my family; the house is bigger, but that space creates more room in which bad things can hide. It's off of 43rd Street and Central Avenue, the cultural hub of black Los Angeles and ground zero for nightclubs and parties. I can smell the remains of all-nighters wafting down the alley on mornings after; I can walk out my door to see the stacked empty bottles behind the Dunbar Hotel and the famous Elks Ballroom. Like a runaway car, my mother's drinking accelerates after we move, and it's not long until the brake lines burst.

In the wee hours of one Sunday morning—around 3:00 a.m.—my mother and Daddy Lonnie stagger back from a night clubbing on Central Avenue. I'm sound asleep, but I jolt upright when they come home: my mother is screaming outside.

I jump out of bed and run to the front of the house to find my mother rolling around in the middle of the street. In the glow of the moonlight, I can see the outline of Daddy Lonnie doing his best to get her off the ground. He tries to pick her up, but she's fighting him, and it's clear that she's dead drunk.

"Leggo of me!" she screams. "I wanna stay out! Don't make me come back on home; it's early!"

With my help, he gets her into the house. She starts cursing and screaming, calling Daddy Lonnie all kinds of names. My heart's pounding so hard I don't know what to do. Is this my mother? What is happening to her?

She keeps up her tirade well into Sunday morning. It's not until she passes out from exhaustion sometime after daybreak that we can all go to sleep. Only as she slowly shuffles off to bed does Daddy Lonnie tell me the story.

My mother had wanted to stay out drinking, while Daddy Lonnie—who, for all of his faults, isn't much for booze, at least not to excess—thought it time to go home. She didn't get her way, so she turned mean and aggressive. That's all he tells me, and I'm left to wonder, is this the first time this has happened? Is it the last?

On future weekends my mother drinks more and more until her antics become nearly regular. About once a month she comes slobbering home up the path, Daddy Lonnie dragging her back from the clubs so she can sober up. Sometimes I lie awake in bed and stare at the ceiling, wondering what I can do to fix things. I wrack my brain for an answer, but once again I'm powerless.

My fortunes look brighter come the start of ninth grade, when I start at Jefferson High. The school is something of a legend around my neighborhood. Just as Central Avenue is the hub of Afro-American Angeleño social life, Jefferson is the nexus of academic and athletic achievement for black students. The school opened in the mid-1910s, and its first students were mostly immigrant Germans and Italians. At that time black residents of the city lived nearly exclusively downtown, filling tenements near Figueroa Avenue and Wilshire Boulevard. For a while Jefferson remained small, but eventually it expanded, beckoning the black populace to it like a flower's nectar does a bee.

The transition was swift. Only six years after opening Jeff named its first black valedictorian: a young basketball devotee named Ralph Bunche. After graduating Bunche matriculated to Southern Branch—a school that came to be known as UCLA—where he played ball for three years before growing up to win the Nobel Peace Prize. I dream I might follow in his footsteps—not to become a diplomat but to play college ball.

Ralph Bunche didn't grow into his own overnight, of course, and for that matter neither did Jefferson. It took two men—a track coach named

Harry Edelson and a music teacher named Samuel Browne, the latter him-self a Jefferson alum—to coax programs out of infancy and grow them from mere shoots cracking the LA asphalt into powerhouses of national renown.

Browne's music department produced Dexter Gordon, the greatest tenor sax player of all time. I know Dexter's father as a doctor with an office down the road from me on Central Avenue—word is that whenever Duke Ellington comes to LA and needs medical help, Dr. Gordon's his go-to man. Marshall Royal, Count Basie's bandleader, got his education at Jeff, too, and years later Etta James, Barry White, and the songwriters who pen "Louie Louie," "Only You," and "Earth Angel" would all also grace its halls.

Samuel Browne knew his stuff, but as strong as he built his music depart-ment, Edelson's athletic department grew even stronger. In the late '30s, Jefferson won title after title in track and field, and its 1937 team was hailed as the greatest high school squad of all time. It produced, among others, such notable alumni as Mal Whitfield, a Texas transplant who went on to win the eight-hundred-meter races in both the '48 and '52 Olympics. Hot on Whitfield's heels came Charles Dumas, a fellow Jeff alum and front-runner for high-jumping gold in '56. Jefferson's football team, too, was a powerhouse. In '51, they were not only undefeated on the season but *unscored upon*—every single game they played, they took the field and proceeded to shut out their opponents entirely.

Not bad for a couple of downtown street kids.

In the years before I matriculated, Jeff's basketball program grew quite strong as well, thanks to the arrival of a young man from South Dakota who brought the team into its own. From what I hear, Coach Larry Han-son's initial recruiting strategy was simple: he went to all the gym classes in the school, found the most athletic kids, and told them that they had a choice of either going out for the basketball team or failing phys. ed.

Within four years they'd won a city championship.

It's while I was still at 28th Street that the Demos took their first bas-ketball title. Their squad was led by a whiz kid named J. C. Gipson, a tenth grader rumored to be nineteen. After leading the school to the crown, he dropped out—hard to blame him, if he really was already old enough to go out to bars at night—and signed with the Harlem Globetrotters.

In my neighborhood, that's considered success.

Lefty and I don't need any of Coach Hanson's famed "encouragement"; all summer we throw ourselves into training and prepping for our first year of high school ball. Carver might not have had an organized team, but Jefferson certainly does, and we're determined to make names for ourselves like Gipson did playing for the green and the gold.

All day, every day, the two of us hit the courts. While playing three-on-three against all comers at South Park, we work on every conceivable shot that we can think of: the layup, the dunk, the jumper, the standing hook. Against the background of those same doo-wop groups with their slicked, congolened hair and the gangbangers and the greasers, we push each other to play harder, to play faster, and to get stronger. Eventually Lefty and I stop playing three-on-three altogether—there's no challenge left to it. We switch to playing one-on-one in a little gym where, despite his height disadvantage, Lefty's strong D makes him the only player I know who has a prayer of slowing me. As a pair, we're firing on all cylinders, and both our games are getting better than ever.

In a white T-shirt and khaki pants I've ironed the night before—Lefty showed me how—I walk to my new high school. The air in south central LA is hot and still—thick late-summer soup. Turning left onto Hooper Avenue, I flow into the foot traffic of all the other students—girls in pleated dresses and saddle shoes; boys with pompadours or cool conked haircuts styled short and plastered down, shining in the sun like smoothed glass—toward the looming schoolhouse.

"Billy!"

I pause. A man stands on the front steps with a clipboard pressed into his hip. A whipped blur passes before my face, and I pluck it out of the air before even realizing what I've done: there's a basketball in my hand.

"Nice catch." The man descends the steps one at a time with his hand outstretched. "Coach Hanson," he says.

I shake his hand and nod, giving him back the ball. "Yes, sir. I know who you are."

"Good," he says, and he puts his arm around my shoulder and leads me into the building. "Come on. Let's get you registered for classes."

From what I'd heard, in high school everyone spends their first day going from room to room signing up for classes, figuring out on their own when they'll have science, English, and so on. But Coach Hanson walks me through the halls, signing me up for a full course schedule himself—and talking my ear off all the way.

"I've heard you have trouble in math," he says, and I nod, because it's true. Still, I wonder where he got *that* from. I can understand that maybe he read some of Brad Pye's press on me, but how did he find out about my math grades?

Coach goes on about the importance of maintaining my GPA, and slowly I tune him out and lose myself in the sights of this massive, windowless school. Students swish by, books tucked under their arms. Locks click shut on metal lockers. The walls, studded with banners, and in one nook a trophy case, serve as testament to the school's greatness. The occasional buff letterman in a gleaming green and gold jacket underscores that point, and each time an athlete wearing one passes I feel a twinge of jealousy.

"And be sure to be there on time," Coach says as he signs me up for my last class of the day.

"Sorry?" I say. "What?"

"I said practice starts at 3:10 p.m. sharp. Which doesn't mean 'arrive at 3:10.' It means you're on the court, in your gym clothes and gym shoes, dressed and ready to go ten minutes after the final 3:00 class bell. If you're late, it's a hundred laps around the gym you owe me. So be there on time." The look in his eye dispels any thought he might be fooling around. "Welcome to Jefferson, kid," he says, and he leaves, leaving me alone to wonder what I've gotten myself into.

As it turns out Lefty is in my last class of the day; whether this is at the behest of Coach Hanson or not, I don't know, but as soon as that final bell rings the two of us sprint together through the halls to get to practice. The school is far bigger than Carver was, and it takes some serious bobbing and weaving to make it down to the locker room with any changing time to spare.

At 3:09 and 50 seconds, Coach steps onto the court with his whistle. He watches the red, sweeping hand of the wall clock creep upward, and once it's vertical he blows one loud, sharp tweet.

"Gentlemen," he says. "Welcome to the team."

And we begin.

As soon as I enter Jefferson, my life becomes about one thing only: basketball. I think about basketball all day long; my mother ups my daily meal allowance to a dollar so I can stay fueled; and even craps fades out of view. There's only one tiny, niggling problem: grades. I need to stay afloat in academics to keep from getting kicked off the team. As it happens this is a tricky proposition.

I never had any tough teachers at 28th Street Elementary. There was the one time Miss Grey stuck me behind the chalkboard and jammed a dunce cap on my head—a real pointed cap, like in a cartoon—but even though I wasn't keeping up, it never seemed like much of a big deal. No one ever pulled me aside and told me to shape up or ship out. And as for Carver, it had been more of the same.

In high school, however, I quickly learn that the teachers expect more than just attendance and promptness; they want effort, understanding, and hard work. After going to all my classes that first day, then the first week, then the first month—and promptly falling behind in all of them— I find myself wishing that I had studied harder growing up. I begin to feel inadequate and underprepared in classes, especially mathematics; algebra is like a foreign language to me. And there's no relief, either. I don't have friends who are doing any better, and with things as they are at home, I can't exactly go to my mother or Daddy Lonnie for help. I begin to pull a self-pity job, working out excuses instead of working out my assignments, and I try my hardest to skate through. The teachers see how hard I'm working at not learning anything, so they begin to get down on me, which just makes things worse. Other students no smarter than me get the clue. They put in the hours and start raking in As and Bs. Me, I just wait on the 3:00

p.m. bell so I can leave class to hit practice, hoping that my diffidence will defend me.

I can't see how much this will come to hurt me. All I can do is pour my heart and energy into basketball.

"Unlike in the classroom, the court will be a place where 100 percent effort and focus are demanded and given at all times," Coach Hanson says, turning on his heels, military-style, "or else." I feel like he's talking directly to me.

He's not kidding, either. Show up to practice at 3:11, and that's it: a hundred laps, no questions asked. Held up by a teacher after class? Too bad. You're late.

Coach Hanson's balls-out work ethic gets drilled into us quick, and Coach backs up his rhetoric with drills designed to kill. Run-and-guns, suicides—these become basic tenets not just of practice but of our lives.

What's a suicide? "You take off from the baseline at the far end of the court under the basket and sprint to the near free-throw line. There you stop, slap the line, and sprint back to where you started. You stop and crouch low to touch that line! Then, about-face and sprint to the mid-court, slap that line, and run back. Then you run to the far free-throw line and back and the far out-of-bounds line and back, stopping and slapping each line every time." It sounds grueling, but the '51 championship banner waves in the rafters. Is that what it takes?

"When you're done and slap hands with your teammate—your partner—he goes. Once he's done, you go again, then he goes again. Every player goes twice." Inwardly, I groan, and then he finishes. "Except for the losing team. Losing team has to do the whole thing a second time over."

When Coach blows his whistle after that little speech, I take off sprinting as hard as I can. I have no problem taxing my body to the point of exhaustion, because as rough as this feels, there's no way I'm doing it over. The sprinting burns our lungs, but no one ever thinks of giving up. We can't. We know what the penalty will be for quitting: a hundred laps.

Day in and day out Coach has us running like men on the lam. It hurts, but it makes us strong, and it makes us mean. I had always been fast, but thanks to Coach my speed reaches the point where I begin beating the senior guards—the "quick" men, the guys three years above me—in running drills. Coach teaches me—teaches all of us—to refuse to be beaten, and I take that message to heart. I hope he can see my dedication, and it turns out he can.

One day after practice he pulls me aside. "Billy," he says. "I'm putting you on the varsity team."

The words ring sweetly in my ears like the call of a bird in the sunlight.

"I know you're only a ninth grader, but I think you can make it all the same. It's going to take a lot of work. Are you ready to work hard for me?"

It's all I can do to choke out a "Yes, Coach," before he sends me off to the showers. I'll be the first ninth grader ever on the Jefferson varsity squad. Lefty is shunted off to JV—a decision I don't agree with, but not one I can do too much about—but we're still excited.

Though the workouts at Jeff are far harder, game days are just like they'd been back at Carver. The stands fill with screaming people, many with some connection to the school but some just regular fans from the neighborhood. Other teams come and visit the gym, and time after time they leave with their tails between their legs. Our conditioning has made us unstoppable and our skill level is unparalleled; other teams don't even have a chance.

There are a few differences from Carver, of course. For one, it's nice to be part of a real team—to have uniforms, to have away games; to be able to slip on the green and gold of the Democrats and to be a part of something bigger. It makes my days feel full, knowing I have something to look forward to once I step on the court.

For another, we have cheerleaders at Jefferson. That's pretty nice, too.

I'll never forget the first time I hear them cheering for me. It's December, and we're playing our rivals from Fremont. I score nineteen points, setting a freshman record, though that's not hard as *any* high point total I tally becomes the new record automatically. Still, Coach subs me out for a breather, and as I jog off the court I hear the cheerleaders scream my name. "Billy, Billy, he's our man! If he can't do it, no one can!"

The feeling that wells inside me is like magic. This is what I've been working toward all along: encouragement. Being noticed. Validation.

Acceptance. Besides Mr. Ward, no one else has ever made me feel like I have someone in my corner before. And to go from such a place of solitary emptiness to having the prettiest girls at school yelling my name—well, it's nothing short of amazing.

That night, Lefty corners me in the dressing room. "Some game you had." We bump fists.

"Thanks, brother."

"I notice those girls were calling your name."

I grin. "Yeah."

I'm tying up the shoelaces on my Converse, and he puts his hand on my shoulder. I look up.

"So, which one are you going to ask out?"

I try to shrug him off, blushing, but he brushes that away.

"Buddy. You just scored nineteen points." His voice becomes slow, deliberate. "You're the new starting center of the Jefferson High basketball team." We lock eyes. "Man up."

When I ask one sophomore cheerleader out on a date that night, I'm surprised—though Lefty's not—that she, without a moment's deliberation, says yes. All of a sudden, and for the first time, I am somebody. And I love it.

My folks never come to my games, of course, but I tell myself it doesn't matter. The stands at our games are packed with paying customers, and knowing that people plunk down their hard-earned money to see me—to see all of us—feels good. Our matches are doubleheaders: the JV, led by a fearless Lefty, plays first, and they have no problems steamrolling other squads en route to victory. And after the opening show is over we come out and mop the floor with our opponents. People pack the stands at Jeff; by the time the varsity game starts our gym is invariably sold out, and would-be fans are turned away at the door. That's how popular we are: people show up early and sit through the JV contests just to ensure they'll have seats when it's our turn.

As in junior high, the schools are segregated along unofficial lines. It isn't like the Deep South or anything, but just like on that bus from Texas, people of different ethnicities get shunted apart from one another, so that when we play Hollywood High or Roosevelt, our opponents are all white, and when we go to Fremont or Manual Arts, every face in the stands is black. It doesn't matter who we play, though; our opponents all leave the courts wondering what hit them. From my early high of 19, I keep up my scoring pace and average 15.4 points per game over the course of the year, even with just sixteen minutes played. Our team solidly sweeps through LA, and at the end of the season we're alone atop the standings in the Southern League. With that we're crowned district champions and given the number one seed into the citywide championship.

The city is broken up into a number of leagues—Southern, Marine, Valley, among others—and every year the top two or three finishers from each league are invited to a single-elimination open tournament. The last few years running the Southern League has been dominant, with most of its league champions taking the citywide crown as well. Some people say that our league rivals the best prep circuits in the country in Philadelphia and New York, the ones that turn out such stars as Wilt Chamberlain and Paul Arizin, Bob Cousy and Dolph Schayes. Whether that's true or not, we do sweep through the tournament, knocking off all opponents before running into Eastern League champs Jordan High in the final.

Despite our determination, it's close all the way. The two teams are neck and neck at halftime. Walking back out from the locker room for the beginning of the third quarter, sweat still dripping down my brow, I scan the stands for my buddy Lefty. Though I don't see him, I do spy the *Sentinel*'s Brad Pye Jr. in the bleachers. This one is going to be big.

Throughout the third quarter, Jordan and Jeff push each other harder and harder. Try as both teams might, though, no one can pull out to a lead. The crowd is split and going wild with each basket: the green and gold supporters of the Democrats explode every time we score, and the blue-and-white-clad fans of the Jordan Bulldogs cheer their lungs out every time they put one in. It's the hardest game I've ever played to date.

The score is tied as we begin the fourth quarter; I'm nervous, but I have faith. We go on a little run to take the lead, but Jordan answers back and pulls within one with just a minute left on the clock. Coach Hanson calls a time-out and brings us all in for a huddle. With the season almost over, we're in our closest scrape of the year, and our dreams of a city championship teeter on the precipice. I've never played for anything so hard before; I want this win so bad I can taste the iron of blood in my mouth.

Coming out of the huddle, we push the ball up the court—and turn it over! The Jordan fans roar as their team pushes it back up the court. They move it around, setting up for an open shot, and they launch one. It's a miss! Sweating, I throw myself between two other bodies and crash the boards; I pull down the rebound and send our team sprinting back in the other direction. Coach Hanson favors a run-and-gun style—he doesn't like us to dribble the ball upcourt on offense like other teams do; instead we utilize a pass-heavy, diamond-shaped system that helps us transition to a quick attack—and, like always, Coach is screaming at us to keep it moving, keep it moving.

The ball ends up in the hands of our big senior set-shooter, a guard named Leo Hill. With a hand in his face, he slips in a jumper—and it's good! Jordan has no time-outs, and they spend the last few moments trying to get the ball up the court and find an open shot, but they can't. The buzzer sounds, and the scoreboard tells the story: 58–55. We've won.

I bask in the glow of adoration I feel from the rest of the school—teachers, teammates, everybody—after winning the LA city title, and I receive the added honors of being named to both the All-Southern League first team and the All-City squad. I'm the only freshman named to either team. I feel as though I am, for the first time, amounting to something, and it's amazing.

That's it. I'm now hooked, and I know it. There's nothing else that I'll ever want to do.

After the season Brad Pye Jr. describes me as LA's high school phenom. "Billy the Kid," he calls me, and like my namesake, I feel unstoppable. Though I've barely turned fifteen, my whole game is above the rim. Word on the street and word in the *Sentinel* is that I can jump, dunk, rebound, block shots, and score at will—I can do it all.

It's a nice thought, being able to do it all. Reflecting on all those times I've felt so impotent in my life—with my father, with my mother, with Gloris Jean—being able to do it all feels like a prayer come true.

Lefty dominates the jv ranks his freshman year just as easily as I tear up the main league, and after school ends we spend the whole off-season working the courts at 51st and Avalon, honing our skills on the blacktop. Lefty is determined to join me on the varsity squad next year, and come fall he does.

The practices my second year under Coach Hanson are as brutal as ever, but they're a different beast altogether from the previous year's. Coach adds tennis to our training regimen—chasing down ground strokes and building frontcourt net play force us to bolster our footwork, and by the time games against opponents hit our schedule, we've got lightning fast feet to match our ball skills and our toughness. And now we're dominating the court in two sports.

We're all so tall and muscular that we're naturally good at serving hard. "You know," the tennis coach says, "you ought to come out for the team."

"Not interested," Coach Hanson speaks for us. When he gets us back into the gym, he assures us that if we even think about dropping basketball for tennis, he'll go back to his old tactic and personally make sure that we all fail phys. ed.

"Now," he says, "let's practice zone defense. Put all that footwork and conditioning to use." And we do. On "D," we swarm; on "O," our M.O. is to run, run, and run some more, and nearly always we run teams right off the floor. It isn't uncommon for us to be up by solid double-digit margins come halftime, and usually Coach makes the first string spend most of the back half of games riding the pine to keep all our games from turning into blowouts.

It's nice being out there with Lefty, having the two of us together on the court again like we'd done all through Carver and our summers. Quickly, the winter of 1955–56 becomes the Lefty and Billy show at Jefferson High.

The Demos sweep through the Southern League like a wildfire once again. We win the regular season title, and once again we find ourselves in the city championship game against the team we took out last year: Eastern League champions Jordan High. Stepping onto the neutral court at Venice High, I'm confident—we're the defending champs, plus I've got Lefty here with me. We won all our games at Carver, and the old one-two punch always worked back then, so why shouldn't it work this year, too?

"Because," notes a man in a trench coat, scarf, and fedora—a scout—as we watch the Bulldogs warm up once again in the odd, expansive confines of the neutral Venice High gym before finals. "Unlike Jeff, Jordan didn't lose any of their big players." He points out two muscled boys who work layups back and forth between them on the floor. "That's Sterling Forbes and Bobby 'Blue' Odom. Word is they've already got scholarships to play at Pepperdine." Lefty and I are sitting on the bench, just within earshot, and though we're trying not to we can't help overhearing what the scout is saying to the man sitting next to him.

"And that other one?" he adds, gesturing toward a lanky, skinny kid with close-cut hair, a boy who looks just like me but smaller, as if he were a clay model of myself that had gotten shrunk down a size in an oven. "That's Bobby Sims. LA city high-jump champ. The Hill's got height, sure"—and at a listed size of six feet seven, I sure do—"but Sims will still get plenty of rebounds. There's no one else on Jeff to help Billy on the boards."

Lefty and I try to push the talk out of our heads before the game begins, and Coach does a good job of getting us fired up to defend our title. But being fired up is not enough. The question is, do we have the horses?

For the first three quarters, my second city championship game plays out just like my first. Jordan and Jeff are neck and neck, and the cheering crowd stands swathed in blue and white and green and gold. But in the fourth quarter something happens: our offense starts to falter. I'm still pouring them in, but our replacement at guard for the graduated Leo Hill, a usually dead-accurate marksman named Robert Guidry, begins to miss. Blue Odom nails set shot after set shot, and Jefferson can't answer. When the final buzzer rings, both Odom and Sterling Forbes have finished with nineteen points in the final, and Jeff loses, 64–57.

Like that, Jordan snatches the repeat out from under our noses and takes the '56 Los Angeles city championship. I'm left with a sinking feeling in my gut. There's nothing left to do but struggle through another five months of classes and wait for summer so we can start working toward next season.

Except for chasing girls, of course.

For a guy like me who has always been shy, the sudden skyrocketing of my social stock is an unexpected but very welcome boon. Suddenly, as an All-City first-teamer and the consensus star of our team, I'm a hero. Lefty's no slouch, either, and having him with me gives me strength. He's calm with the girls, cool, easy; I may be feted, but it's still my best friend who ends up being my male role model and getting me all my dates. Whenever there are parties, he makes sure we're invited; whenever a cute girl wants to go out, he gets her to bring a friend so we four can double date. And it's not just the ladies who treat me special, either.

One Friday night I'm on my way to pick up a girl. She lives in a neighborhood I'm not too familiar with, so I end up getting a little lost, which leads me to cut through a city park so I don't arrive too late. But just as I'm on my way across the fields, I notice one or two guys get up from a little bench and follow me.

By the time I reach the edge of the park, those one or two guys have seemed to grow to four or five, but I keep walking. When I hit the corner, I suddenly realize that I'm surrounded. From behind a tree emerges a pack of six more who block the road before me. Counting the others on my tail who are now closing in, there must be ten or eleven guys quickly forming a ring around me. And under the glow of the streetlight, I catch a glimpse of the flashing glint of a knife, and I freeze. I don't know what's coming, but whatever it is it isn't good.

I can't fight all these guys. And I don't want to get cut up. What do I do? Just as I'm about to dig in and try to make a break for it, though, I hear one of their voices call out through the night.

"Aww, man, it's Billy! Billy the Hill!"

The guy steps forward with his hand extended. I don't know him—don't recognize him at all, in fact—but I coolly give him a high five. Another guy steps forward to high five me, and next thing I know they're all wishing me well. Good wishes all around for the basketball star! The knife disappears, and they step aside and wave me off. As I make it to my girl's house, I still have no idea who they are, but I know this: I'm glad that they're fans of Jefferson basketball.

Despite Lefty's help and the support of thugs citywide, I'm still, at heart, introverted. Brad Pye's belief that I can do it all dissolves when I find myself face-to-face with a beautiful lady—I just don't feel I can talk to other people. Despite my athletic skills, I always feel like I'm on the outside of the crowd looking in, and it doesn't help that I'm the only member of the basketball team without the one piece of armor everyone else has: a letterman jacket.

Lettermans are huge. They're very popular and a big point of pride, and not only at our school. All over Central Avenue, athletes from across the city step out while repping their letterman jackets. They look amazing, and they identify the wearer as a real jock. But though I'm the star of the Jefferson High team and would love to own one, I don't. Daddy Lonnie says we can't afford it. When I want to wear one, I have to borrow Lefty's.

It sounds a little shallow, but it shames me, and I feel the lack of a letterman every time a girl smiles at me. Of course, there's more to women than just asking them out.

I may feel as hopeless at times around girls as I do around algebra, but that ceases to matter once I discover the Move.

The Move becomes my tactic when I can't get Lefty to do the heavy lifting for me. Essentially, I pick a weekend day and head over to the Lincoln Theater, where I get myself a pass for the matinee. The Lincoln puts on a real show: a feature-length movie bookended by live talent acts. It's quite popular, attracting a large crowd of all ages—and both sexes.

The Move is simple: I go to the Lincoln by myself and find a pretty girl all alone. I sit next to her and introduce myself—more often than not she'll know who I am. I'll ask her for her name, wait for the lights to go down, and that's it. Though I may not be smooth-tongued, halfway through the movie we'll be kissing. As "the Hill," I let my reputation do the talking.

Thank you, Brad Pye Jr.

Of course, it isn't all a life of ease. My height makes me stick out even when attention's not wanted, and just like with the bullies at 28th Street and at Carver, one day some guys decide to try to put me in my place.

It's at the Lincoln—a lonely Sunday when I'm hoping to run a Move—when I find myself walking through a row with four other guys seated in it. They've all got their hair slicked back and have leather jackets on, but I ignore them as I hone in on my target because the girl is blindingly cute. Soft, straight hair, a tight-pulled white cardigan—before I even reach her, I already see myself nuzzling up to her neck. Unfortunately, since I'm so big and gangly, when I try to walk around the guys in the narrow row, I accidentally step on one's shoe.

In poor communities like ours, stepping on a man's shoe is a serious affront. So even though it's an accident, to him—and his three leather jacket–wearing brothers—it's a declaration of war.

Before I know it I'm in the middle of a full-on fight. One guy throws a punch that lands square on my jaw; it stings and I know I need to react. I answer with a hard haymaker to the nose, again silently thanking my birth father, and then I shove my way forward like a boxer clenched against the ropes. The amazing part of it is, all five of us are still wedged into this one little theater row. At least they can't all get at me at once.

I take another glancing blow off my chest and throw one more big left hook, and then, just like that, I'm gone. I leap onto the armrest of the seat in front of me, hop onto the seatback, and spring over the people in the row behind, landing in the wide exit aisle. And then I book it out of there.

I throw myself through the double doors into the lobby, barreling into someone carrying a basket of popcorn, just like in a movie. My mind is racing. My heart is, too; I can feel it thumping a conga beat inside my rib-cage. The guys are right on my tail. In the chaos I hear the squeak of a poorly oiled door hinge. I turn to it, and I see my answer: the street. I sprint toward the exit.

Bursting past patrons onto the sidewalk, I don't know if the gang of four is still following me or not, but I'm not about to stop to find out. I'm frantically scouting out the options—Do I sprint down Central Avenue? Do

I head north or south? Should I duck down a side street?—when suddenly a car pulls up in of me.

I immediately assume that the thugs have called in their friends and I'm about to get pounded. But that's not it at all.

Sitting there in the car, staring at me from the passenger side window with a scarf around her neck and a scowl on her face, is my mother. And she looks pissed. "Billy! What are you doing?"

I lunge for the rear handle, throw it open, and dive into the car.

Lonnie and my mom examine me. She must see the mark on my face. "Billy, what's going on? Have you been fighting?" The world seems to be moving in slow motion; all I want is for my mother to stop badgering me and for Daddy Lonnie to start the car. I've never heard of a guy getting beat up in front of his own folks, but I sure don't want to be the first—especially not here, in the middle of Central Avenue.

"No, Mom," I pant. "I haven't been fighting. Let's just go!"

She frowns. "Then what's that on your face?"

I sneak a peek at myself in the rearview mirror. Already the space between my cheek and jaw is swelling up like a ripening orange.

"It's nothing, Mom," I say, shifting my glance from the mirror to the outside window. Those boys, I'm sure, will be barreling out the front doors of the Lincoln and after me any second now. "Are you guys heading home?"

Mercifully, Daddy Lonnie shakes his head and shifts the car into drive. Before my mother can argue we're pushing along Central Avenue, and in that moment I decide to retire the Move then and there. It's too dangerous to wield skills like that off the court.

The Shot

Right after losing to Jordan in the final, Lefty and I decide to go to work, determined that next year we will take the citywide crown. We practice every day, working on all facets of the game, and our dedication and efforts show. We get even better, and just as I grew out of the Y, early summer finds Lefty and me throwing our high-tops over our shoulders and walking away from South Park. The competition just isn't there for us anymore. It's time to move on, and we adopt Denker playground as our new home in which to hone our skills.

For the next step above street ball, Denker is the best in LA, perhaps even on par with the infamous cage at West 4th Street in New York. Local studs of all stripes go there to sharpen their skills, and it isn't uncommon even for pickup games there to draw a crowd.

One Saturday morning Lefty and I are holed up at Denker and hard at work, running a 'round-the-world outside shooting drill and mixing it up with the occasional point of one-on-one. It's only 10:00 a.m. or so, so we still have plenty of room to play.

Though we don't know most of the other guys there, we've seen them all around, having played against—and beaten—most of them in pickup games before. So when the door bangs open and three guys walk in who I don't recognize, I quit for a moment to take a look at the new players.

I'm not the only one. Everyone in the gym seems to be frozen dead once they realize who's just walked in: Guy Rodgers, accompanied by Bill Russell and Wilt Chamberlain.

Guy Rodgers is a star guard at Temple University in Philadelphia and a shoo-in first-round draft pick for the NBA, and still he can't compare to the other two. Bill Russell, after all, is a legend. He walked onto his high school team as a sophomore with nothing more than his leaping ability, and within four years he was able to lead the unknown University of San Francisco to the NCAA title twice in a row. He's just been signed by the Boston Celtics, and he's poised to become a great NBA star.

Of course, as great as Russell is, even he pales in comparison to Wilt.

Wilt the Stilt may be the only man alive who can force Bill Russell into second billing. He's the most imposing, most impressive, and flat-out biggest man I've ever seen. What he—what all three of them—are doing in my little Los Angeles gym on a Saturday morning, I have no idea. But here they are. And they look ready to play.

"Three-on-three?" Wilt's voice rings out like a baritone in a concert hall. He holds up a hand and someone instantly dishes him a basketball.

Russell nods. "All right. Let's choose up sides." And then he lifts his huge mitt in the air and points directly at me. "I'll take the high school phenom."

For a moment I can't believe what's happening. Then it hits me. They know who I am, and I'm about to play basketball with Bill Russell and Wilt Chamberlain.

Next thing I know, me, Bill Russell, and some gym rat are squaring off against Lefty, Guy Rodgers, and Wilt the Stilt. It's three-on-three to fifty points. I'm in awe, and at the same time, I'm in heaven.

Naturally, Wilt and Bill Russell guard one another, and immediately each attacks. They work each other inside and hit each other hard, with free-flying elbows smashing into ribs like pistons drilling the earth around an oil well. They never once call foul; they just hit, bounce, and play on.

We score on a Russell jump shot, then on a Russell drive; next our team-mate throws up a brick and Wilt's team goes on a run, first with a set shot, then a layup, then a dunk. Wilt slams it home over Russell's outstretched arms with authority and taunts him afterward.

It's the toughest game I've ever played, and even though it's just pickup, Russell and Chamberlain both badly want to win. When they see a chance to roll off each other and play help D, they do, and over and over again they launch into the air and turn what look like otherwise sure buckets into blocked shots stuffed back into the crowd.

The crowd's hooting and cheering echo off the walls of Denker and grow louder by the moment. Every point is hotly contested; nobody gives another player an inch. When I get the ball I'm either fighting Lefty hard for free space to shoot a midrange jumper or I'm driving to get him off balance and dishing the ball to a teammate. The other team's making sure nobody posts up inside—Wilt's there to block shots, and Guy Rodgers is itching to swipe the ball away off the dribble—and as for driving the lane, forget it. Wilt and Bill are so strong in the post on defense that I'm the only guy who doesn't get blocked all game. Everyone wants this win, and as it gets to 40–39, and then 46–45, the play gets tighter and tighter.

With us up by one, Bill Russell passes me the ball, and the noise from the sideline seems to fade away. This is it. This is my time. I drive past Lefty and I hear Russell's booming baritone shout, "Shoot it, Billy!" I want to. I will. I'm ready.

It's just at this moment that Wilt Chamberlain ducks around Bill Russell and plants himself directly before me.

I've already picked up my dribble. I've got nowhere else to go. Wilt's mass—I can feel it before I see it—is right on top of me, and wet, hot waves radiate off him like I'm standing between a monsoon and the sun. He's as solid and slick as the wall in a steamed-over shower room.

"Put it up!"

Russell's still yelling at me to pop a shot, and I push Wilt out of my mind. I set myself to jump, and as I do my first thought is, "Uh-oh." I'm in trouble.

As he has his whole career, Chamberlain has smacked away shot after shot today. I'm pushing six feet seven, but he's still got to have half a foot on me. His height is massive, his reach is insane, and the idea of even trying to release a ball at eye level and getting it above his outstretched arms is preposterous. It can't be done.

All the same, my toes press off the ground and I leap. It's too late to go back now. Lefty's rotated onto Russell and Guy Rodgers is guarding his man—a pass will get picked off, and if I land without shooting, it's a travel. I've got to get this shot off.

They say that in moments of great stress, the conscious brain shuts down and the muscles take over and act for themselves. As I'm in the air, knowing that if I release this jumper naturally, it's going to get blocked, my body starts to turn. I'm twisting myself away from Chamberlain by instinct, and as I soar upward I realize what I'm doing: I'm shooting a hook shot. A jumping hook.

Normally, with a hook shot, you're perpendicular to the basket and have the ball out in space, away from the hoop and away from the defender. I know I'm good at it; after all, I nailed hook after hook from beyond the free-throw line that day outside Carver, and Lefty and I have been working on shooting all summer. But you also release hook shots with the inside foot planted, barely coming off the ground at all. You don't launch up in the air and then shoot. That's just not how it's done.

Well, it may not be normal, but if I don't do it I'll get stuffed. Chamberlain has turned into a beast before my eyes. He's chasing after raw meat, and my shot is the steak. So in the air I curl the ball away from the basket, and when my palm passes above my head, I release.

With a flick of my fingers, the ball launches toward the hoop. Before my shot even crests, the crowd begins to cheer. Chamberlain takes off, launching skyward for the block. The mottled noise of the assembled crowd swells, half in awe of my unorthodox lob and half in excited expectation of Wilt throwing my shot halfway toward San Diego.

Watching the Stilt leap, I can see how he got his name. It does seem like he has some sort of extra support in his legs, an inhuman boost that pushes him higher into the air than any man should be able to go. He rises as if pulled by wires, arms high, and I see his palm reaching for the ball as he goes up, up, up . . .

And misses.

The ball, as if lifted by angels, goes above even the reach of Wilt the Stilt. It soars over even his thrusting arms and rotates slowly, gently, toward the hoop.

Then in it. Then through it.

It takes me a moment to realize what has happened. The swish of the net and the roar of the crowd echo dumbly off my eardrums as my brain processes what's just occurred: I've scored. And in the process I've invented a new shot—a jump hook—and sank it over none other than Wilt Chamberlain.

Everyone in the crowd begins to cheer. "Aww, man, that's the Hill!"

"The Hill! The Hill!"

They're cheering my name like I've never heard before; even Mr. Boston Celtic himself, Bill Russell, is laughing and clapping for me. "Did you see that?" he yells. "Did you see that?" He steps over and slaps me five. "High school phenom!"

I'm grinning, my mouth spread wide like I've got clothespins holding it open. I catch a glimpse of Chamberlain—Russell's moved to mocking him now, laughing about how a high school kid got one over the great Wilt the Stilt—and I see anger flash in his eyes. I try to eat my grin, but I can't; all of LA, it seems, is cheering for me.

The game ends not long after that, and I don't even notice who wins. All I can think of is Bill Russell's bellowing laughter.

The Other Shot

"You're a great young player, kid. Keep working hard, and you'll go far."

In the weeks and months that follow, Bill Russell's words echo through my head. With each squeak of my soles, I hear Russell's deep, bellowing laugh of surprise on the hardwood. Day in and day out I work on my jump hook. If Wilt Chamberlain couldn't block it, who will? I hone the shot until it becomes reliable, then perfect, then my new signature move. Each time the ball swishes through the hoop, I see Chamberlain's mouth agape, the basketball giant stunned. For the first time I really believe I've got something. I've held my own with Bill Russell and Wilt Chamberlain—maybe someday I can make it to the NBA.

When I return to school this newfound confidence extends even off the court. First quarter grades are released, and I'm ecstatic to find that I've earned Ds in both basic math and algebra. Ds might not sound like anything to celebrate, but I'm proud of them. At least they're not Fs.

Official basketball practices finally start in late October of my junior year, and I feed off the buzz of being around my teammates again. Word has gotten around town about my shot, thanks to Brad Pye Jr. continuing to write articles about me, and all of us are primed to avenge our finals loss the year before.

Despite my growth Coach Hanson never lets up on us, and practices are as hard as ever. He runs us until we're about to keel over, and when we do he runs us some more. We cover passing and ball handling, perfect our footwork and shooting, and by the time the season begins we're in a class all our own. Every game we play we take by a healthy margin; our home matches are like contests in a Roman coliseum. Our fans scream for blood, and we feed on visiting squads' starting fives, leaving nothing but their empty high-tops on the hardwood. From day one we can feel that we are on a collision course with greatness.

Of course, the higher you rise, the harder you fall.

It all happens during the first round of the city championships. We're playing dead-last seed Huntington Park, and there's not a doubt in my mind that we're going to blow them out of the water. We've already run away with the Southern League and taken the regular season title, and I feel both invincible and unstoppable.

Walking onto the neutral Venice High court again, I notice that something feels different. I can't put my finger on it, but as our team runs through warm-ups, I feel a distinctly different vibe in the air than I usually do. I look into the stands: besides the fact that there's not as much green and gold as we'd get at a home game, nothing seems too unusual. It's not until the very moment before tip-off that I realize what it is.

It's my parents. My mother and Daddy Lonnie are sitting in the stands.

Neither of them has ever come watch me play before. It's an omen, surely. But of what? I don't have time to figure it out.

The ref tosses up the ball to start the game; I tap it with a flick of my wrist to Lefty, and we're under way. We score quickly and easily; the first possession establishes the tempo. Then we score again. Then again.

Late in the first quarter, with us already holding a healthy lead, Lefty goes up for a jumper, and he gets fouled. As he walks up to the line, I take my position along the edge of the paint, bookended on either side by orange-and-gray Huntington Park Spartans. Their center stands between me and the basket; he's almost as tall as me, but much meaner, and I get the sense that he doesn't like how easy we're making it look against them.

"Hey," he says, "Hill," as Lefty puts in his first free throw. "I'm gonna open your eye." The ref tosses the ball back to Lefty for his second shot, and I do my best to shake off the taunt. But as Lefty releases and we all step into the lane to jostle for position, the Spartan center throws an elbow that catches me clean above the left eyelid. Just as he promised, I drop straight to the parquet floor, gushing blood.

Dull pain surges through my forehead; I feel like one of Mr. John Henry's pigs whacked in the forebrain with a sledgehammer. The ref blows his whistle to stop play. His back was to us, watching the free throw, so he didn't see the hit. Despite the brutish play, the Huntington Park thug doesn't get tossed, and I'm the one who's leaving the game, forced to head to the trainer to see to my wound. Our opponent's fans mockingly applaud me off to a chorus of jeers.

After I make my way back to the bowels of the gymnasium with a towel pressed against my forehead, the trainer takes a look at me. He frowns. "Good gash there," he says.

I nod. I have a thick headache. My sense of balance is off.

He mentions the hospital, and I shake my head. I'm not leaving this game. My parents, for the first time ever, are here. And I have a debt to a certain gangly center that I plan to repay in buckets.

"Okay. Stitching you up here, then," he says, and he pulls out a needle and thread. Just like that, he lays me down and sews my forehead back together under the dingy glow of the overhead lights of the concrete locker room.

It's halftime when I make way back into the game. I should just take a break; already Jefferson's up almost twenty points. But the opposing center grins at me, and that flips my switch, fueling my fire. Suddenly I am mad. I am determined.

The other team can't stop me; I pour in point after point. I'm in the zone. When Lefty rips down the rebound after an errant Huntington Park jump shot, I channel Coach's workouts and take off running upcourt. Lefty dishes the ball to John Mason, one of our guards. Mason receives it and sees me streaking just past the half line; with a flick of his wrists he passes to me.

This is how it's gonna be, I think. I'm gonna make a statement now and let everyone know exactly what happens when you mess with Billy McGill. The Huntington Park center is the only defender left between me and the basket on this fast break, and he doesn't stand a chance. This one's in the bag. As I drive with the ball, I feint forward, putting him on his heels. Then I step to my right, gaining separation to pull up for an easy jumper.

As I take off my first thought is: count it. My defender's been faked out badly. I prepare to release a pretty, short jumper as I rise that I can already see swishing through the hoop. This is an easy two points. But right after that thought, at the height of my leap, follows another: wow.

I almost say it aloud to myself: "I don't think I've ever leapt this high before."

The crazy thing about it is it might be true. And I've been getting up. It's not uncommon for me to go up for a rebound and find my armpit level with the ten-foot rim. So when I take off for this jumper and notice that something's different—that I may have, in my anger, pushed myself to jump higher than I've ever leapt before—it's memorable. Indeed, I will remember this moment for a long time.

I release the ball at the apex of my jump, and as I let go I seem to hear something pop. It's a quiet but clear sound, and it's unlike any noise I've ever heard before. It's not painful—at least not at first. But this changes the instant I touch the hardwood.

I land and immediately I flop to the ground in crippling pain. My knee feels like it has been blasted with a twelve-gauge shotgun, and I fall like a sack of rice to the floor.

The hurt is unimaginable. My entire brain is overwhelmed by an intense, blinding anguish. I thought I knew pain before when I was elbowed. Now I'm in agony. I'm on my back on the parquet. I don't even hear the ref blow his whistle; all I can think is that I'm dying. It's like a fire is sending spiraling waves from my kneecap out to my whole body.

Players huddle around me, stunned. They're unsure of what to do. Coach

Hanson slams down his clipboard and rushes across the floor. My team-mates stagger after him, forming a loose and worried circle around me.

"Billy!" Coach screams. He's inches away from my face, and I can barely hear him. "Billy! What happened?"

I shake my head. The pain is unbearable; I can no longer fight back the tears. Through the salty sting and the glare of the gym's overhead lights, I look into my coach's face. The world falls silent, and I can barely speak.

"Coach . . . did I make the shot?"

In the trainer's room Coach has to narrate what happened next because I can barely remember.

"Your mother ran down from the stands." I picture her in her tan dress and hat crouching next to me on the floor.

"Lefty and I, we had to help you up. You couldn't put any weight at all on your left leg. And then we brought you in here."

But Lefty isn't in here. Neither is my mother. It's just me, Coach Hanson, and the trainer. And the trainer's appraising me with the look of a man who's about to shoot a horse.

"I—" I begin. "I have to go back out there—"

Coach cuts me off. He tells me to stay here, that the team can finish the game without me. He puts a hand on my forehead, avoiding my cut, and tells me that I will be all right. Then he heads out, promising to be back in to get me as soon as the game is over, leaving the trainer to go to work on my knee.

The trainer probes my kneecap, and when he squeezes I felt the hurt of it pump through me like snake venom. "You comes down hard on it," the trainer says. He lays his hands on my knee again, and it's all I can do not to scream even at his gentle touch. "This isn't no sprain. You need to go to the hospital." He puts a bag of ice on my knee and begins to wrap it in gauze while I lie and wait.

There, in a concrete closet that smells of must and sweat, I sit shivering under the low-level buzz of flickering overhead tube lights. Every few seconds I hear from what seems like a distant world the cheers of the assembled crowd. I've never sat so far away from a game before, never just listened to it take place without playing in it or even watching. It's a very different experience. All along I keep hoping for my mother to come in. I keep looking at the open door, expecting to see her stomping in at any moment, followed by Daddy Lonnie close behind. I expect her to check in on me; I expect her to take my hand.

She never does. As the minutes tick by, I have no choice but to lie immobile inside as the world goes on without me.

After the game ends Coach Hanson returns followed by Lefty, who carries my street clothes. There's no way I can get off my uniform, though, not over the massive bandage job the trainer has done to keep my knee from swelling. So I ball my pants up in one hand and throw my arms around Coach and Lefty for support.

As I'm led outside, this small kindness dissolves before a maelstrom of questions that flood my mind. Every time my ankle grazes the floor, darts of agony shoot up the side of my leg. Am I out for the season? Am I out for good?

I hobble outside to find, at last, my mother. She stands in front of our car next to Daddy Lonnie. "Where were you?" I want to challenge her. I want to scream, "Why? Why did you pick this game to finally come, to finally care?" I want to blame this on them somehow, and I want Daddy Lonnie and my mother to confess. It's my mother's fault for drinking; it's Daddy Lonnie's fault for never giving a damn about me.

Of course I don't say a word of this. Instead I allow myself to be set into the backseat of the Ford, watching mutely as my city passes by while I'm spirited off to the hospital.

The drive is miserable. Now and again I try to flex my leg, only to find that I can't. What's worse, every bump is agony; I feel each little pothole and dip with the pain of a thousand fiery needles. These are the roads I grew up on; how did I never notice their pocks and ruts 'til now?

When we reach the emergency room I am dropped into a wheelchair by a pair of orderlies. I suffer this silently; if I don't cry out, then the pain can't be that bad, which means I'm fine. I'm not that injured! Of course I'm not!

Before she wheels me into an examination room, the head nurse passes me off to a grizzled X-ray technician who takes pictures of my knee. "Damn," he says, propping me up on the table. One thing I do not want to hear a hospital employee say while looking at me is "Damn." He aims a massive gun at my leg—"This'll let us see your bones," he says, and adds under his breath, "not that we can't see 'em already." After, the three of us—Daddy Lonnie, my mother, and I—sit around and wait for a doctor to show up.

We find ourselves shunted off into a small, concrete room, not that different from the trainer's vestibule at Venice High. The only difference is that in here it doesn't smell like sweat. Otherwise, it feels no less isolated, no less apart from the world.

After an eternity of us not speaking to one another, the doctor strolls in with my X-rays in his hand, whistling. "This," he pronounces, "is the worst knee injury I've ever seen." These are the first words he utters. Great.

"How bad is it?" I ask.

"Bad," he says. I can see his nostrils flare.

"How bad?"

The doctor looks up from the negatives. "Well, you can forget about ever playing basketball again."

As soon as I hear these words, I feel my brain start to dissolve. I have the feeling I'm floating away from my body and watching my own burial. I'm barely seventeen and my life as I know it is over.

The doctor—Dr. Mason, a name I've just learned and just learned to hate—lapses into medical jargon. It's "patella" this and "fibula" that; every word seems to be constructed to be one that I can't understand. Shame overtakes me, and I wonder: what's this guy's problem? This Dr. Mason's got no sympathy. All he's got are big, thick glasses and an oversized white lab coat. Why is he so eager to shoot me down?

I shift from denial to bargaining. He's a doctor; surely he can help me. "Isn't there something I can do?"

The doctor just laughs. His stethoscope dangles low around his neck and I want to strangle him with it.

"You've severely damaged your knee," he intones, and I wonder: who chuckles when giving a kid this kind of news? But when he puts the X-rays up on his light wall, there's no question I'm messed up. What I see of my kneecap looks like a wishbone ripped apart by a pair of tugging kids.

"Surgery is your only option," he says with finality, and then he sits down and lifts a clipboard from a side table, lighting a cigarette by my side.

"Surgery," Daddy Lonnie mutters. "How much is that gonna cost?"

"What's it going to do to him?" my mother spits over Daddy Lonnie, and the doctor exhales a puff of smoke. He looks at me.

"You're going to have to have an iron kneecap inserted. It will be heavy, and it won't flex well, but at least you'll be able to walk normally."

"An iron kneecap just to walk normally?" I mutter.

"Halfway normally."

"Halfway?"

The doctor nods. "You'll probably still have a limp."

"A limp?" my mom asks. "For how long?"

He takes a casual drag. "Forever!"

I can hear my heart beat in my ears. The blood courses so loudly through me I think that everyone staring at me can hear it.

"Okay, Doc," I say. "So—when can I start playing again after this surgery?"

The doctor shakes his head. "Son, you're not listening. You can forget about playing basketball again, okay? Ever."

He says this like he's not signing the death warrant of my dreams, as casually as if he's telling me to water his lawn. Would he be so dismissive, I wonder, if we were richer? If we were white?

While the doctor drones on and on about how I'll never regain full mobility, throwing around words like "flexion" and "incapacitation," I look to my guardians for support. But Mom is lost; she seems on the verge of tears and is taking this news really badly. Daddy Lonnie is even worse: he just sits there in silence. His lips are sealed together like the flaps of an envelope.

I'm big—listed at six feet nine, and in truth at least six feet seven—but inside I'm still just a boy. I'm scared and I'm in pain. Why, I wonder, doesn't

Daddy Lonnie help me? If he's my Daddy Lonnie, where's that daddy part now? Why doesn't he stick up for me?

My real dad would have stood up for me, damn it! Why did this happen to me? Why isn't anyone protecting me? Why doesn't even the doctor care?

And that's when I snap. "No!"

Everyone in the room—Daddy Lonnie, my mother, and especially the doctor—freezes, shocked by the shout echoing from my lips.

"No?"

"You're wrong," I say. I'd pop out of my seat if I could. "All of you. I'm playing ball again. And if the surgery will keep me from basketball, I don't need it. I won't do it."

For a long time the room sits in squashed silence, compressed by the weight of my words. It's eerie, and in those moments my determination breaks. If the doctor were to tell me right now to shut up and mind my place, I would. I'd do the surgery, and that would be the end of it. The end of me.

But that doesn't happen.

"All right," he says, stubbing out his cigarette, and I see a flash of something in his eyes. Is it hate? I don't know. I can see that he's never been challenged before, and certainly not by an overgrown black boy. "If that's what you want, that's what we'll go ahead and do. No surgery. Nurse!"

The doctor pulls open the door, and a petite woman in white pops in.

"Get this boy prepped for a full-leg cast," he says, never for a moment taking his eyes off me.

"Yes, Doctor," she replies, and bows backward out of the room. He follows and slaps the door closed behind him.

No one says anything. My mom is too stunned to move. The echo of the door still rings in our ears, but the three of us remain frozen in tableau, silent and alone.

Sitting there wordlessly between my mother and Daddy Lonnie, I realize I've just told off the man in charge of my care.

Sitting there wordlessly between my mother and Daddy Lonnie, I wonder: have I just made a terrible mistake?

Road to Recovery

The first few days of lying around the house are the worst. It takes all the willpower I have to not to crack and break down over what has befallen me.

With a cast on my left leg from the top of my thigh all the way to my ankle, the urge to scratch exists 24/7. Worse than the itch, though, is the fact that without me the Green and Gold founder. With me out of the lineup our offense falls apart, and we lose in the quarterfinals of the city championship to the rich kids from Hollywood High. It's a huge blow.

Brad Pye Jr. writes a piece for the *Sentinel* saying that I'm out with just a minor injury, in a cast that'll be off in three weeks. Yeah, right. Little does he know. If Coach Hanson didn't tell him, he won't tell anyone, and if Coach won't, I won't either. I ball it up inside me. Nobody else needs to know that I may be out of the game forever.

The one nice thing is learning that, though I'm sidelined, I'm at least not forgotten. Despite missing most of the tournament, I'm again named to the All-Southern League and All-City first teams. The accolades don't stop there: I am also voted the LA High School Player of the Year, which, in a city of two million, feels pretty damn good. Additionally, I'm awarded a spot on the national All-American Second Team and I get my photo in *Parade Magazine*.

Still, it takes me a week of leg pain and feeling sorry for myself before I pull my ass off the couch and return to high school. It doesn't hustle my return to know that Daddy Lonnie won't so much as give me a ride in the mornings. Hell, shattered knee and all, he won't even let my mom give me extra change for bus fare. Every morning I hobble to school with my books.

Finally, six weeks after the injury Daddy Lonnie piles my mom and me back into the car to return to the hospital to have the cast removed. It's a day I've both looked forward to and dreaded all along. My only hope— other than that my knee will be perfectly healed—is that the same evil sawbones of a doctor won't be there to take the cast off.

Of course he is.

Dr. Mason sneers at me as I reenter his examination room. He sends my mother and Daddy Lonnie out and, without so much as a word asking how I'm feeling, begins to chop away at my bandages with a frighteningly loud electric saw. As he cuts through the cast, he a few times presses a touch too far, making surface cuts and scrapes upon my skin out of carelessness. I want to slug him. Finally the cast falls away. For the first time in weeks I am able to see my leg.

It's terrible. My first thought is: whose leg is that? My legs are long, strong, rippled and supple. This is a limp, misshapen tube. It's all gray and withered and still looks like it's been split in two, like a peanut butter cup left out in the rain.

"Told you," says the doctor, shaking his head. "That's never going to heal." Then he calls in my parents.

I lower my head again to stare at the mangled mess protruding from my torso. With my mother and Daddy Lonnie present, the doctor again tries to convince me that I ought to get an iron kneecap inserted. "You'll need it," he declares, "if you even hope to walk halfway normal again." I try to remind him of my goal to return to basketball, after which he turns his back on me, as though I'm too stubborn to even be worth talking to.

When no one's looking I try to put a little weight my left leg, and it's impossible. But there's no way I'm gonna let them throw a locking iron kneecap in me.

As I'm wheeled out of the hospital, the doctor waves me off with the back of his hand. "If you wanna try to play basketball, it's up to you," he says. "But you're just going to get hurt again, probably even worse." He doesn't even finish tending to me, leaving a young nurse to wrap my knee with a long elastic bandage before shooing us away.

He is wrong, I tell myself. My will is strong. He's mistaken; I'll not only be able to walk, I'll recover, return to the court, and play again. I'm sure he's wrong; I'm sure I can.

But what if he's right?

Road to Recovery 2

Even with the cast off I can't quite walk. So for the next three months I crutch around everywhere. I crutch my way back and forth to school. I crutch my way to math class, a pencil stuffed behind my ear. I crutch my way to the first-floor bathroom when I have to take a whiz at Jefferson, and when the bell rings I crutch back home again.

For the first time in my life I look forward to my final exams.

When at last summer begins, I don't have to crutch around anymore. But losing the regularity of school to bring order to my days, I fall into a spiral of self-pity and regret. Day after day I glue myself to the couch, losing myself in a funk that could easily knock me down for good. But Lefty—good friend that he is—eventually comes to my house and kicks my ass straight.

And where does he take me? Right back to school. In the heat of the LA summer, he brings me out to roast under the sun on Jefferson's black cinder track.

"What are we doing here?" I lean heavily on my crutches.

"Starting your rehabilitation session," Lefty says. "You wanna play again or not?"

A bird flies overhead and dives into the shade of a nearby copse of trees. It's so hot out that already a bead of sweat runs down my brow and into my right eye. I nearly lose my balance and fall over wiping it away.

"Of course I do, but—"

"But nothing. You wanna get better, you gotta work. Now get going around this track."

I frown at him. "Lefty, I'm on crutches."

He crosses his arms. He points to the oval. "So crutch."

To think: just a few months earlier hundreds of people paid to sit near me and scream my name. And now this is me.

I open my mouth to try to reason with Lefty, to try to convince him of the utter ridiculousness and futility of his idea—but then I don't. I look around. My father's not here. Daddy Lonnie's not here. My damn doctor's not here. Right now Lefty is the only friend I've got. And if I want to keep him in my corner—if I ever want to get better—I better get moving.

So I do.

Flailing around the track, I quickly heat up, half out of response to the weather and half out of anger and frustration. Having spurned entreaties to join the track team all year long, how ironic that I'm here huffing around the oval in a hundred thousand degree heat, a penguin in a gray sweat suit waddling around on crutches stuffed under each arm. With the sticky smell of fresh-mown grass stuffing my nostrils, I drag myself around the pebbled track, wincing all the while as I pull my gimpy leg along behind its healthy twin. Almost immediately I want to quit. I want to give up. But I can't. I have to finish.

When I finally return to the starting line, covered in sweat and cowering in pain, I'm beaming. I've done it. "Done!" I exult.

Left claps me on the back. "Good." He smiles. "Now do it again."

He's serious. My best friend stares at me with his arms folded across his chest until I again begin to try to drag myself around the track. When I finish he demands another. Then another. He makes me loop the quarter mile again and again, and only after I'm coated in a film of body grease that would make Wilt Chamberlain blush does Lefty finally call it off.

"Okay," he says. "You can stop." Then he adds, "I'll see you tomorrow."
The next day it's even hotter.

I develop blisters on my palms and in my armpits, and both my ankles swell as they fill with fluid. But Lefty won't let me quit. Every day he pushes me to walk the oval more and more, until at last he sees determination take root within me on its own.

And that's when he drops the bomb. "Okay," he says. "Now it's up to you."

I frown.

"I can't be out here every day," he says. "You have to keep on working on your own."

I almost don't. The next day, when I'm all on my own, I take one look at the couch and almost plant myself back on it. But I don't. I wake up, eat a bowl of cereal, pull on sweatpants, and hobble to Jefferson. Wriggling and ducking, I squirm through the hole cut in the school's chain-link fence, then stomp around that track until I damn near drop from the heat. I start a routine, and I do it each day. No one asks where I go.

Time passes. June becomes July, and July bleeds into August. For sixty-something straight days I hobble around that track, and something unexpected happens: I become stronger, inside and out. My gimpy leg grows more stable, and my resolution toughens. It's a struggle, fighting through the intense pain, but I do it. I have to.

Come the first day of senior year, I stroll through the doors like I own the place. On my own two feet, to boot.

As I walk in heads turn. Save Lefty, nobody has seen me all summer long. I've been in isolation, leaving my house only to pull my leg around the school's track like a convict dragging a ball and chain. So when I return to Jefferson at the beginning of senior year, it's with purpose, confidence, and poise. I walk on no crutches and I have no limp. I feel strong; my withered leg has blossomed. I am tough. I am ready.

I am going to be the center again. I am going to play basketball.

"There's Billy!" I hear people gasp. "There's the Hill!" and the faintest trace of a smirk teases the edges of my cheeks.

For a month I strut through campus like Alexander conquering Rome. Young brothers and teachers alike welcome me back to Jefferson. Girls, too, slip me notes and looks, and it's nice to feel the eyes of the cheerleaders, fresh from the summer, on me once again. But though a carefree smile remains plastered to my face, inside I'm focused intently on magnetic north: the first day of basketball practice.

My teammates—the ones who haven't graduated, the ones who had been there last season—look at me in awe. Until now none of them knew if I'd return. And nobody but Lefty knows how hard I've worked all off-season long, pushing myself to the limit to prepare for this moment. Glad as they might be to see me, though, it's when Coach arrives—when he steps onto the hardwood the moment 3:10 rolls around and blows his whistle—that I really feel like I'm back. Despite himself and his stone-faced nature, Coach Hanson can't help but look me dead in the eye and smile.

And then he jams his whistle in his mouth.

That first practice I don't even think about my knee. I push out my fears right at the outset because within the first few minutes we've fallen into our same old routine like the previous season never ended.

"On the line! Suicides! Last place does it again."

Senior season opens, and it's just like old times. Teams come in, get beat, and go home; we roll all over everybody. Quickly Jefferson shoots back to the top of the conference standings, and I become used to the roar of the home crowd as fans pack the stands for our matchups once more. We mop the floor with all of our league rivals: Washington High, Manual Arts, dreaded Fremont—nobody even comes close. As for my knee, it gives me not a lick of trouble. I do wear kneepads, but otherwise that's it—I'm an unencumbered scoring machine once more.

We get wins, and fans and teachers pile on the love; Lefty talks his game and girls line up for double dates. Though there's pain after every time I play—pain that's matched by swelling in my knee that I have to attack before going to bed each night—I push it out of my mind. I am back in the papers and back on top, and it seems like nothing can bring me down.

I should see that it's the calm before the storm, but I can't; I'm too high up to even take in the view.

And that's when it happens.

It's during a scrimmage about halfway through the season. We're playing a mock game, five-on-five with the first string against the second, when I go up for a rebound and feel something give.

In a second I'm down on the ground and clutching my knee—a repeat, full-on, of last year. Pain and fear swell through me—is this it? Is this the one?—and even with my slick forehead pressed low against the waxed floor, this time I hear the sharp blast of the whistle reverberate through the air.

"Practice is over," Coach Hanson says, but the other Demos players stand stock-still, as if unable to move. "Hit the showers!" Coach barks, and all but Lefty hustle off. The ball rolls toward the padded wall, unwanted fruit falling off the apple cart.

Coach rolls me onto my back. "Can you walk?" Lefty's eyes sear into mine.

"I felt something pop," I say. "I don't know."

Gingerly they lift me to my feet.

I attempt a careful step, expecting to instantly collapse to the floor. But the stumble never comes. I take another tentative stride, then another. "It hurts," I say. "But I think I'm okay."

"There's pain?" Coach asks, his fingers probing under the simple covers I wear over my kneecaps—they're green and gold, to match the school colors.

"A little. Not much more than normal."

He frowns. "Your knee's been hurting all along?"

With reservations I admit to this. But though I do, I still don't tell him about the fluid that's been massing in my knee after practices at night; I don't tell him about the hour I spend each morning and night massaging and pressing all the swelling out of the area around my left patellar tendon. If he knows what's happening he may kick me off the team. And that can't happen. So I just nod.

"Some," I bluff. Coach excuses himself.

As I join the other guys in the shower room, the terror that had briefly shown its sinewy face abates. We joke and laugh, and though I am still scared—have I done it? Have I finally torn my kneecap apart as the doctor presaged?—the soap and water wash away much of my concern along with the dirt and the sweat. I even manage to walk home under my own volition, and I don't think about my knee again. It was just a scare, I think. Everything's okay, I decide.

That is, until I wake up in the morning and find that my knee has swelled up to the size of a small gourd.

When 3:00 rolls around I book it to the gym like always. When I get there, though, Coach is waiting for me, and he never, ever arrives before practice begins. As I run toward the door to the locker room, he stops me, and in his hand he dangles a brown leather strap with two iron rods protruding from each side.

"What's that?"

He thrusts the contraption out at me at arm's length. It looks like a restraint for a mental patient. "It's a knee brace."

"But I'm—"

"You're wearing it, is what you're doing."

Something tells me this is not the time to argue. I take it from him and after dressing slip it on my leg. Immediately I hate it. Coach's knee brace is leather and heavy, with two huge bars running up the side to force the kneecap in place and a shoelace string running up the back to tighten it. The rods make me think of my near brush with an iron fate in the doctor's office, or an ancient torture device, and the heavy leather begins chafing me the moment I put it on.

I go to Coach to protest. "I'm not sure I'll be able to move around with this thing on me," I tell him.

"And I'm not sure I'll be able to have you on the court without it," he says. "Now put it on or go home. You've got"—he checks the clock—"two minutes until practice begins to decide."

I have no choice. It's this or nothing. I jam the top of the metal side of the brace down so it won't scrape against me, and then I get ready to play.

Though I hate the brace, it does help, I suppose—it keeps me from hurting myself again at least. What it can't do, however, is prevent those thick pools of fluid from amassing in my kneecap every time I play. Whatever I do after that reinjury—a game, sprints, tennis, cross-training—it doesn't matter. Whenever I put myself through any form of physical exertion, my knee swells like a parade float. So I get into a rhythm. Every night before I go to sleep and every morning before I lift my body out of bed, I massage my knee. But now, after forcing all the fluid away with my big hands like I'd been doing before, I wrap an Ace bandage so tight around the joint that there's no space for the fluid to come back. Whether that's the right thing to do or not, I don't know. Nobody tells me, and I don't ask. Winning is all I care about.

Running Coach Hanson's offense, we tear through the Southern League. Jefferson wins its fourth straight regular-season title, and for the fourth year in a row the Green and Gold earn the top seed into the city championship tournament. It's a feat I'm damn proud of. Not to tell any tales, but it's a feat our student body seems to appreciate, too.

Walking into the tournament, Lefty and I know that this is our last chance for a victory, and this time we cannot blink. Doing extra practice and playing one-on-one the week before the tournament, we agree that we'll accept nothing less than the gold. Our first opponent is South Gate, and though we've got destiny on our side, we're swamped with nervous tension. Still, they're the second seed from the weak Eastern League, and they go down without a fight. In the quarters we have Westchester High, and they're no tougher. Like sharks circling chum, Lefty and I smell blood in the water.

With each win we gain still more confidence. This year there will be no errors. No one can match our hustle and desire. In the semis we square off against Manual Arts, a technical school that's in our division. Though we won the Southern League the year before, they won the city championship tournament, and they come in seeming to think they can handle us.

They can't.

Lefty and I take down Man A like we used to take down rich kids at Carver, and going into the finals, we know we can't lose.

The game is not even close. We trounce Hollywood High, the team that knocked us out last year in quarterfinals after I'd been sidelined, by the lopsided score of 69–50.

For the second time in my four-year career, Jefferson High has claimed the Los Angeles city crown. And for the second straight year, I'm named LA's top prep basketball player, an award even sweeter because I share it with the best friend I've ever had: Lefty Thomas. Brad Pye Jr.'s end-of-season story for the *Sentinel* highlights the two of us together.

Victory

Winning the title and going out on a high note my senior year at Jefferson is outstanding. In addition to sharing Player of the Year honors, Lefty and I are named to the LA All-City first team with Chris Appel, Vern Ashby, and Bob Benedetti. The tough question is: where are we going to go from here?

Despite our successes and awards, Lefty and I find ourselves at a troubling crossroads in the spring of our senior year. We live in the heart of Los Angeles and want to stay at home, but nearby USC has never had a black starter on its basketball team, and both Lefty and I get left out in the cold. In fact, despite the award, not a single major LA college comes knocking at our doors. I even get named to the first-string All-American high school team, but still, none of the local programs—USC, Loyola, UCLA, LA State, or Pepperdine—show either of us any love. What are we going to do next?

Lefty decides to go to school and keep playing ball at a nearby two-year school called Harbor Junior College. But as for me, I have no idea. It's not like I'm forgotten altogether. Every day I receive recruiting letters from across the nation, even from East Coast powerhouses like St. John's and

Temple! But they seem so far away, too far to be real. Why can't I stay here with my mother? Why can't I stay with my family?

I do visit the East Coast, but not for recruiting. Part and parcel of being named an All-American is an invitation to appear on the *Steve Allen Show*, taped and broadcast from Rockefeller Center in New York City. Coach Hanson and I fly there together, and as we soar over the country, I decide that just as there's no way I'm going east, there's no way I'm going to a junior college, either. I was a poor kid who grew up on a dirt farm in Texas; the last and only time I've ever traveled across the country it was on the back of a bus. But look at me now: I'm lounging in a Western Airlines seat next to a window with a curtain, and air hostesses with bouffant hairdos are serving me orange juice. Playing at a four-year school is my next step in the path to playing in the NBA. Do I really want to step back?

The moment we step off the plane and onto the tarmac in New York, we're immediately whisked away to a monolith of a hotel in the shadow of Park Avenue. Though the digs are grand, the show is a bust; Steve Allen is really only interested in the collegiate All-Americans. We teenagers are just the window dressing. Even Jerry Lucas, the famed superstar high schooler from Ohio, gets little more than a passing glance from Allen. Of course, I can't blame Steve Allen. Among the college awardees are Elgin Baylor, Oscar Robertson, and miracle of miracles, my friend from Denker Playground in the flesh: Wilt "the Stilt" Chamberlain.

I try not to stare at Wilt. Actually, the one time I lock eyes with him I think he's glaring at me. So instead I focus on Lucas. I'm six feet nine, but he still looks like a big boy to me. Word is he can take over a game all by himself, and I'm itching to get him onto the court for some one-on-one to find out myself. Too bad that's not on the schedule.

We're in New York three nights, and on the first I'm so tired I go to bed without eating dinner at all. The second, the night right after the taping, Coach and I go out to dinner at famous Mama Leone's. Coach Hanson tells me that he's bringing someone along, and who should end up sitting with us at our table but Jerry Lucas. Without a word our whole dinner becomes a competition—we even race each other to finish our meals.

On my last night in the city, Coach Hanson offers to give me some time to myself, and I find myself roaming the halls of the hotel without a plan when I hear a ruckus. I turn a corner, and there I find Baylor, Robertson, and Wilt all running around like the Three Stooges, trying to hit one another with whipped cream pies. Elgin Baylor looks up, sees me, and gets nailed in the side of the face by Oscar Robertson. That leads to a minor wrestling match, which results in the walls and the carpet covered in cream; Wilt barely jumps out of their way and bumps smack into me.

"Oh," he says. "Look who it is. High school phenom." I can't tell if he's upset at me still or playing with me or what, but next thing I know these guys are inviting me to dinner.

"Sure," I say. "But don't you have to tell your coaches first?"

They just laugh. Stupid kid.

On our way back from eating we pass a hotel with a flag hanging off a pole along its side. The base of the pole's raised about twelve feet off the sidewalk. Robertson, I think, catches me staring, and he dares me to jump up and touch it.

"No way," I said.

"Why not?" he goads.

"Too high," I say, figuring he's just trying to make me look dumb. "No one can touch that." For a moment we stand there, mutely looking up.

"I can do it," intones Wilt.

"No way," says Elgin.

"Yeah I can," Wilt retorts. "I can touch it."

"Bet?" asks Oscar.

"Bet," Wilt says, and before anyone can even come up with terms, Wilt springs off the asphalt and slaps that brass flagpole with inches to spare, hitting it full on through the middle knuckles of his outstretched fingers.

Oscar and Elgin clap and chatter on about his impressive ups, but I walk on silently, in awe. A lone thought plays on a loop through my mind.

If Wilt can get up that high, what does it mean for me that even he couldn't block my jump hook?

Good-bye, LA

I return from New York to find an answer to my recruiting question, although not one I was expecting.

Coach calls me into his office. "Billy," he says, "I've got something serious I want to talk to you about."

At first I have no idea what Coach wants with me. I laugh. "What is it, Coach? Am I failing PE?"

He shakes his head. "No, but you're close. It's grades that's the issue." He then sits me down and proceeds to tell me that I may not be academically eligible to play D-I college ball.

This is a blow and a wakeup call, words almost as gut shaking as the doctor's prognosis for my knee. D-I hoops is the path to the pros; everyone knows that. Is this why I've not been getting any local offers? And what am I going to do if I can't play college ball?

Coach Hanson says, "Go get your grades up at a two-year school and prove that you can handle the academics. Then when you're a junior you can transfer up and play in the big time."

I shake my head. I'm one of the top basketball prospects in the nation, with a hundred-some recruiting letters waiting for me on my mom's coffee table and more coming in by the day. I'm not going to community college. Is something stupid like my grades in math really going to keep me from getting a shot? There has to be another option, right?

I can't run from this problem like I did from the greasers at the Lincoln. But I do find a solution that isn't far off: I can transfer. Turns out, if I transfer to a different school and finish high school there, my transcript doesn't have to follow me when I go to college. I can close out my last quarter of senior year somewhere else and if I make good grades go straight to school.

The plan sounds good—certainly preferable to actually paying for my sins in academics—but of course there's one small problem: I don't have anywhere to go. Talent or no, it's not like Mom and Daddy Lonnie are going to up and move somewhere else just so I can get a fresh start to finish high school, and my grandparents don't exactly live nearby. Through the mist, though, another unexpected option emerges: I can go to San Francisco.

Unlike all of the local colleges, Cal-Berkeley is keenly interested in me. They've hotly recruited me from the get-go, and though they put strong emphasis on academics, they're not above helping me pull something unusual, but above board, if it will help be become a Golden Bear. They're willing to arrange just about anything if it means that I'll play ball, and if it'll help me play ball, I'm willing to do it. So with one quarter remaining in my senior year, I pack up my things and move in with a host family of Cal-Berkeley alums in the Bay Area, enrolling myself in San Francisco's Polytechnic High.

Coming from LA, I expect San Francisco to be a bit of a shock. I don't know anybody, and I wonder what I'm going to do to get by. Turns out I needn't have worried—somehow everyone knows me when I arrive. I think word has gotten around that I've transferred up to Polytechnic to play basketball, and though that rumor's not true, I'm not gonna dispel it. "Hey, the Hill!" people call to me in the halls, and though I don't know a one of them from Adam, I slap 'em high five and move along.

All the same, it's a very different experience for me. The school is small, for one, and actually mixed—the neighborhood hadn't been redlined like Los Angeles was; people in San Francisco talk about racial equality and brotherhood and seem to mean it. For another, my host family actually seems to take some interest in my day-to-day life. Finally, the Bay Area has something that Jefferson never offered me: a mentor and a role model, Earl Robinson.

Earl Robinson, the Earl of Berkeley, is a star player in both basketball and baseball at Cal. He's athletic and lithe, quick and built like a whippet, and black people all over the city seem to know and love him. We meet— he seeks me out once I transfer—and immediately he takes me to Cal's enormous gym to work out. While playing one-on-one with me, he starts selling me on the school.

"Come here. Good education, good sports. Look at me; I play ball for Coach Newell and he lets me play baseball, too."

"Seriously?" Dribbling, I think about what Coach Hanson would have said if any of us had left the team to play tennis or run track.

"Yup. In fact, I just got drafted by the Dodgers," he says. "Starting this summer I'm going pro in baseball."

At that moment I drive to the basket, plowing over and past him as I go up, lift off, and stuff the basketball through the hoop. I land and offer him a hand to pull him up off the hardwood.

"That's good," I say, "because your basketball game could use some work."

As Earl gets up I hear the creak of a stadium chair being moved behind me. I turn to follow the sound, and there I see Pete Newell, coach of the Cal-Berkeley Golden Bears, watching.

Coach Newell is dressed in belted khaki slacks and a polo shirt, and his hair is combed flat and close cropped. He looks older than Coach Hanson but athletic, and the lines by his eyes show a kindly wrinkle. As Newell descends the stadium aisle and makes his way toward the court, he raises his arm and stretches out his hand to me.

"Billy McGill," he says. "Pete Newell. Nice to meet you. Have you put any thought into staying up here and playing for us?"

As the weeks wear on Earl and I become close, and when I'm not hard at work hitting the books—got to get my grades up, the Webbs, my host parents, remind me—Earl and the Webbs' son, Talbert, take me out to hit the town. The Bay Area, Oakland especially, buzzes with a vibrant black nightlife that puts even Central Avenue to shame.

Among other things Oakland is a hotbed for live music, and at the California Hotel we watch mambo legend Cal Tjader play his vibraphone and see Latin greats like Tito Puente, too. I didn't bring my conga drum up from LA with me, but I nonetheless get to be known at some of the mambo clubs in the area. Not for my playing, of course, but for my dancing—when you're six feet nine it's hard not to stick out. In fact, the only time I don't stick out is when I run into Big Jim Hadnot. Hadnot is six feet ten, a high schooler and a basketball player like me, though more of the Bill Russell–style defensive mold than a pure shooter like me. He even goes to Russell's alma matter, nearby McClymonds High. When the two of us brush up past one another on the dance floor, the crowd always parts for us—how can regular folks not part the way when two titans take to the floor?

If only opponents stepped aside so readily.

After three months I finish at Poly with a B average and return to LA. My grades are now good enough to go straight to a real four-year college, but where I have no idea. My mother's no help, and Daddy Lonnie's not either; all they can say is, "Take one of those scholarships and go somewhere." I liked Cal but I didn't love it, and I don't know what to do. Stopping for gas in Santa Maria on my way back to LA, I chance into John Rudometkin. He's a Southern California guy and a stud ballplayer at that, so I ask him for his advice.

"You think about staying local?" he asks. "I'm going to USC." That's when I'm forced to admit that for whatever reason, I didn't garner any interest from the LA schools.

"Hmm," he says. "I wonder why that is. You think they think you're trouble?" He smiles, then he peeks over my shoulder. "Say, where'd you get that ride?"

The car I'm driving is a '49 Mercury with a grille as wide as an oven door. It doesn't exactly belong to me—in fact, I got it in exchange for agreeing to play with an AAU team, though suddenly I don't feel like telling him how I got it. "It's just a loaner," I say. And then I drive back home.

As July turns to August and time begins to grow short, I still have no idea what I'm going to do with myself. Newspaper writers, even Brad Pye Jr., begin to ask awkward questions about why I went up to San Francisco to finish high school and where I'm going to matriculate, and I have no choice but to tell them the real, if partial, truth: I don't know. I'm no closer to knowing my future, in fact, than I was before I left for Poly. I feel entirely lost at sea—and that's when fate sweeps me to a lighthouse keeper in the storm: a six-foot-something LA sharpshooter by the name of Rich Ruffel.

13

"No Coloreds"

Though I don't know exactly what proselytizing is, I suppose Rich Ruffel is doing it. From the moment I meet him he's telling me about Utah and the "U." The guy grew up just down the coast from me, and yet he knows more about Salt Lake City than I know about all of the subjects I've ever studied in school. Hell, within a few hours of talking to him I know so much about the men's dormitories that I can describe them myself. I know about the pines and firs on campus that surround Baliff Hall, and I know about the academic buildings that sit in direct sight of the majestic, stiff promontories of the Wasatch Range. A hundred letters from across the country, and suddenly I'm swayed by a chatty ballplayer who can't stop talking about the Golden Gabriel on top of the Tabernacle.

I tell him I'm interested, and Rich makes the arrangements. Within a week my mother and I are flown to Salt Lake City. But as we settle into the plane on the way to our recruiting visit, she freaks out.

"What's wrong?"

"Bilbo, I don't feel too good."

My mom is nervous about flying. She's never done this before, she tells me.

"Mom," I say, "relax. It's 1958. These things are way modern now."

When we touch down in Salt Lake City, the freshman coach, Ladell Andersen, meets us at the airport. He doesn't try to sell me on the school or blow smoke; instead he drives us straight to the campus. I like him—and it—right from the start.

The campus is both overwhelming and beautiful; it's like Rich Ruffel described but more so. Sprawling trees claim dominion over the grass, and the Wasatch Mountains nestle up against campus like lords of nature. Nothing I have ever seen on the concrete streets of LA have prepared me for this. It's breathtaking.

Ladell takes my mom and me into the Einar Nielsen Fieldhouse, the massive indoor gym where the Utes play basketball.

While I'm marveling at the arena, a smiling, jocular man in a red pullover sweater walks toward us. "Hello, Billy." He shakes my hand. "Coach Jack Gardner. Nice to meet you."

Over the next few hours Coach passionately describes to us the university and the four-year scholarship I will receive, which piques my mother's interest.

"He's guaranteed to get to go to college for four years—for free?"

Deferentially Coach nods, and instantly I can see she's impressed. This is a sharecropper's daughter, a woman who never got anything free in her whole life. I can see the U grow quickly in her estimation.

"But there's more," Coach says to me. "You won't just play. You'll play the style you're used to." He goes on to describe how the basketball team at Utah runs an up-tempo offense similar to the one I've grown accustomed to at Jefferson.

"They don't call us the Runnin' Red Skins for nothing," he says, and as he continues something blossoms in me. I don't know if it's the prospect of playing ball in that big gym, the campus and the pines, or Coach's odd blend of authority and kindness, but whatever it is I have this sudden feeling that the University of Utah is the place for me. I was born to be a Ute, I think.

And then I blurt it out. "I was born to be a Ute!"

Everyone stops talking. Coach Gardner—Hall of Fame coach Jack Gardner—smiles. Ladell Andersen laughs. My mother even smiles—no, she *beams*. That settles it. There is nothing left to discuss. I'm going.

The plane ride back to Los Angeles flies by, literally. I stare out the window into the clouds, my mind racing, thinking of the sincere way Coach Gardner talked to my mother and me and the clear air of Utah. I also replay in my head the videos of the Utah team Coach Gardner played for us in his home. I smile. Seeing myself dressed in Utah red before a crowd like that is a beautiful, captivating vision. So captivating, in fact, that I don't even notice myself unconsciously kneading my left knee as the plane lowers itself to the tarmac.

Rich Ruffel calls me about two weeks before the beginning of fall semester freshman year. "Billy? It's Rich. Pack your stuff."

"Now?"

"Coach wants you to report early to get situated. You're leaving in a few days. Someone'll come to get you."

He hangs up. Three days later a hulking giant drives a hatchback up to my front door and hops out. "Hi," he says, "Dave Costa. I'm a guard on the Utah football team." I thought I was big; he's enormous. He's like a refrigerator with arms. He pumps my fist furiously. "Nice to meet you! You ready? Let's go."

I learn a lot about Dave Costa over the course of our twelve-hour drive to Utah, first and foremost that he's manic—with the exception of breaks to refill the gas tank and pee, we don't stop once between LA and Salt Lake City. En route we pass Las Vegas, and from the road I can see enormous dice leaping off a billboard advertising the Sands. I've never seen such a thing before, and like a dog my mouth starts to water. It's been years since the Carver Junior High bathroom, but the old feeling comes back, and I wonder: could I maybe earn my semester's worth of pocket money before even getting to school? Indeed, maybe I could, but I don't; when I make the suggestion, Dave shakes his head. "Later," he says, and I'm too timid to argue. Instead, we drive on into the night.

When we do arrive at the U, I yank my suitcase—singular—out of the back of Dave's car and let him lead me to my dorm room.

"You'll have a roommate," Dave says. "Jim Thomas. He's not here yet; you'll meet him. He's older."

I'm already old for my grade; I'm a freshman who'll be nineteen before the basketball season begins. "Older?" I ask. "How much older could he be?"

Straight-faced, Dave answers me. "Twenty-seven."

The next morning I wake up hungry and alone and with no idea what to do about it. Luckily Dave comes for me and takes me downtown for breakfast.

I spend the whole drive staring out the window. Salt Lake City is just as gorgeous as I remember it. This time, though, I pay more attention, and I notice an odd fact about this place, something that makes it very different from my hometown: I'm the only brother around as far as I can see.

"Dave?" I ask.

"Yeah?"

"Are there any black people in Salt Lake City?"

He glances over at me with this odd slant in his eye, then he looks back to the road ahead. "Yeah," he says, "there are. But they mostly live around 2nd Street South."

"Where's that?"

Dave pauses before he answers. "On the other side of the tracks."

"Oh."

After a few more minutes of cruising around, we spot a diner ahead. Dave pulls into the parking lot, and we walk in. Stepping through the door, I notice that it's almost empty. There's a waitress behind a counter with a coffeepot in her hand. She's got a farm girl look: healthy, pretty, blond. Behind her, leaning through the cutout pass between the dining room and the kitchen, is a white-shirted line cook with a paper hat. In front of him sit some white-haired old-timers humping vinyl stools in clumps of twos and threes.

It takes me a minute to realize that every one of these people is staring at me.

Dave doesn't notice; he just strolls into the middle of the dining room and seats himself. I follow, making like I don't notice everyone's eyes on me. The waitress's gaze flicks over to the regulars at the counter, and then she makes her way over to our table. The cook has not left the pass; he's still staring at us out the box hole.

"Can I help you?" the waitress says, only she doesn't say it like a person who means it—she says it like she's feeling both aggressive and confused, like something here has gone very, very wrong.

Dave again doesn't notice, and he orders an impossible amount of food, way more than any normal human should consider eating in one sitting: waffles, pancakes, eggs scrambled and fried, a ham steak, and a large malted milk. I guess I shouldn't be surprised; the man is wide as a picture window. I just order bacon and eggs and a glass of orange juice, and as the waitress walks away Dave gets to talking about the football team and how great they're going to be this year.

Ten or fifteen minutes later the food comes. Or at least Dave's food comes. He gets his pancakes, his waffles, his eggs, and his steak, plus a bowl of oatmeal he'd forgotten at first but called the waitress back over to order. My food, however, is not there.

I ask the waitress. "Is there a problem with my order?"

"No," she sneers. "No problem."

The waitress stomps away, and I've got an off feeling. "Gonna go wash my hands," I say, and Dave just nods, hardly looking up at all from his meal.

I make my way to the rear of the restaurant. As I approach the restroom I see a sign on the door that, for an instant, takes me back to a cramped waiting room in a frightening hospital with a devil-faced, angry old sawbones. Now I know what's holding up my order. The sign has two words: "No coloreds."

Just like that it all makes sense. I push past the hateful words and step inside—if I gotta pee, I'm gonna pee, no matter where I am—biting my lip as I wash my hands. I'll have to find somewhere else to get breakfast; that much is clear.

When I walk back to the table, though, to my surprise, my food is there. Dave hardly looks up.

"She wasn't gonna serve you," he says between mouthfuls. "But then I told her who you were." He smiles. "New starting center for the Runnin' Redskins basketball team! Here to win us a title. She said they'd make an exception for you." And then, without missing a beat, he gets back to talking about the Utah football team and their all-star quarterback, Lee Grosscup.

I look down at my fried eggs. "Wow," I think. That's all I can think. They'll make an exception for me.

Wow.

Passing

School begins, and for a while I fear it will be more of what I found in the restaurant. Walking to class one morning I cross paths with a lady holding hands with a very young child. In the middle of the sidewalk the kid stops and points at me. "Mommy, Mommy," she cries. "Look! He's so black!"

Thanks, kid, I think to myself. Thanks for pointing that out.

There aren't many black people around the U—in fact, I've only seen one black co-ed on this whole campus, and we almost avoid each other in hopes of not drawing attention to ourselves. Even my late-arriving roommate, Jim Thomas, works hard to "pass": turns out his father is black. But Jim has creamy, light skin so everyone assumes he's white. He does little—nothing, in fact—to dissuade them of that notion. Keep your mouth shut and don't volunteer for anything, that's his M.O. It's something he learned in the service. That's why he's older than everyone else: he's on the GI Bill. He keeps quiet about the black half of his heritage, because he knows the trouble it could bring. But I don't. No one told me of the sad and unfortunate racism that permeates the culture of beautiful Utah. Nobody told me how Mormon scripture specifically states that black people are descendants of evil, and that black men aren't even allowed to become full members in the lay priesthood of the Mormon Church. But Jim knows. And Jim knows how important the faith is here in Salt Lake, and that's why he makes it a point to pass. But with my skin there's no way I can do that. All I can do is keep my head down and wait for freshman practices to begin.

The Needle

I'd expected to enter the U like a Caesar. Clearly, that was not the case. I thought I'd be a BMOC from the moment I arrived, like at Polytech. But there were still greater hurdles than the subject of race. I didn't know it but it turns out that freshmen aren't allowed to play on the varsity team; there's a separate squad for first-years. And scholarship or no, I have to earn my spot on even that.

Coach Gardner doesn't come to freshman practices. Ladell Andersen runs them on his own, and Ladell's got a far harsher demeanor than Coach Gardner had shown me.

"Okay," he says. "Line yourselves up, double-time. Because today we're gonna start with wind sprints."

I had always thought that Coach Hanson's practices at Jeff were tough; Ladell Andersen makes those look like a cakewalk. "Come on," he yells, "speed it up, ladies!" I push myself, but the stop-and-go drills take a heavy toll. In my life I've never worked so hard at running drills before. A couple of players on the team can't go on; they stagger to the trash cans at the edge of the hardwood and puke their guts up. I myself reach the verge of throwing up a few times but I fight it. I don't want to look weak.

After a few hours Coach Andersen blows his whistle and tells us to hit the showers. I'm in and out quickly, because the longer I linger, the greater the chance of giving up the ghost; my knee has swelled to the size of a grapefruit.

After winning the '58 city championship, I had given Coach Hanson his old knee brace back and vowed never to wear it again. It was big, it was ugly, and it was heavy, all metal and leather, and worst of all it advertised to the world that I was injured. That I couldn't take. I knew that I'd never make it to pro ball if teams thought I was playing on one leg—a crippled horse you don't pump money into; you just ship it off to the glue factory. From then on I wore only simple kneepads. They worked to mask my injury and keep people from catching on, but after playing my knee would balloon to an unbelievable size. It took a lot of work to get the swelling down, and even afterward I'd wake up to a kneecap the size of a beach ball.

Every day I'd play, go home, rub down my knee, and then wrap an Ace bandage as tightly as I could around my kneecap to try to keep the fluid from returning while I slept. It was painful, but it sometimes worked. When it didn't I'd call a doctor and pay him to drain my knee. Thus began my introduction to a life lived by the needle.

The fluid that comes out is the watery, off-yellow color of death, and it scares me like no opposing player ever has. But draining my knee works— at least it got me all the way to college. Sadly, though I tried not to think about it after leaving Los Angeles, it turns out that the needle isn't afraid to follow me over the Wasatch. As I stand in the shower room after my first practice at the U, my knee gets scarily big, and watching it swell, I know I have to do something about it, and fast.

Trying to hide the melon my knee has become, I stagger fast as I can back to my dorm room. I reckon I better try and wrap my knee to push out the swelling, but it's so full of fluid that I can't even get my pants leg back down over my knee to wrap it.

Clearly I'm in trouble. Big trouble. And if I don't do something it'll get even worse.

I get up off the bed and hobble into the dorm lobby. I stagger toward the pay phone and look for a doctor in the yellow pages.

There are hundreds.

With no idea what to do, I close my eyes and stab the page with my finger. I open my eyes and look down. My finger rests on the name of one Dr. Clegg. His office is in downtown Salt Lake City.

I slip a dime into the slot and dial.

"Doctor's office."

I freeze. What do I say? How do I explain to some stranger what's going on?

"Hi," I begin. "Look, you don't know me, but my name is Billy McGill and I'm a basketball player at the U? We had our first practice today, and my knee is all full up with fluid. It's pretty painful. I think I need to get it drained."

There's a brief pause, and then the voice on the other end of the line asks, "When can you come in?"

Again I freeze. How am I going to get there? And when I do get there, how am I going to pay?

Slowly, I tell myself. One thing at a time.

"I—I guess I can find a ride with someone or other around here right away. But look, I gotta tell you—I don't have no insurance or anything."

"Don't worry about it," says the voice. "Just get here." Relieved, I place the receiver back into the cradle. Now I just need to find someone in the dorm with a car to rush me downtown.

The whole way to the doctor's office I'm worrying. What am I gonna do if the doctor says I need to pay him on the spot? I don't have any money. And what if he's a racist bastard like the diner waitress or that Dr. Mason who first set my knee? He'll probably kick me out when he sees I'm not white.

I get out of the car after we park and walk up to the building, nervous. I open the door, and the creak of the unoiled hinges echoes unnervingly in the pit of my stomach. I expect the worst. Stepping over the threshold I feel a biting wind at my back, as if shoving me forward into the depths.

So I'm surprised when I enter to find before me a kindly looking, bespectacled man in horn-rimmed glasses who smiles when he sees me.

"Billy," he says. "I'm Dr. Clegg. Welcome. Let's have a look at you."

I hold up my hand up to protest, to remind the doctor that I can't pay—I don't want to get treated and then have something come up afterward, like maybe the receptionist didn't tell him or there's some change of plans—but Dr. Clegg waves my concerns away.

"Don't worry about it," he says. "Let's worry about getting you healthy. Now come on, follow me into my examination room."

This settles me. Dr. Clegg certainly doesn't seem racist. He's just matter-of-fact and to the point. He takes a look at my knee and admits that it's a mess. But he also says he can help, and he tells my ride to head back to campus, that he'll make sure I get back okay.

"I can drain your knee," the doctor tells me. "But not before you tell me how you did this."

My first few minutes in the office settled my nerves, but when the doctor demands that I tell him my story, fear floods over me once again. My blood turns to ice and my breath shortens; I can feel the heady thump of my heart behind my ribs. I haven't told anybody how bad my knee still is. Not even my mother. I can't tell him, this stranger—can I?

I stare into the doctor's face. His cheeks are lined, but his eyes are kind. They make me think of the pastor at the church my father, my real father, used to drag us to on Sundays when I was a kid. And as I see the kindness in the doctor's eyes, a dam breaks within me. The floodgates open, and I confess.

Despite my fears, I tell Dr. Clegg everything. I tell him about the jumper, and I tell him about the meanness and indifference of Dr. Mason, and Daddy Lonnie's inaction in the face of them. I tell him about the improvised sessions of rehabilitation on the track, the summer draining—all of it.

It's amazing. I've never told anyone about what happened to my knee before. I've been so afraid I'd lose my scholarship and my shot that I kept it bottled up inside. But for some reason I just trust Dr. Clegg and let it all out. And when I do I feel uplifted.

The doctor seems to understand. From my knee he drains a syringe full of what looks like turkey gravy being sucked up through a baster. "Go home," he says once we're done. "Give it a rest for a day, maybe two, and then see how it feels." He calls me a cab and pays for it up front himself. As I'm about to get in, he adds, "If you ever need to come back to see me, don't worry about money. Just give me a call."

It's another kindness, and I do take the doctor up on it. I see Dr. Clegg two or three times a week for the rest of the year, and then onward after that as well. He never charges me, never utters a word. He just helps me get healthy enough to play, and for that, I'm grateful. But I never play unburdened by pain again.

The team practices don't get any easier after that, but I am at least able to push through. Ladell Andersen's assistant coach, Ted Berner, divvies us up into two teams for scrimmages, and I quickly earn my spot as the starting center on the freshman first team. Joe Aufderheide is the starting forward on the first string, and although he's a good jump shooter, his favorite stat to collect is assists. So next thing I know Joe's getting the ball and feeding me in the paint, time after time. He's great on D, too, a real bruiser on the boards, and soon he and I fall into a groove. It's just like old times at Jefferson.

In the season-opening frosh-vs.-varsity scrimmage, the whole school seems to show up to at the field house. I've never played before so many people before, even at the LA city championships, and it's breathtaking. Our freshman team actually beats the varsity squad—albeit with a cushion of points spotted before the game began—and that generates a buzz. Ute fans start arriving early to take in the freshman matchups before the marquee varsity games, and one university alumnus even takes to meeting me in the Baliff Hall parking lot for weekly "chats." We sit there for an hour or two, listening to the radio, and when we're done he hands me a hundred dollars. "For you," he says. "For your time." I don't question if these gifts are illegal or improper. I just take the money.

With my newfound comfort on the court and off, I start to get into a rhythm in my classes. I'm still avoiding math, but when my report card arrives for the first semester my grades are good enough that I remain academically eligible, and that's all that matters.

We win nearly every freshman contest we have, setting us up for what I hope will be a big end-of-season victory against Weber State. Weber State's isn't actually a freshman-only team: Weber is a two-year junior college; as their school is comprised entirely of freshmen and sophomores, they compete largely against other junior colleges but also against freshman squads of big universities like ours. This gives them an advantage over us on paper—they've had more opportunity to build chemistry playing together, and they've got guys with an extra year of real college ball experience—but we don't care. I certainly don't, anyway. I've been playing older, more experienced guys my whole life, and it's never slowed me down.

But all that ends when we run straight into an indestructible wall by the name of Allen Holmes.

Holmes is Weber State's superstar; everybody calls him Sweet Al. Their squad is known nationwide for being quite strong, and Al himself is seen as a pro-level prospect. The *Utah Chronicle*, our campus paper, has already hyped this contest as the key matchup between the two top young players in the state.

On the sidelines before the game, Coach Andersen pulls us all aside to give us the skinny on the Weber State squad. "Billy," he says, "Sweet Al will probably be guarding you. We'll need you to overpower him to have any chance of scoring inside."

I look over to the Weber State squad and see a lanky, wiry, whippet-shaped kid about half a foot shorter than I am. He's standing underneath the boards and throwing elbows cartoonishly at imaginary defenders as he grabs the rebounds in his team's shooting drill.

"Him?" I ask, incredulous. No one in Utah has been able to stop me, and I haven't been stopped inside by anyone all my life. This little guy thinks he's going to slow me down?

Ladell Andersen nods. I chuckle.

We break huddle and step onto the court. The ball goes up and I win us the tip; jogging down the court I think to myself that this kid Holmes doesn't have a prayer of stopping me.

As the game goes on, though, I change my tune—the way he shuts me down, maybe Sweet Al has something akin to a direct line to heaven.

Never in my life have I been bossed around on a court by an opponent the way that Sweet Al does to me. He is skinny but hard, and he uses his elbows and knees to knock me around, shoving in front of me when the guards have it on offense and digging into my ribs when he boxes me out under the backboard. He dictates my play in a way that no one else has ever been able to do, and by halftime I'm floundering.

And as for his offense, he's like Lefty, except even better. His high, kicking shots swish through the net one after the other with hardly any misses. He's so fast, too, that though he guards me with ease when we're on offense, I can't D him up in return. Single-handedly, Allen Holmes takes me apart, and the Utah freshman squad, stunningly, loses.

Though it's tough to end freshman year with a loss, I try to stay positive. My jump hook shot has become both deadly accurate and near unstoppable. Teams put two and sometimes three players on me when I have the ball to try to tie me up, but when I can't move one way or the other I either go straight up and pop the jump hook without even a dribble or dish it off to a teammate cutting into the lane for an easy layup. My scoring ease makes me a force to be reckoned with, and in recognition I not only make the first team All-Utah freshman squad but am named the Utah Freshman of the Year. Of course the pain in my knee slowly mounts and the joint itself blows up more and more after every game, but thanks to my oversized kneepads my secret is safe.

Still, I prefer winning championships to awards, and who ends up winning the NCAA championship? The University of California at Berkeley, the very school I at the last minute snubbed to attend the University of Utah. And their starting center, Darrall Imhoff, was a walk-on player from the city of Los Angeles who earned the starting spot uncontested when there was no other big man to vie for it.

Oops.

When Dave Costa and I drive back to LA at the end of freshman year, we pass through Las Vegas again. I see the signs on the side of the road once more, and this time I won't be denied.

"Dave," I say, "pull the car over. Let's go shoot some craps."

I'm half surprised when, to my delight, Dave agrees.

The lights and the buildings of the Strip are even more amazing up close than they are from the road, and when we leave the car with the valets at the Sands, I wear a grin as long as the Strip itself. We stroll through the glass fronts like we've broken the bank already, and skirting the blackjack tables, roulette, slot machines, and money wheel, we make our way straight for the velvet pit.

Stepping up to the craps table, I'm momentarily at a loss. The playing area is huge, and there are all these bets—come, don't pass, field—that I have no clue what they mean. When I played dice at Carver, it was seven and eleven, craps and the point, and that was it. Plus what made me so good at craps when I was a kid was the way I rolled. I knew how to massage the dice off the tile and the back wall to hit the points I wanted. I don't know if my long reach and tight grip will be enough to nullify the long, soft felt tables here in Vegas, but with this charge running through my blood, damn it, I'm willing try.

The stickman pushes me the dice. I lay my money down. Here's the come-out roll.

"Seven!"

The assembled gamblers—mostly men, some with smartly dressed women dangling from their shoulders—cheer, and I'm pushed back my winnings. Riding high on emotion, I decide to let it all ride.

I roll. "Another seven!"

Again the crowd cheers; I'm winning. It's just like basketball, and the pull of strangers' adoration is just as strong here as on the court.

I shoot at that smoky table for hours, throwing hard but hitting the back wall soft so the dice don't always break. I win my share, but really it's the other people, the big bettors, who make money off my hot hand, and they love me for it.

Most of them, anyway. While I'm taking a break, I hear two old gamblers muttering over by the johns.

"What's he doing here, anyway?" one asks.

"Don't look at me. Thank Governor Sawyer and his integration program. I mean, I don't mind having Sammy Davis around or anything, but one of them shooting craps at the table? It's ridiculous."

That's when I look around and notice that I'm the only brother in sight. You know that moment when you realize you've just caught someone talking about you? This is it.

Suddenly, I understand. This is why Dave Costa wouldn't stop here on the way to school. Just a few months ago my black money wasn't good enough for these casinos.

The moment I realize this, I pick up Dave and my winnings and make my way to the door. The big money men—the ones who rode their stakes on my back—clap for me as I leave. They don't tip me out or anything, though I don't expect them to. That's not the kind of thing that the rich do for people who bring them their bread and butter.

Sophomore Year

I return to LA to find that in my absence my mother and Daddy Lonnie have moved once again. We're back on the east side, near where I first lived with my natural father and far from south central.

The U gets me a job with an area alum named Harry Guss, who owns a big electronic parts business. My work's pretty menial—sorting electronic odds and ends and making sure they're stored in the right bins—but it pays well enough, at least, that I'm able to buy myself a proper winter coat. I'd never owned or needed one in LA, but there's no damn way that I'm gonna spend another year in Utah suffering under the weight of eight layers of sweaters.

As boring as my job is, at least it's less bad than my mom's. The city finally closed down the pressing plant where she'd been slaving away all these years, which is a miracle. The chemicals gave her headaches and a hell of a cough. Of course, the miracle of closure is sullied by the fact that without the plant my mom is near forced out of work. With no other options, she's reduced to cleaning houses to make a paycheck. We just can't catch a break; for us even the silver linings of clouds are quick to tarnish.

Now and then I make my way back to Denker to train and play, but far more often I choose to rest my knee instead. I've not been truly challenged at Denker since Bill Russell and Wilt dropped in, anyway, so instead of hitting the court I catch up with Lefty by hitting the floor. On weekend nights Lefty and I head out and go mambo dancing. It's a different kind of motion between us now, but still it feels smooth and right.

Summer flies by in a blink, and next thing I know Dave Costa's parked outside my door again. This time Daddy Lonnie is there to see me off. He gives me a hug on my way out—really stiff-armed and awkward—and I think we're both glad when it ends. All the way to Salt Lake City Dave's back to telling me about football, but all I can think about is the start of hoops practices in October.

I remember from my first year how quickly I showered and dressed after our freshman games so I could sit in the stands to watch the varsity play. I marveled at how crisply they moved, how clean their passes were, and how smooth was their shooting touch. And now I'm poised to be one of them.

We enter the preseason seeded in the top ten nationally; sportswriters are saying Utah has a shot at the title. Of course, they're saying the same thing about Cal-Berkeley, too.

I can hardly concentrate at Utah until practices finally begin. I'm excited to see we've got another fresh face in the group: Sweet Al, who's finished junior college and is now at Utah as an upperclassman. Tryouts blow by, and during them there's little interaction between the players and the coaching staff—we scrimmage, we run their drills, and we're told when to show up and when to leave, but otherwise they're removed entities, shadows up in the stands. Once cuts are announced, though, they make their presence known. Coach Gardner blows his whistle. Monkeying-around time is over.

"Okay," he says. "Listen up. I expect each and every one of you to work to make this the best team in the nation. This will involve personal sacrifice, both on and off the court." He points out the 1944 national championship banner hanging in the rafters. "You know how we won that title?

By attacking at all times—in practice, in training, and with every aspect of our being."

It's moving, and I find that I can't help but admire this great man. I'd always liked Coach Gardner from the first time I'd met him and saw how well he treated my mother. But now I'm ready to step into battle for him.

It's a good thing, too, because Coach Gardner's practices are even tougher than Coach Andersen's were. Eternally we sprint and run, forced to push ourselves harder and longer than we ever have before.

"Rebounding time," he says. "Who's toughest? Get the boards. Fight for 'em. Go."

Coach throws a ball at the rim. There are five us: veterans Gary Chestang and Jim Rhead, my man Joe Aufderheide; senior center Carney Crisler, and me. Getting the ball under the backboard is a challenge: who wants it most? As it falls from the rim we attack it like starving rottweilers fighting one another for dinner.

This is what we go up against in our first practice: each other. My teammates are beasts, unwilling to give anything less than their all, and anyone who watches our practices knows that these battles Coach arranges for us are designed to make us get tough or die. Jim Rhead is a pure animal on the court, and he wants every rebound that comes off the boards. Gary Chestang letters for the Utah football team in addition to playing basketball, and he plays hoops with the same tenacity he flashes when tackling opposing running backs. Joe Aufderheide is a fighter himself, and as for Crisler—well, Crisler knows about me. He's a senior, the captain, and the starting center; it's his last year. I'm coming for his spot. I'm the Utah Freshman of the Year, the guy who led the freshman squad. Out of everyone, he attacks the loose balls—and me—hardest.

When regular season begins the Ute faithful come out in droves. Though Carney Crisler's still in the lineup and I have to start games on the bench, by ten minutes in the Ute fans are chanting my name. It's music to my ears, and when I hear the crowds at the Einar Nielsen cheering, "The Hill! McGill! Put in the Hill!" it buoys my spirit, the cheering making me forget the pain, the draining, the showering in private, and all the work it takes to get the fluid out of my knee. Every time I step onto the court, the fans cheer and I smile. And every time Crisler steps off it, a water boy gives him a towel to wipe off his sweat, a towel that he invariably slams straight to the hardwood.

Mad though Crisler may be, he can't deny the rhythm that Sweet Al and I have when we're on the floor together. If I get the ball in the middle with no clear shot, I gently loft a no-look pass right behind me, like a housewife leaving a pie out on a windowsill. Right as I release it Al's there to collect, and with his forward momentum he takes it straight to the hoop without even a dribble and lays it softly in.

Through the first half of sophomore year, we roll through the Skyline Conference. We're not really tested until we hit the road, flying to Carolina for the 1959 Dixie Classic. We'll be playing, among others, NC State, North Carolina, and a host of East Coast teams, and our opening round matchup for the tournament is slated to be Duke.

We disembark at Raleigh-Durham airport, where we hop on a charter bus to the team hotel. Coach Everett Case from the host school, NC State, has made reservations for all of the teams, but when we get there we're told there's no space.

Coach Gardner is livid. "What do you mean there's no space! We just flew all the way across the damn country!"

"That may be," loudly answers the hotel manager, arms crossed, a plug of chewing tobacco in this mouth. "But we can't let all of y'all into our hotel with them two black fellers on your team."

Sweet Al and I exchange worried glances with each other. This place may be dangerous. We offer to sleep on the bus. But Coach Gardner's all class, and though he knows the lack of rest will take its toll the next morning, he packs the team back into the wagon and drives around all night looking for a hotel that will host us. "If they won't take every one of us, they don't get any of us," he proclaims. "No hotel's good enough for just a few Utes." And indeed, though we're sluggish and slow the next day, something real happens: our team is formed. We are blown out by the Blue Devils, but we easily take the last two games of our tournament and head back to Salt Lake City with renewed drive and passion. We're together now, a unit, a team, and together we've got something to prove.

Luckily, we don't have long to wait to do it.

Ohio State

The true test of our Utah squad arrives in late December when Ohio State University comes to town. Ohio State is ranked number one; they're undefeated and are led on court by the man touted by some to be the best sophomore player in the nation: Jerry Lucas.

I have a thing for Jerry Lucas the way Chamberlain has a thing for me. I've wanted to play Lucas since the day we met in New York City. Despite all the accolades I've received, he's always been held just a little bit higher. The newspapers are touting this matchup as the blowout battle of the top-two big men in the country, and to win it would mean everything to me.

Every night before I go to sleep I say my prayers just as I did when I was little. And on the eve of this matchup I pray that by daybreak my knee will have healed. Still, it's a surprise when come the morning of the OSU game, I awaken to find that my prayers have been, at least temporarily, answered. There is hardly any fluid in my knee, and the pain is gone. For the first time since I was a teenager, both my knees are of equal size, and my left knee feels pain-free, newborn. Pure. Perfect. It's as though the injury never happened.

osu is going to be in trouble.

Huddled in the locker room, Coach paces before a chalkboard covered with Xs and Os. "It's more than just Lucas," he cries. "They've got John Havlicek. Larry Siegfried. Bobby Knight." As he rattles off our opponents' names, spittle forms and foams in the creases of his lips.

All of osu's starters are likely NBA guys, which means shutting down their scorers will be tough but key. Their number two man behind Lucas is Havlicek. Hav has been a scoring machine all year, which is why it's no surprise when Coach assigns his coverage duties to Sweet Al.

Joe Aufderheide would have been the more natural choice—after all, Havlicek is six feet five and two hundred pounds, a man with a body oversized for even a lumberjack. And Aufderheide is both taller than Sweet Al and has a bit more heft. But here's the thing: Sweet Al is a defensive genius. When he was at Weber State he stopped me cold, and if he was able to cross me up, he's likely going to be able to work some magic on Havlicek as well.

Joe Morton, our star guard and the heir to the Morton salt fortune, is set to match up against Siegfried—a tall order, but since Morton's an important cog in our offense, he's got to be on the floor one way or another. That really only leaves Jerry Lucas to stop.

"McGill!" Coach calls my name from the center of the locker room, and both Carney Crisler and I look up.

"You've got Lucas. Keep him out of the inside."

Crisler and I lock eyes. He is riding the bench. That means tonight against osu will be my first varsity start.

My world slows. I'm elated. I'll be matched up on Jerry Lucas. With the biggest game of our careers on the line—playing host to Lucas's number one team in the nation—my name will be called over the loudspeaker as the starting center for the Utah Runnin' Redskins.

Coach Gardner puts his chalk down and backs toward the door. "Make no mistake, gentlemen," he says. "This is a big game. And it's ours to win. So let's go out there and do it."

I'm so excited that I fail to notice that all but one of us stand and cheer, rushing toward the open mouth of the locker room entrance. The one man left? Carney Crisler, who turns and plants his foot so hard into the front of his locker that he leaves a dent in it the exact shape of a size 15 Converse.

By the time we hit the floor to the roaring applause of the Utah faithful, the osu Buckeyes are already well into their pregame warm-ups. I watch them. Like us, they wear red and white, and like us, they've got some swagger. In fact, they may have more.

Our trainer, Lynn Bywater, pulls me aside while we watch their layup drills. "You know," he tells me, "they were talking trash about you guys in the showers."

"Oh, yeah?"

"Yeah," he says. "I'm handing out towels and Lucas walks into the shower room, points at the low spigots, and says, 'Who showers here? Midgets?' Then he laughs like an idiot, and all his teammies do, too."

I seethe. "Midgets, huh?" I look over at Lucas. "We'll see," I say, "we'll see."

From the beginning it's a seesaw battle, with the lead trading back and forth. Havlicek, despite having Sweet Al on his hip, makes the first basket of the game, and when Lucas gets the ball next, he scores on me. That riles me up, and he knows it—so when I get the ball, I fool Lucas with a fake and dish off to Sweet Al, who lays the ball up easily into the basket for our two points.

The fans explode, and on our next possession, when I get the ball at the free throw line, I take a big step to my left and let loose this time with a sweeping jump hook, hitting nothing but net. The fans stomp their feet and the cheering grows louder.

Our two teams are evenly matched, potent offensive machines. Lucas is hitting all of his shots, but so am I—I'm in the zone. I just can't miss. Lucas and I go shot for shot, scoring points at will on and over each other like our lives depend on it. Sweet Al, too, is doing his job on O, but that's where we have the edge: he's also doing his job on defense. Havlicek notched the first basket of the game, but after that, for all his skill, he can hardly get close to the ball. And when he does get it, Sweet Al is on him with a fury of hands and elbows. Havlicek's opening two points mark the high point of his night. Larry Siegfried picks up Havlicek's slack some for OSU, but by halftime we're still ahead. When we leave the floor the scoreboard reads, Utah: 49; Ohio State: 44.

In the locker room we're charged. Sweet Al's loud and boisterous, slapping backs and slapping hands, and even I, shy and reserved as I usually am, am getting into it. Coach spits a speech of brimstone that lights a fire underneath us, and when I tell the team what Lucas said about us before the match, it pumps us up even more. Coming out of the twenty-minute break, we're all feeling charged and excited, ready to get out there and kill some Buckeyes.

All of us, of course, except for Carney Crisler, who still hasn't seen the floor at all.

He hasn't even gotten a towel to spike.

When we retake the court for the second half, the Utah fans erupt again. They cheer for us before the refs even find the game ball; they can feel the same energy we do. We've prepared for this, all of us; if I'm not getting the rebound, Gary Chestang, Joe Aufderheide, and Jim Rhead will be snarling right behind me and fighting for it. Lucas may be shoving his weight around, as nobody can stop him, but we've got four against one out there.

Sweet Al continues to cut up Havlicek like a piece of paper on offense, and on the flip side of the court, Havlicek cannot get loose. It's as if Sweet Al is part of Havlicek's skin. He's running a defensive clinic. It's unreal. Havlicek has never, I'm sure, experienced someone guarding him like Sweet Al. I know what he's going through, remembering playing against Al my freshman year, and for a moment I almost feel bad for him.

Almost.

As the end of the second half draws near, we're still up by five points. It's a slim margin, and the victory is so near we can feel it, but the Buckeyes will not cede ground.

I score with three minutes left; Lucas scores with two and a half. I score on our next possession, and Lucas scores again ten seconds later.

With the clock winding down, Jerry Lucas and I are matching basket for basket and rebound for rebound, pushing the low roar of the crowd into a frenzy. Our lead dwindles to three, but then Sweet Al drops another bucket and puts us back up by five. Finally Ohio State misses one, and we know we're close. In the last few seconds we players on the court can't hear anything; the cheering has grown so loud that's it's just a throbbing pulse of noise.

"Ten!" The din is barely differentiable.

"Nine! Eight! Seven!" The fans count down.

"Six! Five! Four!" Ohio State is trying to foul us to stop the clock, but they can't. None of us are holding the ball long enough to let Ohio State get us to the free-throw line.

"Three! Two!" Sweet Al tosses the ball in the air. I glare at Lucas. He's hanging his head.

"One!"

The buzzer sounds. The scoreboard reads, Utah: 97; Ohio State: 92.

That's it. We've done it. We've beaten the number one team in the nation.

It's the first time osu has been defeated all season, and the roof of Einar Nielsen is about to blow off from the cheering. I can actually feel it inside my eardrums—it hurts, but it's good. As my teammates begin jumping and hugging one another, I can't resist taunting Lucas. "Still think we're a bunch of midgets now?"

As the official scorers rise from their table, Einar Nielsen erupts into a madhouse. The crowd floods the floor. In the mayhem my buddy the booster reaches out and pumps my hand, a heavy lump in my palm. He shouts in my ear. "Great game, Billy!"

I open my fist. Inside it is a hundred dollar bill.

I can't believe how brazenly he's openly flaunting the rules. I could get kicked off the basketball team for this. I look around, though, and I see that everyone is too jacked up to notice or care.

I surreptitiously slip the money into the waistband of my shorts.

After winning the whole squad—heck, the whole city (save Carney Crisler)—is on a high. So Sweet Al and I decide to kick up our heels and celebrate. Usually when we go out it's to 2nd South, Salt Lake's hidden black neighborhood across the tracks. But after beating osu and becoming the new kings of Salt Lake, the only thing to do is to really step out. We decide, freshly laurelled conquerors that we are, to go out to the nice restaurants and the nice bars, the places where people like us wouldn't normally go. Where we wouldn't normally be welcome.

The places where white people go.

We step up to a pretty Italian place with white tablecloths. "I don't know," I confess to Al. "Are you sure about this?"

He smacks the back of his hand at my chest. "Come on, Hill. Don't worry about it." I accede, but I'm worried—I can't forget the diner incident. All the same, we walk in, and immediately we're seated.

"See, Hill?" says Sweet Al. "Nothing to it." And just as quickly as we're shown our table, Sweet Al wanders off to the bar for a drink and to charm the manager.

Alone, I'm nervous again. Mine is the only black face in the dining room, and it's unsettling when a young, pretty waitress comes over to bring me breadsticks and a cocktail, on the house. I thank her quickly, but once she leaves, I wish she were back so I wouldn't have to be alone. I ought to be on a high—we just took down the mighty OSU! Still, the longer Al's away, the more I find I'm straining to try to maintain a brave face in front of all these strangers.

Some minutes in, as I'm starting to contemplate getting up and heading for the door, I hear a female voice from the table next to me. "You're Billy McGill," she says. "Billy the Hill."

I turn and look at her. She's beautiful. Lustrous, demure, and pouty. She's got skin like porcelain and hair as dark as buttery chocolate syrup. Immediately I'm stirred by desire—a desire that's muted by the man who sits directly across from her, close enough to touch, a man I can only assume is her husband.

I nod. "Yes, ma'am."

"That was an incredible game," she says.

She's an incredible woman. "Yes, ma'am."

She turns to me from across the thin aisle between our two tables. I hold my breath as her torso twists to face mine; her leg swivels toward me, opening, for a moment, the space under her dress.

"Amazing," she says. "I loved watching it. Every second."

I nod. "Mmhmm." Where's Al?

"It really did it for me. All that passion, energy, excitement. And that climax at the end! Unreal."

I'm gripping the table hard at is corners now, and it's only half because I don't know what to do with my hands. What is this woman doing, and with her man right there besides?

"Can I get you anything?" she offers. "A drink, maybe?"

Meekly, I lift my glass. "I'm all taken care of," I say.

"Would you like something else then?"

I glance over at her husband—maybe it's just her boyfriend? Her uncle? A friend? Whoever he is, how is he letting her talk like this? "No," I say. "Nothing comes to mind."

The hell it doesn't. I may be shy, but I've been a star athlete since the ninth grade—I know what to do with a woman. I'm shaking my head, but all the while I'm thinking, "Boy, what I'd really like is her." She's got this amazing body, and she's no simple girl like the coeds at the U. She's a round-bodied, full woman, and it's all I can do not to stare.

"You're sure?" she says.

I pick up my cocktail. "Yes, ma'am." I take a sip.

And that's when the bomb explodes.

"Nothing?" She uncrosses her legs again. "Not even me?"

I start to choke on a piece of ice. No one ever accused me of being smooth. I finally swallow it down, and I manage to gasp, "Excuse me?"

She leans over farther, exposing to me the thrust of her bosom. "I said, what about me? Would you like to have me?"

Al, I think, where are you? And what have you gotten me into now?

Tragedy in Triplicate

Over the course of sophomore year Sweet Al becomes a treasured friend. The two of us grow as tight as Lefty and I had been back in the day, spending all of our time together. If I'm not in class, on the court, in the student union eating, or in my dorm room sleeping, chances are good I'm hanging out somewhere with Sweet Al.

When the weekend rolls around and we've not got a game, the two of us go spend time with our own at Porters and Waiters, a club owned by Sweet Al's family in the suburb of Ogden. Though we could go anywhere, Porters and Waiters is special to us. The club itself is just a long, dark room with a bar running along one side. It's narrow, with a janky juke box, a small dance floor, and no booths; there're just a few tables and chairs arrayed across the wooden slats on the ground. There are probably a hundred other gin mills just like it. But the thing is, this place is ours. We can spend a Friday or Saturday evening drinking orange juice (me) or cocktails (Sweet Al) and meeting some of the few people in Utah who look like us and can relate to who we are.

Lowell, the sumo-sized man at the door, becomes a dear friend. Though it's Sweet Al's godmother, Annabelle Weekly, who owns Porters and Waiters, it's Lowell who really runs the place. Even when I have a little spending cash in my pocket, my money's no good here. Lowell sees to that. And when a cute lady sidles up to the bar without escort, she's steered to us. Lowell sees to that, too.

In the aftermath of Ohio State the Utes evolve into a national powerhouse. We take the Skyline Conference without trouble, finishing league play with thirteen wins to one loss and a season record of 26-3 overall. Heading into the NCAA championship we're a top seed in the Western Division bracket, and our first opponents are John Rudometkin and USC.

We have the horses—this much is certain. Between the quick guard play of salt heir Joe Morton, the tough inside games of Rich Ruffel and Jim Rhead, Joe Aufderheide's passing, my infallible shooting, and the staggering all-around play of the magic Sweet Al, there's no one in the tournament who can beat us, and we know it.

The USC game is held right near our home turf, on neighboring BYU's court in Provo. Naturally, many of our supporters come out to cheer us on—for us it's practically a home game—but surprisingly, quite a few Southern California basketball fans make the trek out from Los Angeles to watch as well.

My family, of course, is not among them.

We win the tip and go up early. Carney Crisler is still riding the pine and seething, and I'm pouring in buckets like I'm mixing paint. The Trojans start putting two or three men on me at a time, but I'm on a tear: I beat Wilt the Stilt in high school and now I've beaten Jerry Lucas, too; my basketball is the best it's ever been and I simply refuse to be stopped. When they put two defenders on me, I shoot a jump hook over them both. When they add a third to swat at the ball from behind, I dish it out to Aufderheide or swing it around to Sweet Al for an easy two-pointer. USC's good—they've got Rudometkin, after all—but not good enough. After we coast in to an 80–73 win, Rudometkin comes up to me and shakes my hand. "See you made your decision okay, Hill," he says. I just smile.

The next game of regionals is against Oregon, and it's more of the same.

Nobody can beat us; we know it. After Oregon will come defending champs UC Berkeley, and once we beat them, we'll head to Daly City, California, for the 1960 NCAA Final Four. It's just an easy win over the lame-duck Ducks that stands between us and destiny.

Tip-off comes and I easily get my hand on the ball, flicking it to Joe Aufderheide. Just like that we're off and running.

We score the first points and gain a lead early, but our halftime lead is tenuous, and for whatever reason Oregon just won't quit. It doesn't help that we're playing in Seattle, just hours from Eugene, and the crowd seems heavily canted toward our opponents—and the refs along with them. Time after time, call after call, the whistle blows in favor of Oregon. Every fifty-fifty ball is theirs, and what's a charge against our offense when we're driving the lane is a blocking foul on us when we're playing defense. One after another our starters foul out, and Oregon begins to mount a comeback. The fans get louder, and our tickets to the national championship, which in my mind had already been punched, disintegrate before my eyes. Carney Crisler even gets real minutes on the floor for the first time in weeks as I, too, exceed the foul limit and am forced to sit out. Time winds down, and unbelievably, we're behind. The final score reads, Oregon: 65; Utah: 54. We're stunned. Just like that our season is over.

We end the year ranked sixth in the AP polls, but we should have gone out on top. With us absent, the national championship game becomes a joke that goes easily to Ohio State—Ohio State, the team that we bumped off with poise just three months earlier. It could have been us. It should have been. And the team that practically gave it away in the finals— by a score of 75–55—was the team that beat Oregon the very round after we choked away our championship chance: defending champion California-Berkeley.

As a consolation prize (for them, not us) Berkeley's coach, Pete Newell, is picked to helm the U.S. basketball team for the 1960 summer Olympics. So impressed is he that he takes, among other players, both starting centers from the NCAA championship game for the gold-medal squad: Darrall Imhoff, the young Californian from his own team, and a still-younger kid from the Midwest named Jerry Lucas. Now I'm twice as mad as I was.

It should have been me.

I remain angry about the loss, and junior year I show up at school with blood on my tongue, a man on a mission. I've spent all summer on the courts working on my game and bulking up, adding size to help fight through double and triple teams. The extra weight plays hell with my knee, but I don't care. I'm not about to see our Utah team crumble again, and I'll carry us all the way to the championship myself if I have to, whatever the cost. And as it turns out I might just have to. Our team re-forms down a man.

It happens during a drive back into Salt Lake from Ogden. Sweet Al is the passenger in a two-seater convertible, feeling the wind rush through his hair. The driver's been drinking, and the car slips into the shoulder of the road. It shouldn't be a problem, but overcorrecting, the driver swerves back toward the median and crashes.

Not wearing his seatbelt, Sweet Al launches like a stone from a catapult, his body splaying across the brush on the roadside. For a moment he feels okay, and he tries to brush away the cobwebs from his brain and rise. But he can't, because his femur is sticking straight up like a flagpole through a fresh hole in his jeans.

It's two months before Al comes back to school in a wheelchair. "I'm okay," he tells me, but it's clear that he isn't. He can't even walk, let alone play basketball; this is the kind of injury that is career ending. I tell him so, and he laughs.

"They said the same to someone else I know, Hill."

"Yeah, but I did that myself," I remind him. I wasn't thrown out of a two-ton vehicle doing sixty.

He shakes his head. "I'll be back."

I don't believe him.

"I will! I've got a really good doctor," Sweet Al insists. "You know him. Dr. Clegg."

"Dr. Clegg?"

"Yeah, didn't you know? Dr. Clegg is the team doctor! He's an alum of the U. He does all of the athletes. Coach Gardner sent me to him."

Suddenly I understand why, for the last two years, I've been having my knee drained whenever I need it, free of charge. That random pick from the phone book was guided by providence. Any other name my finger had fallen on and my career at the U might have been over before it began. But I just happened on the one man in Salt Lake who performed free medical work on all the varsity athletes.

Whether I knew it or not, God's been in my corner this whole time.

I just hope he sticks around.

Girls

Despite Al's crippling injury, the world keeps turning and the team survives. And for the third year in a row a new black player arrives on the Utah court: a guard from Indianapolis named Bo Crain. All these black players at the U: seems I'm something of a trailblazer.

This Crain kid is good, and we're still the team to beat in the Skyline Conference, but still, it's clear there's a long road ahead. We graduated a lot of seniors and lost Sweet Al; the preseason college polls all had us in the top five in the nation, but they didn't know about the accident. We do. What's more, the still-fresh memory of last year's season-ending loss hangs around all our necks like a yoke, and we have much work to do before we can hope to throw it off again.

Though Bo's not quite Sweet Al on the court or off it, the two of us nonetheless become fast friends. We start to connect in our preseason games, and as we learn each other's tendencies and moves, we become greater and greater fixtures on 2nd South together as well.

At the clubs Bo meets this beautiful girl named Karen, a jazz pianist and singer who really brings them in. It doesn't hurt that she's usually the only white girl in our part of town. Watching her, I'm amazed at her talent and voice; she makes me want to grab congas and form a band. Watching her, all Bo notices is her long hair and her body; she makes him want to grab something else.

Bo manages to woo Karen and convince her that he's something special. Pretty soon they're going together. Their relationship is torrid but rocky, and in short order I find myself regularly playing the confessor to my roommate, listening to his problems and doling out advice the best I can.

And there are plenty of problems indeed. Because, see, Karen is white.

For a black man to be dating a white girl is almost unbelievable. Just two years ago Dave Costa had to shield me from the disappointment of being turned away at the Sands and I couldn't get served in a diner. Now Bo's not only become a regular at the white clubs downtown but has bagged their headlining chanteuse. Still, he feels constantly under pressure about it, and he does his best to keep the relationship a secret. Instinctively I understand why, but I don't really get the picture until later that season.

One Saturday game day morning I'm getting breakfast in the student union at the U—eggs and pancakes, bacon, sausage, and toast—when a girl I don't know approaches me.

"You're Billy McGill, right?" I look around. There aren't any other six-foot-nine black guys in earshot. She extends her hand with confidence. "Melanie," she says. Her hair is fiery red and streaks all the way down to the crook of her back. "I'm from Canada," she adds, like that explains everything.

"Oh," I reply as I take her palm in mine and shake. "I'm from LA." Because what else am I supposed to say?

"Well," she says, "good luck tonight. Maybe I'll see you after the game."

I walk off to find a table, fully expecting never to see her again—that was the most awkward conversation I've ever had. So it's a bit of a surprise when Melanie comes over when I'm finishing up to give me her number. "For after the game," she says.

That night while I'm playing I notice her up in the stands cheering for me. If Bo can do it, so can I, I figure. So after showering I give her a call.

When I pick up Melanie that unseasonably warm evening, she's wearing a beautiful dress, and her hair is swept above her neck. She's stunning—fresh as a just-painted portrait—and as she keeps exuding confidence, all but taking over our date, I come to realize that I quite like her.

As it turns out Melanie quite likes me, too, and I'm reminded of the Lincoln when we kiss. I'm more than happy to take her hand as I walk her home, and as the evening winds to a close I'm happy to go to sleep with her smell all over me.

The next morning I wake up grinning to the midday sun.

The day after that I wake up to a phone call.

It's a bitter winter Monday morning when someone knocks on my dorm room door. "McGill!" his voice echoes. "Phone call."

Clad in my undershorts and wrapped in my quilt, I stagger out of my room to pick up the waiting receiver of the hall phone in my dormitory lobby. "Hello?"

"Billy?" asks the voice on the line. "This is Dr. Olpin."

Dr. Olpin, president of the University of Utah. Without thinking, I stand up straighter.

"Good morning, sir."

"I was wondering, Billy, could you come by my office this morning around 10:00?"

I have a class this morning. And Coach Gardner is adamant that we not miss class. But when the president of the university calls, you hop to. I tell Dr. Olpin that I'll be there, and after showering and dressing in my best, I begin hoofing it across campus through six inches of sudden snow to a towering building I've never stepped into before.

Dr. Olpin's office smells of pine needles and leather. Overflowing bookshelves of burnished wood line the walls. Surrounded by the oversized chairs the man himself almost looks small.

I've never seen Dr. Olpin before—I'd always imagined him to be massive. But he's not. I tower over him when he stands to shake my hand.

"Billy," the doctor begins, "have a seat." I do. "How do you like it here?"

"Here? At the U?" He nods. "I love it here."

I begin to detail how I became enamored of the campus when Rich Ruffel described it to me and how I fell in love with it again when I first visited. I talk about the Wasatch Range and the basketball team and how much I love being a Ute. I even tell him about blurting out that I was born to go here while I was just visiting with my mom. As I talk I scan the diplomas on the walls. Some are from the Mormon Church.

"Good," Dr. Olpin says, "I'm glad you like it here. We all are. We love having you be a part of the Utah family.

"But here's the thing, Billy," he continues. "Some people in the greater Salt Lake community are a little bit . . . old fashioned. They have very deep-rooted and ancient values, and for them it can be hard to accept change."

I just nod. I have no idea what he's talking about.

"Sometimes, in a family, it's important to respect the values of the elders, to keep from rocking the boat. Now, we all love what you've done here," he says, and he rises, walking up to the window. "We love what you've done for the school. I personally am very proud to be able to say we have a Negro as one of our own here in Utah."

"Uh-huh."

Abruptly, he turns his back to the window and faces me. "But, you see Billy, I got a phone call this weekend. A few, in fact. And for some people in our city, it's hard for them to get their heads around the more . . . progressive aspects of our collegiate campus."

"Uh-huh," I repeat. What is he talking about?

"So you see, Billy, if you want to be a full part of the community, of the family, you have to adhere to its guidelines. One of them, for good or for ill, is that some precepts have to be abided by. Is that pretty clear?"

It isn't. I don't get it, and I want to ask him, "What are you talking about?" But I can't do that, obviously. Instead I raise my hand.

"Yes, Billy?"

"I don't understand. Is this what the calls were about?"

Dr. Olpin clears his throat. "The calls, Billy, concerned your social life and your presence outside of campus." He clasps his hands behind his back and begins pacing. "You see, Billy, when you leave campus, you're a representative of this school. And members of this town have certain . . . expectations about what kind of behavior should or should not be accepted."

The force of it hits me like I've just been smacked in the face with a basketball. All of a sudden I understand: if I want to stay at the University of Utah, dating white girls is not allowed. What he's saying is that people called to ask him who does that Billy McGill think he is, dating a white girl and bringing her out to a movie?

"I think I get it," I say, and though I try to keep my cool, I just can't. "In other words," I blurt out, "people love me when I'm scoring points on the court, but the rest of the time they want me the hell out of their sight."

Dr. Olpin comes to me—there's compassion in his face, but it's not enough. I feel confusion, hurt, and rage, and I feel the burn of tears start to sting the corners of my eyes.

"Billy, what you have accomplished, both for yourself and for the school, is impressive. You should hold your head high. But, unfortunately, there are people here in Utah that still cling to the old ways. The majority of the people here in Salt Lake and the state of Utah genuinely love you, and when I say I'm proud to have you here I mean it. But certain things . . . there are certain things that you must realize you should not do." He puts his hand on my shoulder. "Are we clear?"

He still won't say what he's talking about, even though we both know. And he means well—he's trying to protect me from forces that do exist, whether they're right or they're wrong. But will I bow to them? Will I play ball? Should I? I don't know. And I don't have time to figure it out, either, because Dr. Olpin is already shaking my hand and showing me the door.

Slogging back across campus in the cold, I don't want to believe that prejudice still exists toward people like me. But shamefully, I know it still does. Bo's got no trouble because he keeps his thing on the down low, and Jim Thomas had no trouble because he could pass. Me, I didn't. I stuck up like a rusty nail, so I get the hammer.

"Billy," Bo tells me later, "you've got to keep it on the down low."

Well, I'm six feet nine. How am I supposed to do that?

A few weeks later I'm awoken by another early morning knock on my door. Bo gets up and answers it; the visitor says only, "I need to talk to Billy." When I see who it is I know immediately why he's here.

Since meeting Dr. Olpin and talking with Bo, I've been confining my social outings to Porters and Waiters for safety. The first girl I meet there is a family friend of Sweet Al named Susan Washington, and immediately I'm interested in her. Of course there's the little issue of her having a boyfriend, but conveniently I ignore that—I figure, at least she's black; good enough!

Which explains why this man is now sitting in my dorm room at 7:00 in the morning.

"Jerrod," I begin, but he holds up his hand. It's a small enough community that we both know each other, and we both know what's been going on. Bo does, too, and he excuses himself from the room.

And as soon as the door closes Jerrod whips his hand from the folds of his coat and pulls out a gun.

I'm sitting in my bed, swaddled in blankets and wearing only my boxer shorts. My roommate is on the other side of a heavy oak door, and a man I hardly know has a snub-nosed revolver pointed at my chest. He tells me, "I am going to kill you," after which the only noise I hear is the gentle hiss of wind outside the window. It may still be winter, I don't notice being cold.

They say that when you're about to die your life flashes before your eyes. Looking down the barrel of Jerrod's pistol, I see a crazy mélange of imagery, my life running backward. Meeting Susan. Dr. Olpin. Losing to Oregon. Dave Costa. Being born to be a Ute. Hurting my knee. Shooting a jump hook over Wilt. Meeting Lefty. Dunking. Mr. Ward. Seeing my father for the first time. My mother. Gloris Jean.

As I try to refocus on the present, I notice Jerrod's still talking, and the butt of his gun is beginning to shake. Maybe, I think, I can get out of bed fast enough to grab his arm and snatch the pistol before he can fire. I start to spring, but I pause. What if I can't? Do I go for it? Do I dare take the risk?

I start to lose perception; my heart starts pumping hard. The adrenaline courses through my veins as fight-or-flight kicks in. I press my back against the wall, and I lower my knees to prepare to leap. I wonder, can I make it? Is he too close, too twitchy? Will my knee give?

Forget fear, I decide—I'm going for it. I put my weight on my hands, ready to dive, ready to put all my money on the table and roll the dice and pray that I don't hit craps. I'm about to dive when suddenly his voice cracks. His shoulders slump. Just like that, at the moment of truth, I see him give.

My heart is still pounding out a conga rhythm, but Jerrod lowers the gun. He raises his hand to his face. "I love her," he says. "She's my whole life." Deliberately, his hand—his gun hand—slides back into the folds of his coat.

"I'm not going to shoot you," he says, rising. "But if I ever even hear of you seeing her again . . ." He doesn't finish his sentence. He doesn't have to. Instead he opens the door and leaves.

For the first time in what feels like hours, I exhale.

When Bo comes back into the room later, I tell him what has happened. He urges me to call the cops, but I stop him.

"Are you crazy?" he yelps. "You're going to let that nut walk away?" He can't believe it, but I am, and I have a couple of reasons. First of all, Jerrod was right: I shouldn't be messing with another man's girl. And second, I can't spend all day talking to cops and dwelling on what just happened. I've got to focus: we've got a game.

Junior Year

After the incident with Jerrod I decide to devote all of my attention for the rest of my junior year to basketball. Sophomore season we had the horses— we all knew it—and to have exited the postseason so early, with so little to show for our great record and all our hard work, was a serious letdown.

But as low as we feel, Coach Gardner won't let us wallow in it. From the moment season reopens he's down our throats and forcing the highest effort and the best play out of all of us. Sprints, drills—he never lets up on us, and he's determined to get the whole team refocused and thinking as one unit.

It's easy to say but hard to do. Our first game of the year is against Loyola Marymount. They're a small, private school from my hometown that we should beat—but we lose by twenty-one points. After that we lose to Stanford in Palo Alto. Maybe Coach was wrong, we think. Maybe we are done. We're 0-2 and we slip out of the national rankings. Still, Coach makes us fight, and to our surprise we win our next game by a whopping fifty-five points.

The fifty-five-point victory propels us into another win, then another, and next thing we know we win six straight games at home and are back in the national picture. As for the fans, they're great the whole way—they never once lose faith in us; they always pack Einar Nielsen and cheer just as loudly as they ever had. The press's preseason predictions start to feel real, as though we are indeed a force to be reckoned with. After our two season-opening losses, we go on a 20-3 run, leaving us with a record of 20-5 overall and 12-1 in the Skyline Conference with just one game left to go.

Our last scheduled matchup is against Colorado State, whom we've beaten once already. They're 11-2, and all we have to do is beat them—at home—to take the title. It seems almost like a given, like destiny. But we've been in situations like this before, when it seems like a sure thing. And just like last time against Oregon, against Colorado State we fail.

On the strength of their stingy defense, the Rams manage to eke out a 49–50 victory over us, making both teams 12-2 in in-conference play and 1-1 against each other. That leaves us tied at season's end. We're going to play a one-game play-off for the title and the chance to progress into the NCAA postseason tournament.

It's decided that the game will be held at neutral ground, at BYU, and we travel to Provo with a sense of surety and inevitability that actually pushes us forward. Before the game Coach circles us all together in the locker room, reminding us that this is what we all came here for, that this is what we want and even owe to ourselves: another season victory, another conference championship. Another berth into the NCAAs and another shot at the title.

Before the game I see my dear friend Sweet Al sitting in the front row, unable to play but still there to cheer us on. It is in that instant that my drive to win takes over.

We will not lose. I won't allow it.

Game opens, and from the first possession we do our best to control the pace, driving the ball up the court every chance we get. Colorado State plays a defense-first game that's tailored to slow down our high-speed, high-scoring, run-and-gun style, and they do manage to keep the game close, but we simply refuse to be beaten. Even though the game doesn't progress the way we'd like to dictate it to—neither team scores even thirty points by half—we still never once lose the lead. At game's end the score-board reads 55–51, with us on top, and though it's ugly, that doesn't matter. All that matters is that we finish on top. We've won. Even if we are a horse with a broken leg, we're the league champions once again.

Winning Utah another regular-season title feels great, but it's nowhere near enough. We won the conference last year, and what of it? We still exited the playoffs with a whimper. This year, I'm determined that we'll go far.

I'm enjoying my best season yet at any level, averaging twenty-seven points and thirteen rebounds a game so far, and I'm named Skyline Conference Player of the Year. But it's not enough. Going into the postseason all I'm thinking about is the bitter taste of last year's lopsided loss to Oregon, and all I'm focused on is helping the Utes storm through the '61 NCAA championship tournament.

Well, that, and my knee. With more and more of the scoring burden being placed on me throughout the season, my knee's been getting worse and worse this year. Where I used to get it drained maybe once a week, I'm now visiting Dr. Clegg every second or third day, and when we have multigame road trips I always end them with serious swelling and a severe drop in output by the last game of the stretch. I just can't keep pushing myself as hard as I used to with all the swelling and fluid that sloshes around in my leg. So with the NCAA tournament ahead—a stretch of games without a single home date among them, night after night on the road—I try to mentally and physically prepare myself. I knead my knee constantly. I wrap it tightly in an Ace elastic bandage whether the joint seems to need it or not. I ice. I rest. And above all I rein in the demons in my mind, the deep-seated doubts and the difficulties of keeping secrets, focusing only—only—on the games.

School slips by the wayside. School doesn't matter. Winning, now, is the only thing that counts.

We go into the NCAA tournament seeded first in our region. This affords us a first-round bye, meaning there're just two games we'll need to win to make our way to the Final Four. Our first opponent is Loyola Marymount University—after last year we take nothing for granted. Coach Gardner primes us for the game, working us into a rabid rage over our loss to Oregon the year before to make sure that this time there are no mistakes.

It works. The contest is never close. We win by the lopsided score of 91–75. The win puts us into the Western regional championships.

In the shower as we wash up after our victory, everyone's laughing and snapping towels. We've got the biggest game of our careers ahead, but we're all trying to stay loose. Our next opponents will be Arizona State. "We got this in the bag," says Joe Aufderheide.

"When's our game?" I ask, looking forward to some R & R.

He laughs. "You serious, Hill? Tomorrow!"

I freeze. They keep laughing, but all I can think is that I won't get a day off to rest. I won't get a chance to let my knee drain before what may be the most important match of my life to date.

The next day the ref throws the ball in the air, and I miss the tip-off. It's not that I want to come out slow against ASU, but there's nothing I can do. Hampered by my knee problem, I have to settle for the shots I get inside, as there'll be few soaring jump hooks from me today. I can't get over the hump—for every bucket we score they match us, and we just can't pull away. Their inside players, too, seem to have free rein—with me hobbled, Sweet Al out, and the weight of a long contest the night before, it's all we can do to force ASU to work for their buckets, even if we can't keep them from putting the ball through the hoop.

At half we're virtually neck and neck with the Sun Devils of Arizona State, and that's when I start to worry. What's going on out there? Their center is taking advantage of me on offense, scoring over and around me with ease—am I letting my team down? Doubt begins creeping into the edges of my view. But that's when Coach Gardner buckles down on us.

"Don't play like you're afraid!" Coach yells. Hearing his voice arouses pride in me, awakening all of us from our slumber. "They're nothing compared to you! Nothing! So go out there and play like it!"

At times like this I could kiss the man. Coach Gardner knows how to inspire a team and make guys like me want to win.

Stepping out of the tunnel late in halftime, a smile creases the corners of my face. Even with the hobbled knee, I've got my swagger back—we all do. I push through the pain. My team fights for the boards. And when the buzzer rings the scoreboard reads, Arizona State: 80; Utah: 88.

We've won. We're headed to the Final Four.

It's the fulfillment of a dream: playing on a national stage, matching up against the best in the country. Of course, there's another bump in the road: we leave for Kansas City straightaway from Portland, Oregon. This means, again, that I won't have a chance to get my knee drained, and as I've played two tough, close, back-to-back games against punishing, demanding opponents, my knee is more full of fluid than it has ever been in my whole life.

How can I keep a watermelon halfway down my leg a secret? I don't even shower with the rest of the team. I can't: in the locker room I can't get the kneepad off of my left leg, and I have to cut it off when I'm alone back in the hotel room I'm sharing with Bo. It's a good thing I brought extras, because my knee is so swelled up that it would be obvious to even the most casual onlooker that I have a major problem. As I cut away at the fabric, I peek furtively at the door, looking up over and over and ready to hide should someone try to enter.

Three days later we're taking the court in Kansas City at the semifinals of the NCAA championships.

Our opponent in the semis is Midwestern regional champ Cincinnati; the other side of the bracket boasts St. Joseph's from Philadelphia and defending champs Ohio State, featuring my old nemesis, Jerry Lucas.

In the run-up to the semis our whole attitude has changed. Coming into the matchup with Cincinnati, the consensus among members of our team is that we're nothing short of unstoppable. We're cresting, at the height of a two-year run together marked by dominance. Our combined two-year record is 49-11. We've beaten a national number one; we've won our conference in back-to-back seasons; we've overcome racism and injury and at last advanced to the NCAA Final Four. The championship spotlight shines brightly upon us. We can do this.

Stepping out onto the floor against Cincy, we're all feeling strong and confident. My knee is nearly locked in place from all the fluid surrounding my kneecap, but nobody knows that save me, and everyone else is raring to go. Between Bo, Joe, Rich, and the rest of the guys, our roster is tough top to bottom. Besides, all Cincinnati has is Paul Hogue. As good as Hogue is, he's no Jerry Lucas, and we had no trouble bumping Ohio State off.

At the tip-off, Hogue goes up. I go up.

I start going down. Hogue keeps going up.

From the outset Hogue shows that he can outjump me. He gets over me to take the first few rebounds, and I just can't do anything about it. It's like I'm carrying a weight around on my ankle—like I'm back on the Jefferson track hobbling around. Instantly I realize the problem: with all the fluid coursing through my knee, I have no strength in my lower body at all.

This is going to be a problem.

As it turns out, Cincy has two advantages that we didn't take into account. The first is home-court advantage. Ohio is just a few hundred miles from Kansas City, close enough to drive, so the fans are decidedly tilted in their favor. The second and larger issue is that Cincy's got a player we can't contain. With my knee shot I can't get nearly as high off the ground as Hogue, nor can I keep pace with him as he runs up and down the court. Hogue vs. a fresh me would be fine. Hogue vs. No-knee McGill is anything but a fair fight. What's more, there's no one Coach Gardner can put in to match him, either. I've played nearly every minute at center since we beat Ohio State a year and a half ago, so there's nobody on the bench who's got the experience to run our offense in the middle or anchor our defense, especially with Sweet Al out of the picture. It's a bitter pill to swallow, but the fact is that Paul Hogue is single-handedly picking apart our squad. Our dreams and will are not enough. We do our best to stay in it, but there's not much we can do—with each passing minute our national title dreams fade to the steady beat of an executioner's drum. In the end Cincinnati erases us, 82–67, and I take it so hard I can't help but cry.

osu—damn osu—wins their matchup, of course, so our third-place consolation game is against St. Joseph's. From the moment we take the court for warm-ups I can see that though we're both out of contention, this is not going to be a cakewalk for either team. They're dishing passes to each other crisply and cleanly even in their layup drills, and it's obvious they want to win it.

Well, hell. I do, too. If I'm not gonna end my season with a championship, at least I'm going to end it with a bang.

From the opening tip the Runnin' Redskins push the ball up the court. We pour on the sauce, nailing bucket after bucket—it's like our shots are guided by a higher power. We have over fifty points by the half and nearly one hundred at the end of regulation time. Normally that's plenty to win it, but here's the interesting thing: it isn't. Despite the clinic in scoring we put on, Utah never pulls ahead—the game is back and forth the whole way because St. Joe's is scoring just as fast and furious as we are.

At the outset the fans don't much seem to care at all. We're the consolation match, and really, they're all waiting for the finals. In addition, we're a pair of coastal schools, and the hometown midwestern crowd is itching for their local Cincinnati vs. Ohio State finals matchup. So though both our squads come out ready to kill, the fans, at first, are stifling yawns.

All that changes, though. When our two teams—the Western and Eastern champs—come out swinging, ready to brawl, the crowd starts to pick up interest. When the third place match turns into a knockdown, drag-out, street fight of a basketball game, they respond. And as the game ends—tied at the finish of regular time, the crowd takes to their feet. They can see we're out for blood, and they're chanting and screaming as loudly as anyone at Einar Nielsen ever has.

The score is deadlocked, so we play overtime. At the end it's still tied, so we play another extra period. Then another. Then another. After every extra frame, the score is, amazingly, still tied, and we push our third-place match into a quadruple-overtime bout, the longest single game that's ever graced the NCAA championship tournament. For four quarters and three straight overtimes, the St. Joseph's Hawks and the Utah Runnin' Redskins battle over and over to an absolute standstill. A draw.

The crowed is ecstatic. We players are exhausted. By the time I'm finally ejected in the second overtime, just as most of the other starters have been, for going over the foul limit of five, my knee is hugely swollen and incredibly painful. It's so stiff that I don't even take a chair because my knee's so rigid I can hardly bend it; it hurts less to just stand courtside.

When the time finally expires St. Joseph's and Utah have set multiple tournament records, including longest game and highest combined point total. At the last buzzer, the final score reads 127–120 in their favor, and though it's a tough loss, at least it was a good one. The fans—indifferent at first to our efforts—applaud all of us as we leave, and that feels good.

Also there remain three small consolations that boost my spirits as the year draws to a close.

The first is that Cincinnati ends up winning the championship. Turns out even Ohio State, with Siegfried, Lucas, Knight, and Havlicek, doesn't have an answer for Paul Hogue. I'd rather it was us hoisting the trophy, but at least it wasn't OSU again.

The second is that I'm named second team All-American for my play throughout the season and leading the Utes all the way to the cusp of that sweet, promised land. That's quite an honor.

The third is that, despite coming up short in the four-overtime score, we end up winning third place in the nation anyway. St. Joseph's players are caught accepting banned booster money, and every one of their wins is vacated. It isn't the way I would have written it, but we take the bronze by forfeit.

I think about the hundred bucks I got after OSU and the use of that Mercury in 'Frisco. Everybody takes a little money here and there, don't they? So I shouldn't be worried, right? Or was it just that St. Joe's got caught?

One Last Summer

"You think about what you're gonna do after Utah?" Lefty asks. It's summer and a sunny day, and we're playing one-on-one, alone, in a little outdoor park. Birds fly across a cloudless sky.

"I don't know," I say, but of course I know what I want. Lefty does, too. I can't fool him.

"You going to go pro?"

I pause in mid-dribble. There it is. I swallow hard. "You think I can?"

"You serious?" Lefty lowers his hands, breaking his defense. "Look, Billy. Think about all the guys you know. Wilt? Bill Russell? We ran with them. Where are they now?"

"The pros."

"Oscar Robertson, 'Big O'? Bobby Sims, Darrall Imhoff? Where are they?"

"The pros."

"That's right! And you balled with them. Hell, I'm angling to go pro. So why shouldn't you?"

The pros. Playing pro basketball. What Lefty says is true—it's what I want and what I've always wanted: to play in the NBA. I've just never said it out loud before.

My whole life, everything I've ever wanted or loved has been taken away from me. My family, my home, any girl I've ever had. All of them, somehow or another, have slipped from my tenuous grasp. So maybe I've been afraid to admit this one dream to myself because if I admit that I care, that might make it the next thing in line to be taken away. But it's true. I want to go pro. I want to play in the NBA.

Lefty's still looking at me, but now he's smiling. "So? You gonna go for it?"

I nod.

"Good," he says, swatting the ball out of my hands and making me in that moment recall my old friend Earl Robinson from Berkeley. "Then let's get back to work. Because you need to work on your offense."

Senior Year

I return to Salt Lake City that fall a re-created and reinvigorated player. I'm that much tougher mentally and physically, and I've got a goal now, one that I've worked toward all summer long: making the NBA.

Over summer practice consumed just about every hour of my time. I worked as hard as I had ever before, like that little, awestruck kid in the YMCA with Mr. Ward, and it has paid off. My game is at another level. My jump hook has become unstoppable; I can shoot it from anywhere on the court. And since no one else even has a jump hook like that, there is simply no defense for it. Guys try to hop up and block me, but nobody ever manages to do it. I even start taunting guys for trying. "Wilt Chamberlain couldn't block my jump hook; how the hell do you think you're going to?"

When practice resumes we've got most of the same squad from last year's national semifinal team coming back, and we've all matured that much more, too. Bo Crain's muscles are that much bigger. Aufderheide looks that much meaner. And at point guard we've got a lightning-fast California boy: Ed Rowe, a guy who talks just as fast as he plays. He can shoot, he can dribble, he can pass; he's got it all.

I enter the year determined to go out on a high note. The jump hook will be my ticket to the pros. This is the year I'll play my way into the NBA. I push my classes to the side of my mind; I'll get back to them later. I have yet to fulfill my basic math requirement for graduation, but who cares? I've got plenty of work to do on the hardwood and don't need to get bogged down in numbers. Besides, points beat percentages. Free throws beat fractions.

I just wish there was something I could do about my leg.

As it has more and more these last few seasons, my knee constantly fills with fluid. I have to get it drained two or three times a week, and the pain gets more severe each day. Whereas the fluid used to emerge clear into the needle, it begins first to grow cloudy, then shows streaked tinges of cherry red, a sign that the cyst or whatever it is is now filling not just with pus but with blood. Over time the weight—the mental pressure—of this injury continues to build. With the exception of Dr. Clegg, I've still not talked to anyone about my knee injury, and carrying that load is a burden. I've hidden the knowledge of my pain like a horrible, dark secret in the deepest recesses of my mind, and now that I'm so close to realizing my dream—playing pro basketball in the NBA—the notion of disclosing my weakness is unthinkable. I have to hide it every day. I can't trust anyone with my secret.

And this is the mental state I'm in when I meet a guy named Manny.

Manny Zavotas is my buddy and an outcast like me: a swarthy, dark-looking Greek kid in lily-white Salt Lake City. He's one of my few friends who doesn't play ball; we meet around a pool table at the student union and from there we just kind of click. He's friendly and warm, and he doesn't ask questions—instead he just listens, and he even helps as my wingman with girls. When I have a date, he arranges to pick them up and, no questions asked, he brings them straight to my dorm so we can meet in private, away from prying eyes. Are they white, brown, red? It doesn't matter. No date, no movie; we just get down to it in private, where no one can see or complain.

How's that, Dr. Olpin, I think, for clinging to the old ways?

Despite the growing debilitation of my injury and my reversion to prowling for forbidden lambs in my senior year, my basketball game soars higher than ever before. I score at will and I rebound with ease. Every school we play against tries any defense they can think up to stop me, but it's to no avail because Ed Rowe always finds a way to get me the ball. We take down Colorado and we take down Utah State; come late in the season we've already all but clinched the Skyline Conference again, and the only hurdle left between us and the title is our rival from up the road: Brigham Young.

We've beaten them once already, but winning this game on BYU's home court in Provo will allow us to clinch the regular-season championship for a third year running. Provo's a two-hour drive from Salt Lake City, and the whole way there I sit alone in my bus seat, staring out into the darkness of the Utah winter.

I'm supposed to be gearing up for the game, but I can really only think about my injury. As I stroke my damaged knee I think to myself, what if my father had been there? I don't know where the thought comes from, but one minute it's just there, and once it's in my head it won't leave. I picture what it would have been like to have my dad in the stands for all my games at Thomas Jeff. I then imagine what might have gone differently with my rehab had he, a professional athlete, been there to guide me through my rehabilitation. He would have defended me against that evil-eyed doctor and figured out a way for me to get well, really well, that's for sure. But he wasn't there, and he didn't. And now I've got this lump instead.

By the time we finally arrive in Provo I've worked myself into an emotional frenzy. As we walk from the bus to the indoor court, we're ringed by screaming BYU fans. They're letting us know how they feel about us: not good.

"Get outta here, ya damn Utes!"

"You're going down tonight!"

"You can't stop the Cougars! You can't stop BYU!"

I block them out of my mind like I always do. But then one heckler in the crowd makes it very, very personal.

"Get the hell out of Provo, McGill, you dumb, black-ass nigger!"

I'm already full of confusion and rage from my thoughts about my father. But that comment just flips a switch inside me, and as I fixate on what I've just heard I get angry. Really angry.

"Black-ass nigger," I chant, repeating the epithet to myself. "Black-ass nigger, huh? Black-ass nigger?!" Within moments I'm such a fury of emotion that all other thoughts have been pressed away; all I can think about is destroying BYU. My knee, which I'd been absentmindedly rubbing throughout the bus ride to Provo, suddenly feels just as good as it had the morning of the game against OSU—as fresh as it had been before my injury.

BYU is in for a long night. There's no doubt in my mind.

I stride out to center court amid a roaring sea of Cougar navy blue, and all my emotions come to a head. Ed Rowe steps over to me and says, "Billy, be ready. I'm going to get you the ball tonight." And I just nod. To some people, no matter what a black man accomplishes, he's nothing but the color of his skin. Well, tonight I'm going to show them. Tonight, I decide, BYU is about to feel some pain at the hands of this black-ass nigger.

The two hours of the game soar by in what feels like an instant. I take the first possession after the jump ball and immediately put in a bucket. My knee feels blessed by an angel; I unleash shots with deadly accuracy from all over the court. I'm angry, I'm hard; I'm playing like I'm sixteen years old again. All the fans in Cougar blue are forced to watch me launch sweeping shots, going straight up with a dunk, a layup, a jump hook. Over and over again the ball hits nothing but net, and when halftime rolls around I've scored thirty-five points, almost more than the whole BYU team combined. But it's not enough.

When the second half begins I'm playing for everyone: my parents, my fans, the NBA scout I'm sure is in the crowd, my teammates, my roommates, myself. BYU has no idea how to stop me. I've ceased to be a man and have become a force of nature.

As we huddle up and take towels and water during a time-out, Ed Rowe slyly approaches me again. "Billy," he says, "did you know you've already got fifty-four points?" I shake my head. I didn't. I just wanted to take the court and crush 'em. "Well, let's see if we can get you to sixty."

The ref blows his whistle, signifying the end of the time-out. Like Carney Crisler, I spike my towel to the floor. I lock eyes with Ed. "You think you can get me the ball three more times?" He nods. "Then I'll put it in."

We get the ball, and Ed Rowe proves good to his word. Through double and triple teams, he manages to feed me inside. I put in a layup: that makes fifty-six points. A jump hook: fifty-eight. Finally, with three minutes left, I gently kiss a finger roll off the backboard; it toilet bowls around the rim, then gently swirls down and in to give me an even sixty.

When the time buzzer sounds the scoreboard reads, Utah: 106; BYU: 101. I've scored my sixty, which I later find out is the most any player in the state has ever scored in a single game, and more important, we've won.

Job done, we shower and proceed back toward the bus to return to Salt Lake City. Curiously, I don't hear any comments about being a nigger on the way back.

When we return to the Utah campus the Ute faithful swarm me. News has spread like wildfire that we beat BYU and I poured in sixty points, and everyone's ready to celebrate. Once Bo and I manage to make our way through the crowds, we pick up Sweet Al and head to Dave Freed's ball-room downtown to catch Cal Tjader and his Latin band play mambo. We just want to enjoy the show, but as we settle in people in the crowd start chanting out, "Sixty! Sixty!" and "The Hill! The Hill!" and it's all I can do not to lower my head and blush.

In my moment of glory it's tough not to feel for Sweet Al. I want to tell him that I know what it's like. I, too, have been injured; I know what he's going through. I know what it feels like to be hardly able to walk, let alone play. I know the fear that grips him, that maybe he's done forever, and I'm on the verge of telling him—but before I can I'm pulled away by none other than Cal Tjader himself.

From a slip of paper, Tjader reads into a mike, "Billy McGill has just scored sixty for the Utes!" People in the crowd clap and cheer, and again I hear my name called—"The Hill! The Hill!" A spotlight shines on me from up in the ceiling, and slowly, reluctantly I rise.

"Now," Tjader continues, tossing the slip of paper aside, "how about this. Would you like to hear the Hill play the congas?"

I thought I'd heard cheering before, but that makes the roof pop off. "Come on," he calls, "get up here and play!" and before I know it I'm slotting myself in behind Amado Peraza's big, beautiful, twin turquoise congas, and I'm in heaven. Sixty points scored against BYU plus playing with one of the best Latin percussionist groups of all time? It's the best night of my life. When it all ends, I still intend to have my heart-to-heart with Sweet Al. But somehow, despite my best intentions, I never seem to find the time.

23

A Bad Bounce

I'm on a high after BYU, but coming off that win, with us in the middle of another conference championship season, tragedy, as it inevitably does, strikes.

One of the role players on our squad in 1960–61 was a tough nut from New York City, a senior named Barry Epstein. Partway through the year he got a bit homesick, and it turns out he went back to New York for a visit with his folks. Only thing is, he let a booster buy him the plane ticket. The NCAA traced down the money, and even though Epstein's not even at the school anymore, they announce that his stupid move costs us—not him, but *us*—the right to go on and play in the NCAA tournament. The very tournament we barely missed out on winning the year before, the tournament all of us on the team are dying to win in our last shot at glory, we're now locked out of. Because of him.

The news is all over the *Utah Chronicle*, and when we hear it it's a dagger in our hearts. This is it: we're going out with a whimper, and not for lack of heart or effort or the failure to bounce back from Sweet Al's accident, but because of the misconduct of a guy who isn't even still on the team.

"There's no reason we couldn't have done it again," says my roomie Bo when we learn the news, punching his pillow. "We could have gone to the Final Four. Hell, we could have gone farther." All the sportswriters agree: we're in the top ten of every national poll. But it doesn't matter. We'll never know. As I blink back the anger every one of us feels, I try not to wonder whether I was, in my own way, at fault. After all, I accepted money and favors. How different was that?

Besides, of course, the fact that I never got caught?

Last Hurrah at Utah

It's hard playing the remaining games of the season knowing that we won't be in the NCAAS. Most of our last few games are very physical; I think because that BYU game has pushed me over the top. I'm leading the nation in scoring, and everyone we play knows it. Thus there's extra incentive to stop me. Of course, my style isn't a rough-and-tumble inside game; it's about finesse, so trying to shove me around doesn't make much difference. When teams send in their hatchet men to rough me up, it doesn't hurt my scoring line. Although it does hurt my body.

As the season ends the needle nightmares worsen, but I get used to playing with the pain. My defense is shaky, but my jump hook has become so awesome there's not much other teams can do.

Time rolls by, and with one game left in my college career, I wake up at 5:00 a.m. and walk outside the dorm into the predawn air. The cold wind hits me in the face, and it feels good. Looking out over the Wasatch Mountains, I think about how great it's been here at the U. I look out at the range and smile, glad that I've been blessed to be a part of this. Of course, some slice of me is already looking to the future, looking to the road ahead.

I go through the same old little rituals, the ones I've perfected over the years. I walk over to the student union and eat a big breakfast. I call my mother before lacing up my sneakers. And then, after resting most of the day, I settle in and wait for the pregame meal, when the coach will talk Xs and Os as we prepare for our opponents, knowing that this will be our last hurrah.

Listening to our defensive assignments for our final opponent, Wyoming, we're all a little shaken up. It's a weird feeling knowing that despite everything working right, despite having fired on all cylinders all through our years together, despite claiming another conference championship, win or lose this will be our last game together.

When we walk out onto the floor for our pregame warm-ups, the cheer that greets us is deafening. Einar Nielsen Fieldhouse is packed, and the whole stadium bleeds Utah red. During the game I'm in the zone. I'm not thinking; I'm just playing. My shots are falling and my knee feels good; besides that there is nothing else. Before I know it it's halftime, and we're back in our locker room. I think we're winning, but I'm more concerned with looking around and remembering this place, this moment. Right there—there's where Sweet Al used to dress. That corner, that's where I first heard I'd get a start. In that locker, there's that huge dent where Carney Crisler damn near put his foot through the door.

Second half begins, and Wyoming still has no idea how to stop our offense. Sometimes it feels like their whole team is guarding me, but it doesn't matter. When they collapse on me I dish to my open teammates for an easy basket. When they start respecting that outlet pass again, I resume going up to the hoop. With a few minutes left Coach subs me out so I can watch the last few minutes of the game, listening to the fans scream our names and call out their love and respect. When the final horn blows we've won by a landslide: 94–75. I've scored another massive total, fifty-one points, but that's it. My Utah career is at an end.

On the heels of the win a deep sadness sweeps over me. I've just played the last game I'll ever play at the U, and I'm torn to know I'll have to walk away. But as I go to leave the floor I notice something odd: the stands are still full. The fans are still clapping, cheering, and swaying; only a handful of people have gotten up to depart. The defeated Wyoming team slinks back to the visitors' locker room, but everyone else remains. It goes on for two minutes, then five—our whole team is standing, waving to the crowd, and expecting the noise to die down, but it doesn't. Finally, in the midst of all this adoration, two men get up and walk past me onto the center of the Einar Nielsen Fieldhouse floor: Coach Gardner and President Olpin.

What are they doing up there?

Someone brings them a mike, and for a moment the crowd quiets. "That was a great win," says Coach, and the crowd roars in agreement. I can barely make out anything he says after that, but whatever it is it's got to be great, because all of the Ute faithful cheer in exuberance every time he stops speaking. Finally Coach passes the microphone over to Dr. Olpin, and Dr. Olpin—of all people, Dr. Olpin—begins to say nice things about us. About me. I catch only snippets, but what I do hear is wonderful.

"Leading scorer of all time at Utah . . ." He's talking about me!

"Led us to our fourth straight conference title, a record . . ."

"All-time leading rebounder . . ."

"School record for points per game, and a national record all-time for a center . . ."

It's amazing. Accolades flow from his lips like water down a river, and the more he lauds me the more the crowd applauds. An assistant makes his way down to the floor, and he joins our coach and our school president. He holds in his hand what looks like a massive board, and Dr. Olpin calls me to join him on center court.

I look to Ed Rowe. Ed nods. I walk out onto the floor.

Dr. Olpin looks at me, and he smiles. "In honor," he says—and now I can hear just fine—"of the greatest player our school has ever known, we have a special award."

He's talking about me. The greatest player ever? I still can't believe this is happening.

"Today, we are retiring the number 12 in honor of Billy McGill!"

The crowd erupts, and I can hardly believe what I'm seeing. Through a shimmering film of tears of joy, I see a jersey—my jersey—being hoisted up into the rafters next to the school's championship banner, Utah and the number 12 wafting in the breeze as cables tug it up to the sky. Then Dr. Olpin holds aloft the board the assistant brought: it's a glass case with my jersey matted and framed inside. Dr. Olpin calls me over, and in front of everyone he gives it to me. It's like a dream. The moment touches my heart and burnishes my soul in a way nothing else ever has in my life.

All these years of work, of hurt, of pain, mental and physical, of grit, of discrimination, of injury, of determination—they all pay off in this moment. It's the highlight of my career. I shake the president's hand, and I hug my coach. I wave to the crowd. And just like that, it's all over.

Welcome to the Big Leagues, Kid

Leaving Utah, I'm proud of what I've accomplished. I have not only broken the color line at a historically all-white school, but I've been accepted and, more than that, feted. I've been publicly lauded by the president of the school, and I've broken every record before me. My 15 rebounds per game is the highest average ever by any player at Utah. My 1,106 total rebounds and 2,321 total points are also each a new high-water mark. The 38.8 points per game I scored in my senior season is not only the highest ever by a Utah player but also the highest ever by any center in the history of NCAA basketball. Not Bill Russell, not Jerry Lucas, not George Mikan or even Wilt the Stilt can match that. I'm leaving the U as the most prolifically scoring center in college basketball history.

I know that there are people—some even my teammates—who don't think I always ran my hardest or always gave it my all. I do my best to ignore them, although that's about as easy as ignoring the cold winds off the Wasatch. Was I sometimes less than my best? Well, obviously. I didn't score sixty points every night. But there's more than that, too, and I know it. Still, what could I have done? I never could admit that I was barely able to leap off one of my legs. That might have silenced my detractors, but it would have killed my dream. And now, at last, that dream has come true. As I prepare for my final days at the U, I get the phone call I've been waiting on for years: I'm going to the NBA.

The Chicago Zephyrs—an expansion team, the youngest club in the league—open the 1962–63 season by making me the number one pick in the NBA draft. All those seasons of keeping my knee a secret and playing through the pain have paid off. No one knows I'm a racehorse with a hitch—no one but me, anyhow—and now I'm about to go pro.

When the angels would laugh at us, they answer our prayers.

The team gets in touch and makes arrangements to fly me out to Chicago to sign my contract. They offer to let me bring someone, and since Coach Gardner is a little busy for this kind of thing and I can't imagine bringing my mother, I bring a friend. Not one of my teammates, of course—why would Sweet Al or Bo want to watch me sign a pro deal while they get shunted off to the sidelines? Instead I bring the number one problem solver I know.

"Manny," I say, "Manny Zavotas."

We arrive at the office of Dave Trager, the team owner. I can hardly temper my excitement. Manny's practically got to hold me down as we walk into the Loop skyscraper, and I'm already mentally swatting away opponents' jump shots as the two of us ride the elevator to the top of the building.

When we're ushered into Mr. Trager's private hall, my first impression is to be blown away by the size of it. I'm a big guy, too; it takes a lot to impress me. But this office does. The room is appointed in gleaming wall shelving, which rings an extra-long desk that stretches twenty feet across the heart of the room. Framed paintings splash the walls in color. It's the room of an emperor, which makes its occupant all the more incongruous to me.

In the middle of the room behind the emperor's desk sits a ratty-looking man with a gray moustache. He smokes an acrid cigar, and the impression he gives, in stark contrast to his grand environs, is of an actor playing the role of the crooked landlord or shady insurance salesman.

He swivels in his leather chair—for him it's almost comically oversized—and exhales a thick puff of smoke, which hangs low around his greased head. I try not to think ill of him, despite the picture he presents. I just want to hear him say, "Billy, congratulations. You're in the NBA."

He does not say this.

"Who are you?" he asks me curtly. He does not rise from his seat.

"Mr. Trager," I say, approaching him, hand outstretched. "I'm Billy McGill."

He still doesn't get up, instead eyeing me from top to toes. He speaks from the side of his mouth. "I thought you were supposed to be built like a brick shithouse?"

I lower my hand and place it back in my pocket. Mr. Trager does not tell me that it's nice to meet me.

This is not going well.

After calling in his general manager, Frank Lane, and telling his secretary to summon the team photographer and have him wait in the outer room, Trager removes a sheaf of papers from a drawer by his thigh and slams it down on his desk. "Sign this," he says.

"What is it?"

"It's your contract. You're getting seventeen thousand dollars per year, two seasons guaranteed." Another puff of smoke billows across the table. It feels fetid in my lungs.

I look at Manny, dumbstruck. "Mr. Trager," he pipes up. "That seems quite low."

"It's league average," says Trager. "We're not paying you more than our stars." He pauses then adds, "Take it or leave it."

Manny interjects again. "But he's the number one draft choice."

"I know goddamn well who he is; who do you think picked him?" Trager shouts.

"And this is all you think he's worth?" Manny asks. "Have you seen Billy play?" Lane, the GM, seems to shrink against the wall. I'm a little concerned—after all, Trager's the man. He works on the top floor of this building; he owns the team. Is it such a good idea to piss him off? What am I going to do if he tells me he's changed his mind?

"This is the deal: seventeen thousand dollars a year for two seasons. Take it or leave it," Trager repeats. "You can sign or not, I don't care."

Manny looks over to me, and I shrug. He grins and turns back to Trager. Ever the hustler, he's full of ideas. "If you don't think Billy's gonna be worth more than this to your club, don't pay him all this cash. How about we start with league minimum and then give him an extra twenty dollars for every point he scores this season?"

Trager slams his cigar into a bronze ashtray. "Look," he says, "this is not a negotiation. This is how much money he's gonna get." He turns to me, jabbing a finger in my face. "Now, do you want to play basketball or not?"

It's a lowball offer, and everyone in the room knows it. But the sad fact of it is, I want that money. My family needs it. And I want to play in the NBA. Trager holds all the cards. So I sign the contract.

The photographer's called in, and as he takes my photo I try to force myself to smile. All the while I'm telling myself that seventeen thousand is far more than Daddy Lonnie ever made in a year, and I should be happy. At the same time, though, I wonder: would Mr. Trager be railroading the national scoring champ like this if the color of his skin were white?

Before I even make it home, both the *Utah Chronicle* and the *LA Times* have printed articles about my signing. "Terms [of the deal] were not disclosed," they both read, "but Trager said the 22-year-old McGill pocketed 'one of the best contracts ever signed by a collegian entering the monied ranks.'"

Yeah, right.

When I return to Salt Lake City I do three things in quick succession. The first is to buy a car, a 1962 Austin Healey convertible. It's cream colored with a black ragtop and black leather seats; it's gorgeous, and I'm proud of it because it's the first thing I've ever been able to call really mine. The second thing is to send some money home to my mother and Daddy Lonnie. And the third thing I do, almost immediately, is to stop attending school.

Deep down I know dropping out is dumb, even as I'm doing it. But it's so easy to rationalize to myself.

"I'm a pro ball player now. What do I still need college for?" I stop going to lectures or taking exams, allowing myself to flunk out of all of my second-semester senior courses. I can't see the folly of this; all I can see is my name in lights. Who needs remedial math with seventeen thousand dollars in their pocket?

Once word gets out that I've signed with the Zephyrs, my phone starts ringing off the hook. Big Jim Hadnot calls me from California and asks me to ditch the NBA to play with the Oakland Oaks of a newly formed rival group: the American Basketball League. "We'll get you thirty-five grand, minimum," he says. "That's got to be more than what you're making in the NBA." It is, of course, but I don't tell him that.

"Why would I play anywhere but the NBA?"

"Because the ABL is *paying* everyone better than the NBA. Even the refs!" He goes on. "Our team owner is Pat Boone. You know, the singer? He's got cash to burn. And it's still pro ball." Sensing I'm unimpressed, he adds, "We've got some of the best talent out there."

"Oh, yeah? Like who?"

"George Yardley. You know him?"

"Of course I know him. He's washed up."

"He was also the first guy to score two thousand points in a season."

I snort. "Okay. Go on." Yardley, I know, is thirty-four, a dinosaur in basketball years, and he's been retired for two seasons.

"We've got Connie Hawkins out of Iowa."

"The one who got kicked out of college ball for point shaving?"

"That's the one."

"Who else?"

"Well, these two other dudes."

"What two other dudes? Do I know them?"

"I think you played against 'em," Hadnot says. "They're from Ohio State. Larry Siegfried and Jerry Lucas?"

Lucas. The receiver turns to ice in my hand.

"Come play with us," Hadnot cajoles, and now that I know who's in the league his offer is a bit tempting. Double salary and the chance to beat Lucas twice—that'd be nice. I almost want to tell him to give me some time to think it over. But really, I don't. Even if I'm getting paid short of what I'm worth, I've long since made up my mind where I'm going to play: the NBA.

Training Camp

Training camp for the Zephyrs opens about eighty miles northwest of Chicago in Burlington, Wisconsin, and when I arrive I'm feeling good. I've spent a fair bit of time these last few months lifting weights and working out, trying to prep my body for NBA play, and though my knee is still bothering me, I feel strong.

Our living quarters, which are spartan as army barracks, sit just across the street from our practice gym. On reporting day, before practices begin, Coach Jack McMahon gathers us all to elucidate what he demands and expects from us. Looking around, I recognize some of the faces—there's Terry Dischinger from Purdue, a rookie like me who was the Zephyrs' second-round pick, taken tenth overall. Then there're Walt Bellamy, U.S. Olympian and 1960 gold medalist, and Si Green, who was good enough to be selected before Bill Russell in the '56 draft. There're a lot of guys, in fact, many of whom are damn good. But the roster's going down to only twelve men, which means there'll be cuts. Looking around the huddle in that moment, I'm suddenly glad for my two-year guaranteed deal, meager as the attached figure may be.

"Listen up, men," begins Coach McMahon. "I'm gonna make this easy. I'm the captain of this ship, which means that what I say goes. It's my way or the highway. If you cannot do what I say, when I say it, then you should pack up your bags and leave right now."

Well, his inspirational style is certainly different from Coach Gardner's. Gardner made me want to play for him. This guy makes me want to stuff my ears.

"I'm coming off a nine-year pro career," McMahon warbles. "I won three straight Western Division championships with the St. Louis Hawks as well as one NBA championship. Can anyone else in here say that?"

No one answers.

"I've learned more about this game than some of you will ever know. So shut up and listen." McMahon goes on to lambaste us for having turned out the worst record in the league the season before. I'm tempted to raise my hand and point out that many of us in camp weren't even on the team last year, but the venom McMahon spews makes me keep my mouth shut. I don't want him to direct his crazed wrath at me. What's even crazier than his tirades, though, is that most of the old veterans on the team don't even seem to be paying attention! In fact, Woody Sauldsberry and Andy Johnson, the only other black faces in the room, are ignoring Coach McMahon outright and laughing with each other!

This is what I've been dreaming of all these years?

We're told to report back the next morning to start two-a-day practices. On the way out the door, all the players snake into a line. As each player reaches the front a man in a suit with a briefcase hands him an envelope. I'm not sure why, but I don't want to get called out for screwing up already, so I just slide in at the back. It's not until I get mine and open it that I realize what it is.

It's money. He's handing out stacks of money.

Why this is happening I don't know, but I damn sure know not to question it. I take the cash like everybody else, then walk silently but directly back to my room—and only once the door's closed behind me do I count it.

There's four hundred dollars in there. To me it's a small fortune.

That night I find Sauldsberry and Johnson in the rec room of our dormitory huddled over a little pool table. They're laughing and joshing one another again, and I get the feeling that these guys might be trouble. Still, they're brothers like me, the only ones I know who talk the same language. I remember how hard it was starting out as the only black face at Utah, and I don't want to go through that isolation once again. So I ramble on over.

"Hey there, rookie," offers Johnson. "You spend all your money yet?"

I shake his hand nervously and don't answer. I wonder if he can sense that I still don't know why that guy handed me all that cash in the first place—or that I've got half of it stuffed in my sock right now.

"Lay off him," says Sauldsberry, and I'm glad for his help. So I ask, trying to sound casual, what all the money's for anyway. Andy Johnson laughs and reaches for a pool cue while Sauldsberry answers me. "Per diem."

"We get all that cash every day?" I exclaim, and Johnson laughs again.

"Naw," Sauldsberry says, "that's for the whole camp. For food and stuff like that."

"Four hundred dollars? For two weeks?" I've never had anyone hand me that kind of cash for nothing in my life. Hell, even when that alum pressed a hundred on me after we knocked off Ohio State, the money wasn't just for showing up.

"I know, right?" Johnson stands up. "And they only give you one pair of socks for the whole time here, too. Cheap bastards." He takes a shot. He misses.

"Listen, kid," Sauldsberry says. "You need to watch yourself. There're a lot of sharks in this league. You go down here, nobody's got your back."

"Yeah?"

"Yeah," he says. "It's every man for himself. It ain't like college. You can't trust no one here for a minute."

"You notice," Johnson says, "how there were so many guys out there today? Coach is gonna cut at least half of 'em. And some won't deserve it."

"Coach seems to know what's up," I parrot. "Coach won three straight Western Division championships and an NBA ring." Now it's Sauldsberry's turn to laugh.

"Yeah, sure he did," he says. "He won three division championships. But he didn't mention the five years before that he spent in the basement with the Hawks and with Rochester.

"And," he adds, stepping lightly now around the perimeter of the pool table, "the Hawks cut him in 1960 to make room on the roster for me." He takes his shot now, sinking the nine ball. "Or did he neglect to mention that too?"

I'm shocked to hear this kind of talk. "But—but he's the coach."

"Yeah," Sauldsberry sighs. "He's the coach. And he's what we've got. But it ain't like he's the king of the game. He ain't even king of this team."

Why is Sauldsberry talking about the coach like that? My frown draws out Johnson again; it's his turn to sigh. "The real power's in the owner's box, kid. With Trager." He shakes his head. "And Trager, he don't like us too much."

"You got that right," says Sauldsberry, who produces a triangle and begins pulling balls out of the pockets to rack them for a new game.

"What do you mean?"

"I mean he doesn't like our kind," Sauldsberry replies.

"He doesn't care for niggers," says Johnson.

I shake my head. Is it like the Salt Lake diner all over again? It can't be.

"Oh, no?" says Sauldsberry, sensing my denial. "Then answer me this, Mr. Number One Draft Pick. How come Trager's only paying you seventeen thou a year when he's paying white-boy second-rounder Dischinger forty?"

That gets me. I freeze. I hadn't told anybody what I'm getting paid. How did he know?

"I'm just running this down to you," says Sauldsberry, "'cause I want you to know what you're up against. Trager here is a con artist, and the NBA is a cutthroat league. Someone here will always be out to get you. And teams here are only gonna carry as few black players as they can and still manage to get on by."

I'm silent, shaken.

He goes on. "And don't ever get hurt, either. Management don't expect black players to get hurt. If you're black getting hurt is like signing your own death warrant."

Instinctively, I reach down and rub by knee. Sauldsberry's just confirmed the thing I've always feared. I thank my lucky stars I've never told how bad it is.

"Besides," Johnson adds, "we already got a center. We got Walt Bellamy. He was Rookie of the Year last year; he pulled down 31.6 points per game—in the pros—while you were still shaving your whiskers in college. You think you're going to get any playing time? They don't need you on the court. You're not even gonna get five minutes."

"Easy," says Sauldsberry.

"Why do you think they drafted you in the first place? You're their side-show!"

"Easy!" says Sauldsberry, but it's too late. It's true, they have a future Hall-of-Famer in Bellamy already. What, I wonder, is their plan for me?

"Listen, kid," Sauldsberry says, putting his arm around me. "Don't let it get to you. Just stay focused. Play hard. Give it your best."

But it's too late. I've receded into my shell.

"C'mon," he offers, trying to undo the damage he and Johnson have done. "Hey, rookie, calm down. How 'bout this? You play craps at all?"

The magic words. Just like that I snap out of my funk. A light goes off like the flickering of a cracked bulb hanging over a tiled, seventh grade bathroom, and I smile.

Exhibition

As it turns out Sauldsberry and Johnson are right about a couple of things. Without question that lump sum of cash we got on the first day is all we get for the whole training camp. And undoubtedly there are a number of sharks in this league. And I'm one of 'em.

After four hours of playing craps our first night, I manage to take every penny that Woody Sauldsberry and Andy Johnson have. Every time I win—and I win quite a lot—I snatch up their money right off the pool table, and I allow myself to laugh.

"That it, boys?" I taunt. "You done?" Their pride gets in their way of their judgment, and time and again they lay another ten or twenty on the line. They might be wise in the ways of pro basketball, but they don't know beans about dice. I don't win everything in one go, but within three or four hours I've got it all.

Eight hundred dollars is a nice bonus, and it's twelve in all if you count my own per diem. How's that for remedial math?

The next morning I'm awoken by pounding at my door. "Come on," says a grizzled voice. "Wake up. Let's go into town and get some break-fast." I open the door and it's not Dave Costa. It's Woody Sauldsberry and

Andy Johnson. They need me to go with them; without me they can't pay for their food.

I accede, and for the rest of our time in camp I take the guys out to breakfast every day. I don't want them to go hungry, but I'm not about to give them all their money back, either. It's their fault, I figure, for messing with the top dog. In craps as in basketball, when I hit the zone, there's almost no shot I can't make.

I've had dreams of playing in the NBA my whole life. But when our first day of real work begins—the morning of our first preseason two-a-day— it's a nightmare. If Sauldsberry and Johnson were goofing off and trying to show up the coach yesterday, today it's a different story. I've never before in my life run drills like we have to run. As at day one at Utah, a couple of players throw up from the physical effort. The majority of players are simply not in shape for that type of brutal workout—myself obviously included. By the end even Bellamy is doubled over, and he's supposed to be the big star.

It hurts, but for a moment it feels a lot like the first day at Jefferson or the first day at Utah—we're in pain, but we're going through it all together. This is how teams are built, right? I'm expecting camaraderie. I'm expecting hand claps on the back and understanding. But what I get is the cold shoulder.

Sauldsberry and Johnson were right. It's a lesson that's hammered home on this very first day: there is no one here to look out for any man but his own self.

When McMahon at last blows his whistle after hours of training to end the morning practice, it's a mercy. I slink back to my room while the other players are showering at the gym—with these guys I don't want to leave myself exposed.

Once I'm safe in my little hole, I drop onto my bed and begin to undress. It's not until then that I realize just how rough-and-tumble McMahon's bang-up calisthenics were. What I see once I pull down my pads makes me do a double take.

My bad knee is more inflamed than I've ever seen it, even more than after the four-overtime game against St. Joe's. In fact, it's so full of fluid I can't bend it at all. In my whole life it has never been this swollen.

I stumble to the bedside table to find the yellow pages and call a doctor, but then I realize: there isn't a phone.

Since I'm already mostly undressed, I whip the rest of my clothes off and hobble into the bathroom for a quick shower. I try to put on some fresh clothes after, but my knee has swelled so much more in the twenty minutes since stepping into the shower that I can't even get my left leg into my pants. I have to pull the blade off my shaving razor and cut the bottom half off my jeans just so I can get them on. Then I juke my way over to the phone in the front hall of the dorm to find in the telephone directory a doctor who can see me right now.

There's no phone book.

Briefly I panic. What do I do? For a moment, I consider going back across the street and finding Coach McMahon, but remembering what Sauldsberry and Johnson said stops me. I remember the sneer on Trager's face and how McMahon reports to that man, and in that instant I decide there's nobody who can solve this problem for me but myself.

I get into the Healey ragtop—it's rough going at first, and I'm forced to lean in and take the top down while bent over the steering wheel just to get the room I need to slip in. But once I'm in the seat there's another problem: I can't flex my left leg enough to shift out of first gear. That leaves me with no choice but to putter down the streets of rural Wisconsin at ten miles an hour, scanning desperately for a doctor.

I should count myself lucky, though. At least I don't have to put the car in reverse.

After a few minutes of cruising down the main drag of Burlington, I find a doctor's office. I pull into the parking lot and drag myself in, and as it happens he's able to see me right away because he isn't busy at all. Is that a good sign or a bad one?

With my pants one leg long and one short, I look like a jester. The nurse helps me hobble into an antiseptic examination room in the back of the office. When the doctor—a slight, dark man—comes in, he doesn't even finish introducing himself before his eye catches sight of what's growing from my foreleg. He stares at it.

"That," he says, "is the single most inflamed knee I've ever seen in my life."

Great.

Immediately I'm hoisted up onto a big metal table. The doctor begins making preparations to drain my knee, and I feel like a thoroughbred about to be shot.

For most of my life the fluid in my knee has nearly always been clear, or at worst cloudy. Starting senior year at Utah there'd sometimes be a thin trace of blood floating through, darkening the extract like a squeezed marionberry in a glass of seltzer, but nothing more. But as I watch this doctor with his turkey baster needle, I can tell immediately that this is different. This is very bad. The liquid spewing forth from my kneecap is yellow and thick, and I don't need a college degree, let alone a med school one, to know that I'm in serious trouble. Viscous, gravy-colored pus does not belong in a kneecap.

When it's all over I return to the front desk and pay—my days of freebies are officially over—and as I'm leaving the doctor pats me on the back. "I've given you some cortisone in addition to the draining—just give it a day or so to let it take effect," he says. "Make sure you don't run or put any strain on your knee, and in a week you'll be fine."

I stop with the door open, half in and half out of the frame. "A week. Yeah, Doc. Sure." As if I have a choice.

Within four hours I'm back on the court.

My knee feels like a quivering pile of jelly, and it gives easily under my weight, even during soft shootarounds. I shouldn't play, I know—I recall what happened once before: a solitary, skinny kid in sweatpants crutch-waddling around a track all alone—but Sauldsberry's warnings echo through my head. I can't let them know I'm hurt. I'm going to play. I must.

In front of all the assembled tryouts, Coach calls out the starting lines. Naturally, Bellamy's named the first-team center, and I'm matched up against him on second string. Looks like Andy Johnson was right. Coach apparently hasn't considered running me alongside Bellamy as a power forward at all. Bellamy's two forwards on the starting string are Sauldsberry and Terry Dischinger.

"White, second-round pick Terry Dischinger," someone whispers in my ear. I turn and look. It's Andy Johnson.

Just before tip-off I glance into the stands. Trager is up there.

I try not to focus on the boss's boss and keep my attention on the task at hand, but it's hard. My mind's swimming, and I'm worrying about playing time and no-cut contracts, bonuses, and white-player favoritism—if there is such a thing—and next thing I know there's no time to think about any of that because Bellamy's coming right at me.

The man's like an ox: powerful and immovable. I press into him with my chest and the back of one hand, hoping to corral him and force him to pass it off, but instead he takes a few dribbles, fakes to one side, dropsteps with the other, and scores easily with a power move to the basket. He pushes through me like water—slowed, but only just. And it's all I can do not to crumple down to the hardwood.

A glance at the stands shows me that Trager's clapping, and I want to show him that I can score, too. But when we head downcourt and I post up inside, the pass never comes. Instead one of the guards throws up an off-balance shot from twenty feet out. It clangs off the backboard. Bellamy takes the rebound. And like that we're back on defense. Running back upcourt, I wonder why I didn't get fed the ball—didn't the guards see how open I was? And then as one swipes at Dischinger, fouling him, it hits me: these guys are trying to play their way onto the first string themselves. Some of them, in fact, are probably still just trying to make their spot on the team. They're not gonna pass it to *anybody* if they can help it; they're gonna try to make shots to get noticed. Hell, as a center playing inside, I may never even get to *touch* the ball.

His next time downcourt Bellamy bowls me over again. He goes up and I try to go up with him; I'm halfway to launching myself in the air when my bum knee pulls me down like a weight belt. Bellamy gets by easily, and he lays in another two-pointer. Before the ball even touches the floor, he's talking trash, letting me know my place on this squad.

"You sit down, rookie!" he yells.

It's going to be a long afternoon.

When the horn finally blows and the scrimmage ends, I'm thankful as a pig in the confines of the soft, warm slaughterhouse, waiting at last for the merciful hammer. I've just been beaten like I never have in my entire life, and with resignation I make to slink off in the direction of the exit. But someone won't let me leave.

It's Trager.

"What the hell is wrong with you? Hah! I'm talking to you! What's your problem?"

I look up, and the team's owner, that rat-faced bastard, is standing there, leaning over the railing and screaming at me.

"You're worthless! What's the matter with you? You're supposed to be this big great machine, and you're nothing! You hear me, Mr. First Pick? You're nothing!"

I already feel miserable, and this man, my boss, unleashing his horrible vitriol on me in front of all these other people just makes it even worse. It's the first time I've ever really failed at anything, and though I know it's not my fault, there's nothing I can do. I'm ashamed. I'm riddled with conflict. I want to tell Trager about my knee, and at the same time I want to clamber down into a hole and disappear. I want to jump up into the stands and beat that man mercilessly. I want to cry. All these things I want to do at once, but I can't. Instead all I do is stare.

My confidence is shattered by the game. It doesn't help to find, back in my room, that my knee is so full of fluid again that I can't bend it. I don't know what I'm going to do. I shower and wrap my knee like I'd done all through college, hoping that the wrapping will help push away some of the fluid. For hours I lie still staring at the ceiling, wondering what's going to become of me. I've never been so demoralized. I feel like I've descended into hell.

Is this, I wonder, what my dad felt like when he lost those fights at the Coliseum? Is this what it felt like to come home and find us gone?

I awaken the next morning to the harsh buzz of the alarm clock. Hopeful

1. The only photo I have of me with my father: he's teaching me to box on the front lawn. I couldn't have been more than ten years old when this photo was taken. (Courtesy of Billy McGill)

LOS ANGELES
City
CHAMPS
1955

2. (*opposite top*) Me with my mother, with Daddy Lonnie standing nearby. He was dapper. She was beautiful. (Courtesy of Billy McGill)

3. (*opposite bottom*) Our first city championship when I was still a bashful ninth grader. (Courtesy of Billy McGill)

4. (*top*) My senior year high school yearbook photo, signed and made out to my mother. (Courtesy of Billy McGill)

5. (*opposite*) Me practicing my jump hook. (Courtesy of Billy McGill)

6. (*top*) Our 1958–59 University of Utah freshman team. Notice how one player looks very different from all the rest. (Courtesy of Billy McGill)

7. Shooting a jump hook over Jerry Lucas in our victory over Ohio State my sophomore season. (Courtesy of the Special Collections Department, J. Willard Marriott Library, University of Utah, Salt Lake City)

8. Playing a Cal State–Los Angeles squad that apparently didn't know what to do against me. (Courtesy of Billy McGill)

9. Me getting up over an opponent while at Utah. (Courtesy of Billy McGill)

10. Laying one up in my sophomore season at Utah. (Courtesy of the Special Collections Department, J. Willard Marriott Library, University of Utah, Salt Lake City)

11. A University of Utah press photo taken after the first time I made All-American. (Courtesy of the Special Collections Department, J. Willard Marriott Library, University of Utah, Salt Lake City)

12. The Utah starting five in 1960: Sweet Allen Holmes, me, Joe Aufderheide, Ed Rowe, and Rich Ruffel. (Courtesy of Billy McGill)

Bill McGill UTAH 12 All American

1959-60

13. (*top*) Another University of Utah press photo taken after the first time I made All-American. (Courtesy of the Special Collections Department, J. Willard Marriott Library, University of Utah, Salt Lake City)

14. (*opposite top*) Our 1959–60 conference championship team. They put me right next to Carney Crisler. Little did they know. (Courtesy of Billy McGill)

15. (*opposite bottom*) Me stuffing an opposing college player while Ed Rowe looks on. (Courtesy of Billy McGill)

Skyline Champions
59-60

16. A photo from my junior year of college showing the height difference between me and the smallest member of the team, Neil Jenson. (Courtesy of Pat and Neil Jenson)

17. Me and Neil Jenson again. (Courtesy of Pat and Neil Jenson)

18. Laying one up in my junior year at Utah. (Courtesy of the Special Collections Department, J. Willard Marriott Library, University of Utah, Salt Lake City)

19. Looks like a glamour shot, doesn't it? From my junior or senior year at Utah. (Courtesy of the Special Collections Department, J. Willard Marriott Library, University of Utah, Salt Lake City)

20. Popping a jump shot my senior year. (Courtesy of the Special Collections Department, J. Willard Marriott Library, University of Utah, Salt Lake City)

21. Shooting a jump hook my senior year while drawing a foul. (Courtesy of
the Special Collections Department, J. Willard Marriott Library, University of
Utah, Salt Lake City)

Utah's Record Smasher Faces Final Battle

by DAVE SMITH
Chronicle Sports Editor

Name any Utah casaba scoring record and chances are All-American Billy McGill has broken it.

Utah's 6-9 center is undoubtedly one of the most spectacular hoopsters to come out of the school's annals.

As a sophomore McGill was named to every All-Conference list in the book and actually gained some third team All-American ratings.

McGill again gained All-Conference honors in the 1960-61 season. That year he totaled 862 points for a 27.5 point game average, the fifth best in the nation on National Collegiate Athletic Bureau records.

AS A JUNIOR the U.S. Basketball Writers Association named him to the 1961 LOOK All-American squad, and he gained second-teams honors on both the United Press-International and Associated Press national squads.

Some of the Conference marks he set last year include most field goals made, best field percentage, most total points, and most points per game average.

McGill has already bettered his last year's records and has set some new standards.

ALTHOUGH Saturday's game results will have to be tallied before the final record goes in the book, "The Hill" seems certain to set the single game scoring mark with his 60 points scored against BYU. Before Thursday's game with CSU he ...

scoring mark of 404 points by 74 points.

McGill's old average points per game mark of 28.9 points has swollen to a 39.8 point average.

The All-American will set virtually every Utah individual scoring record. The only one he will miss is the season rebounding record, which he set last year. The Utes played five more games last year than this.

McGill is a great sportsman as well as a great scorer. In his entire collegiate career he has never had one act of unsportsmanlike conduct (and there have been times when others would have seen plenty of reason to react).

McGILL'S TALENT with his hands lends itself well to fields other than basketball. He is a master at the bongo drums, which he says help his rhythm. His ability has helped him earn above average marks in his major, fine arts.

Free Skiing

Those interested in serving as gatekeepers for the National Alpine ski meet should contact coach Pres Summerhays in the fieldhouse. Free ski passes will be issued to those participating.

FOR RESULTS—
Chronicle
Classified Ads

BILL (the Hill) McGill has broken just about every scoring record in the Skyline annals.   The 6-9 Redskin great threatens to shatter a new mark every time he touches a basketball.

22. Indeed, I did seem to break records every time I touched the ball. I finished at Utah having averaged 38.8 points per game my senior year—still a record for NCAA centers—and with lifetime totals of over 2,300 points and 1,100 rebounds in just three seasons played. The only other players to score that many points and pull down that many rebounds in just three years of college ball? Elgin Baylor, Oscar Robertson, Jerry West, Elvin Hayes, Kareem Abdul-Jabbar, and Larry Bird. Not bad company. (Courtesy of the Special Collections Department, J. Willard Marriott Library, University of Utah, Salt Lake City)

23. My team photo while with the Knicks. (Courtesy of Billy McGill)

WESTERN   DIVISION   CHAMPIONS   1964–65

24. The '65 Lakers squad. We lost in the finals to the Celtics. (Courtesy of Billy McGill)

and fearful at the same time, I unwrap my knee bandage like a poor child opening his only Christmas gift.

Joy overwhelms me. To my surprise the swelling has gone down, the cortisone has taken effect, and the fluid in my joint has dissipated. There's a little give and a little pain, but no more than I'm accustomed to.

I'm back.

I push through the dreaded morning conditioning practice, thankful that my knee doesn't blow up as it did the day before, and by the afternoon scrimmage I'm hungry to play.

Trager and his posse arrive to watch us again, but this time I'm smirking. This time I'm going to put on a show. Yesterday I may have been dominated, but today I'm feeling good. At the behest of Trager, Coach has given the second-string guards specific instructions to get the ball inside to me today. As we line up Bellamy steps into the circle with this big, cocky smirk on his face. He thinks he's gonna crush me again. But I know something he doesn't.

On our first time up the floor I'm fed the ball inside. I receive the pass at the top of the free-throw line, throw one quick shoulder-fake to juke my defender, and then go straight up with my jump hook.

It ripples straight through the net, not touching rim or backboard at all. Bellamy thinks it's a fluke, so the next time I do it the exact same way. That sinks as well. The third time I get the ball by the free-throw line Bellamy's ready; he knows my shot, and I want him to. He's trying to block the jump hook, and I want him to go for it—I want to show that even if he knows exactly what I'm going to do he doesn't stand a chance at blocking me.

The ball's in my hands. I go up. He matches me.

Bellamy's arm lashes out like a whip, his hand extending toward the ball. But to Bellamy's great surprise my shot flies over his outstretched arm, and the ball, barely spinning, drops leaden, dead, through the hoop.

Bellamy's shocked. I am not. And that's when my heckling begins.

"You can't stop me!" I jibe, and it's not just a boast. It's true. I let him know exactly where I was going, and he planned to feed my shot back to me for lunch. But he didn't. He couldn't. He couldn't stop my jump hook, and that is a fact that neither of us can now deny.

I shoot jump hooks over Bellamy all throughout the scrimmage, and Bellamy can't stop a one. I can't get inside on him—he's got me by two inches, forty pounds, and a healthy leg—but it doesn't matter because I've still found a way to beat him. From that day on we'll hate each other; I know this. It's sad but true; it's like Carney Crisler and me all over again. But at least I've shown them all why I'd led the nation in scoring.

And at the end of practice Woody Sauldsberry comes up and pats me on the back. "You did it, man," he says. "You showed 'em."

Even Trager throws a compliment my way. As I'm leaving I hear him yell, "That's what I'm talking about!" And I can't help but smile.

When training camp finally ends we all pack up our things and go back to Chicago. For me it's not a long job. Just as in college, all the possessions I own fit into one bag. It's a good thing, too; the Healey convertible hasn't got much trunk space.

Exhibition season opens against the St. Louis Hawks. Their big players are superstar Bob Pettit, Len Wilkins, Chico Vaughn, and an old acquaintance from *The Steve Allen Show*, Zelmo Beatty. Coach McMahon tries to get us all amped up for the opening game—unsurprisingly, he doesn't mention anything about his own lackluster history with the team—and despite the fact that McMahon is still no Coach Jack Gardner, by the time we make our way from the locker room to the floor in our warm-up suits, I'm ready to get out there and crush our opponents.

A little Twin Towers action would be killer; Bellamy and I are both such strong scorers that there's no way any team could stop us if McMahon played us both together. But our coach never gives it a go. Instead he plays Dischinger and only Dischinger, and all along I'm stuck riding the pine. I hardly see a minute of court time. Now I feel like the Carney Crisler.

"Look at the stands," Woody tells me when I confess my frustrations to him. "Look at the faces out there. Who do you think they want to see? You? Or someone who looks like them?"

I gaze into the sea of midwestern seats at the faces of the paying fans. It's impossible not to see that nearly every one is white.

Is it true, I wonder? Is that why only Dischinger plays? He was very good in college, no question, but I damn sure was, too. I've got two inches on Dischinger, and I'm a scoring machine. But McMahon has thirty-something plays drawn up, and more than half are rolling picks designed to help Dischinger get open for a shot. Is Woody right?

I don't want to believe it. Over the course of the exhibition season, I see some of the second-stringers—white second-stringers, to be sure, but second-stringers just the same—buttering up McMahon whenever they can, and as we progress through loss after loss it seems that they start to get more and more playing time. So maybe that's the key—not the color of my skin but my ability (or lack thereof) to swallow my pride and kowtow to Coach McMahon? The thing is, every time I even consider playing along McMahon does something so obnoxious and ridiculous that I can't bring myself to do it.

By most halftimes we're down by double digits at least, and Coach McMahon storms into the locker room on a tear. "You're pathetic!" he screams at us, and he's all swelled up and puffed like a steamed cartoon character. Half the guys hang their heads the moment he enters the locker room. Me, I just want to turn my back on him, and in that I don't imagine I'm alone. How am I supposed to kiss up to a man like that?

I get just one chance to make an impact during preseason, and that's because Bellamy is being made to look foolish by the Philadelphia Warriors and their star center, the single greatest player in the NBA: my old friend Wilt Chamberlain.

Wilt and I have a lot in common, and it's not just because we keep crossing paths. Wilt was an early bloomer like me: he was six feet tall at the age of ten, and he was grazing seven feet even in high school. Like me, he led his prep team to a league title every year he played, and he won two overall city crowns for his school. Just as I did, Wilt left home for college and headed toward the heartland; he played his college career at the University of Kansas. There Wilt was showered with racism and abuse even while playing college ball, both while traveling and at home. He got the expected catcalls and epithets from opponents, but he was also forced to confront "No coloreds allowed" signs in lily-white Lawrence, Kansas, even as he racked up points for the local team, just like me. Finally, after two All-American nods, Wilt the Stilt left college without a degree to pursue the big time—the NBA.

The similarities between us end there, though. Wilt's been the highest-paid player in the pros since his rookie season, and me, well, I'm not exactly in the same boat. And as to our stature, Wilt is widely recognized, along with Bill Russell, as one of the preeminent players in the pro game; I've still yet to make a name for myself outside of the NCAA ranks. So when McMahon subs out the foundering Bellamy to let me hit the hardwood, I know I have to give it my all, for the tea as well as for my own sense of worth.

I pull off my warm-up jacket and step onto the court. It's hard to believe, but Wilt seems to have grown even bigger than the beast I remember from when I first matched up with him at Denker Playground. He's got Guy Rodgers with him on his squad again—Rodgers has ended up a Philadelphia Warrior, too; how's that for fate?—and as soon as I step to him on defense, cocksure Wilt starts yelling for the ball.

"Send it in!" he screams. "Get me that rock!"

I know this game. I've seen it already from Bellamy. Wilt, like Walt, thinks that he can just come inside and dominate me, that I'm going to play like some soft, cowed rookie. Well, if he thinks that, he's got another think coming. The first time Wilt touches the ball, when he spins toward the basket to shoot, I rear back and hack him. He wants to intimidate me? Well, how's some of this: I tomahawk swat him right at the joint between his hand and his forearm.

It's a real wrist breaker of a foul, and the ref whistles me for it and sends Chamberlain to the free-throw line for two. But Wilt doesn't for a second consider walking over for his shots; instead he barrels at me, going for the throat.

"What the hell you think you're doing?" he screams. "You don't foul me! You never foul me! You rookie! You don't do nothing!" He's so worked up, the refs have to come over to pull him away.

Though I know I should be nervous, the situation strikes me as so funny I can't help but laugh. Here I am, fresh off a month on the bench, and there's Chamberlain yelling at me, for what? For aggressive play? "Oh, I'm so sorry," I jibe. "I didn't know you were so delicate, Mr. Superstar."

For me it's nothing personal—I love the guy as a ballplayer—but I want to show him that my high school performance against him was no fluke: I can hang. Of course, though, with a team full of second-stringers on the court, I never get a chance to shoot, and after the buzzer ends I'm back on the bench.

When the final roster is released the week before regular season games begin, I see to no surprise that I'm listed as the second-string center. Even Woody Sauldsberry's now a second-stringer, having been bumped down in camp. But Andy Johnson—the team's third-leading scorer the previous season—has been cut from the roster altogether.

When I hear I go to Woody. He has little to say.

"We ran three black players last year too, Hill," he says—the unspoken addendum being that with me the Zephyrs picked up another black face, so somebody had to go. And just like that Andy Johnson's NBA career has been squelched.

It's a scary thought. Regardless of skill, anybody—anybody—can be sent packing in an instant. And in this league black players are doubly vulnerable.

The Season Begins

For our first regular season game we all meet at our home court, the dilapidated Chicago Coliseum; from there we'll go as a team to the airport to
fly to New York and play the Knicks. I pull up to the ramp leading under
the building to where the players park their cars, but I can't get in. An old,
beat-up Chrysler is stalled out and smoking right at the apex of the ramp.
At first I'm thinking, "What kind of hobo came and parked their car here
right before we've got to head out to a game?" Then the front door opens
and I realize that the driver of this jalopy is Bellamy.

Jesus. If Bellamy—All-Star, Rookie of the Year, likely Hall-of-Famer
Bellamy—holds such a tenuous position that he is reduced to driving this
hunk of junk, what does that say for my chances?

They say the first game is an indicator of how a season's going to be, and
in our case it certainly looks true. We lose the opener by two, and it's
downhill after that. Eventually—starting about ten games in or so, after
we've dragged ourselves out to a 2-8 start—the fans start calling my name,
demanding that their top draft pick gets to see some court time. Finally
the pressure gets to McMahon and he starts slotting me in at the tail end

of games—five minutes at first, then, as I prove I can produce, seven minutes, then ten. It's frustrating having to wait to see floor time until Coach caves to the weight of fans' demands, especially as when I play, I play well. But there's nothing I can do about it, and it doesn't make a difference anyway; I'm on a team that's tailspinning, and without court time, what can I do to save it? The one perverse benefit of it all is that since I play so little my knee actually has a chance to start healing again.

When we run into the Cincinnati Royals in the middle of the season, my outlook is buoyed by an old acquaintance: "Big O," Oscar Robertson himself.

· "It's a shame," he says, "that they don't play you more, especially after how you tore it up in Utah. With your skills there's no reason you couldn't make Rookie of the Year. If they played you," he adds.

"Of course," he goes on, "you wouldn't have much competition, especially after we missed on Lucas."

Hearing the name of my old antagonist gets my attention real quick. "What happened to Lucas?"

"The Royals tried to snag him with their territorial pick, but he didn't come. He got paid a ton of money to sign on to play in that other league. The ABL."

"He did?" My mind flits back to Bellamy's smoking car, to Jim Hadnot's offer, to my own lowball contract.

"Oh, yeah. Forty thousand or something to play for some club named the Cleveland Pipers. I don't know. Word is they have a ton of cash from their owner, some rich shipping magnate. Guy named George Steinbrenner."

Oscar pulls the towel from his neck, not noticing the daze I've just fallen into. "Well, Hill," he says, "take care of yourself. Get into that post when you can, yeah?"

He walks off, and I'm left there thinking, damn. Smoking cars, no playing time, an arena that's falling apart. Is this really the big leagues?

I should have taken the money.

Over the course of the ever-downward spiraling season, McMahon's reticence to play me evolves into a kind of disrespect, and then dislike, both of which become mutual. He alienates the whole locker room, but since he only subs me in when he's goaded into it by the fans, he saves for me a special brand of animus.

One night, after another blowout loss, a stranger approaches me in the parking lot to commiserate. "It's a shame," he says, "what a raw and dirty deal they're giving you, not letting you play." Unsurprisingly, I immediately like this guy. He introduces himself—"Tony Banks," he says, and he shakes my hand—and something about him reminds of my old buddy Manny.

I nod. "Hey, I'd love to play more, too. No doubt about that. But McMahon doesn't put me in 'til the fans call for me, and that's not something I can control."

Tony Banks smiles. "You sure about that?" I cock an eyebrow. "You wanna come out and meet some of them?"

That night Tony takes me to a south side spot called Flukie's. I quickly learn that T.B. is like a god there—everybody knows and likes him, and by extension everyone gets to know and like me, too. Even though I don't drink much, Flukie's becomes a welcome refuge for me from the stresses of red-faced McMahon screaming at me and the rest of our team when we're losing, which is almost always, as well as the general disappointment of being forced to ride the pine. It's not as though the place is the Ritz, but still, it's more comfortable than where I live. Zephyrs' management gave me zero help in finding a place when I first moved to town, so I ended up bedding down in an apartment-style prefurnished place with a TV, stove, and refrigerator. It's okay, but it's pretty drab.

Of course, none of the girls from Flukie's ever seem to complain.

One day about halfway through the season, McMahon bursts into the locker room and begins berating us as usual. He's moaning about how we're not playing hard enough and how we're nothing like the player he was. "How the hell can I motivate you lazy bastards?" he demands, and for me that's the last straw. Lazy? He hardly ever even puts me in to give me a chance to play hard. As a matter of fact, even with my limited minutes, I've been leading the league in shooting percentage since Christmas, but I still hardly get to play! Finally I can't take it anymore, and as Coach McMahon yells at us, I pointedly stand up and turn my back on him, which enrages Coach McMahon.

"McGill!" he screams. "Turn your ass around! I'm tired of looking at your backside!" But I don't. He screams louder. "McGill, you turn your ass around right now!" But I ignore him.

It's dumb, maybe, stoking the flames of an emotional firefight with your own coach, but it feels damn good. For the next two weeks every time he barges in at halftime, every time he starts yelling at our whole squad without even having played me, I just go ahead and flip around, not turning back 'til he's gone. If I wasn't playing much before, this doesn't help; for those two weeks I hardly see the court at all. But by the end of those weeks our demoralized team has performed so abysmally that Coach McMahon gets the ax, and Slick Leonard, a fellow player, is elevated to interim player-coach. I couldn't be happier.

I like Slick—he's a bit of a gambler like me, though cards, rather than dice, are his game—and once he takes the helm the fortunes of both me and the team improve. For the last two months of the season, I finally get my share of minutes and start scoring points, and we even win a few games. Life is good again.

With McMahon gone, the only real negative force left in my life is the bitter sweep of the Chicago winter, which bites especially fiercely when you drive a convertible. Though I hate to do it, after much deliberation I trade in my car for a black Cadillac Coupe de Ville.

Of course, I don't think of it beforehand, but driving a Cadillac in Chicago comes with its own issue: not draft but graft. My Healey was noticeable, but the Caddy is downright flashy, and that causes problems. As soon as I start driving it on Chicago's south side, I find myself getting pulled over far more frequently than I ever had before.

The first time, two black cops emerge from a freshly waxed patrol car, crunching through a fine layer of snow to talk to me. "License and registration," they demand.

I pull out my ID, and I'm relatively sure that once they recognize who I am they'll let me off—I mean, not to boast, but I'm Billy "the Hill"

McGill, number one NBA draft choice. However, that's not what happens. Instead the cops tell me to step out of the car and follow them into their cruiser. I don't know what I've done, but I grew up in south central LA, and I do know that when the police tell you to do something, you hop to.

As they guide me into the backseat I try to engage them. "Is there a problem?" I ask.

"Yeah," says the chubby one. "You made too wide a right turn onto Cottage Grove."

"Too wide a turn?"

"It's punishable with a ticket and a fine," chimes his partner.

"What do you do, Mr. McGill?"

I look at them through the metal grate separating the backseat from the front. "I play basketball," I say, as if they don't know. I'm eighty-one inches tall and am wearing gym shoes and knee socks. What else would I be, an accountant?

"Well, that sounds like a demanding job," the first cop says. "Listen, a ticket, a fine, possibly going to court—all of that sounds like quite a hassle, don't you think?"

"Yeah," says the second cop, "it does. Basketball player, you probably travel a lot—maybe it would be easier for you if we just settle it right here?"

It takes me this long to realize what's happening: I'm getting rolled. These cops, black cops in my own neighborhood of Chicago, are hitting me up for cash.

I've got no choice: they're police, so I give them what they want. But when the cops pull away, leaving me outside my car, I grow angry. I can't believe I've just had to bribe the police. How unfair is that?

As it turns out, not half as unfair as when it happens again.

Thus begins a fortnightly habit: every first and fifteenth of the month—every payday—I get pulled over as I turn onto Cottage Grove on my way home. It's like clockwork: I get my check from the team, I cash it and send a big money order to my mother, and then on the way to my place I get pulled over and squeezed. It happens for three months straight until finally I can't take it anymore. This time when I'm pulled over, I don't even wait; I step right out of my Caddy and walk straight up to the driver's side window of the cop car. I pound on the glass. The cop looks surprised.

"Okay, buddy. Here's how it's gonna be. I'm heading to the police station and telling your commanding officer exactly what's been happening since I bought the Caddy. Or this ends right now." I then pull out my billfold, peel off a bill and toss him a single, crumpled dollar, which bounces off his chest and rolls down to the floorboards. "That's your last payoff. You pick," I say. Then I turn around, walk back to my car, and drive off.

I never get stopped by the Chicago cops again.

When season ends—we close out with a loss to Oscar Robertson's Royals that leaves us with a record of 25-55, worst in the West and second to last in the entire league—I'm all too eager to pack up and head back to my mother's house in Los Angeles. Meeting T.B. has been a bright spot, but other than that I can't wait to get out of this place.

I pack my car and head toward the setting sun—back home, toward California. It's springtime now, but the weather is brisk; I drive with a big, long maxi coat on that wouldn't be out of place at Flukie's. It's fly. I'm also wearing a floppy, soft-brimmed felt hat, with the brim tilted at the side. Very loud.

Near the southwestern edge of the state, as I cruise along Route 66 out of Illinois, I decide it's time to stop and fuel up for the long drive ahead. After filling up my gas tank I pull into a café off the highway.

As I pull into a space the stark contrast between me and my surroundings barely registers. The other cars are simple suburban models like De Sotos and Chevvies; nothing fancy. The other customers all wear collared shirts with plain tan slacks, dungarees, or pleated skirts. My car, clothes, and shoes are as loud as the blast of static from an off-tuned radio.

When I walk through the front doors of the restaurant thirty pairs of eyes turn their gaze on me. I stride along the tile, making my way toward the counter and settling in atop a vinyl stool. Ten minutes later I'm still fiddling with the mirrored napkin dispenser and the salt and pepper shakers, waiting to order. I snag the waitress—blond, blue-eyed, one of those corn-fed types—as she tries to breeze by me on her sixth trip past.

"Excuse me, miss?" I say. "I'd like to order."

For a moment time stands still. The waitress—Jean, by her nametag—balances a coffeepot discomfitedly.

"It's—" she whispers. It's almost as though she's embarrassed. "We don't serve colored people."

Her cheeks blush as she finishes blurting it out, and as I'm left sitting there, awed, she scurries off, five years ago all over again. It's 1963, John Kennedy is president of the United States, and this café doesn't serve colored people.

In a case like this Jesus would turn the other cheek. A younger Billy might have, too. But I don't.

"You don't serve colored people? Well," I roar, rising to my full height, "I don't eat colored people!" Half the patrons dump their faces into their meals. The other half just as quickly look up from their plates to stare at me.

In a rage, I knock a bottle of ketchup to the floor, where it explodes, and stomp toward the front door. I yank it open, hard as I can, and as I leave I yell out at the top of my lungs, "All of you can kiss my black ass!" It's a good thing the door doesn't have a central pane of window glass, because I slam the door so hard that it would have spiderwebbed and shattered everywhere.

I look over my shoulder as I storm away into the parking lot. Every one of the patrons I see wears a stare that says, "Nigger, if I had a gun, I'd shoot you where you stand."

I managed to make converts out of them in Utah. Is this how it's going to be everywhere else in the country?

I slide into my Coupe de Ville, yank the door shut behind me, and peel off. The lights of that diner in my rearview mirror are the last I see of Illinois.

Good-bye, Zephyrs

When I get back to LA I start having recurring nightmares. In them I go into the bathroom to brush my teeth, but when I look in the mirror I don't see my own reflection in the glass. Instead Coach McMahon's red ugly mug stares back at me and laughs. He shouts Trager's words. "What the hell is wrong with you, McGill? You're worthless! You can't play a damn! I said, what's the matter with you, McGill? You're nothing! You're nothing!"

I wake up sweating. I'm so distraught over the course the season took that it's weeks before I can bring myself to step onto a basketball court again, even though I had a good rookie season.

Yes, I averaged only ten or so points per game, whereas Bellamy and Dischinger did much more scoring. But they played more! Me, I hardly got subbed in at all. They played forty-plus minutes per game, and I only got to play seven or eight. It was like a self-fulfilling prophecy, with Coach McMahon's dumb logic—I wasn't given time to play because I wasn't scoring as much as the other guys, and since I wasn't scoring as much I didn't get time to play. But I scored half as much as they did—and they played *five times* as many minutes! I actually scored twice as many points per minute on the floor as either of those other guys, putting points on the board faster and better than any other player on the team.

Once I get past being angry at having sat on the bench so much this season, I turn back to my old self, going to all the LA hoops spots and nailing jump hooks and crashing the boards like always to stay sharp. I start lifting weights so as not to let guys like Bellamy think they can push me around inside; perversely, being forced to sit so much with the Zephyrs gave my knee a lot of time to heal and offered me a lot of reserve strength to work with over the long summer break.

I make it a point to get myself in top physical shape to prepare myself for the morning conditioning and two-a-days that I know are coming. I awaken early and run alone on the beach as the sun breaks the horizon each morning. It's amazing to see the world rouse itself from its slumber, and as I run, upping my distance on the sand each day, I can't help but smile as I remember the little penguin-crutched kid I was, waddling his way alone around a cinder track. This is much better.

This is gonna be my year. I know it. I just know it.

As fall camp draws near I learn that the permanent hiring of Slick Leonard as coach is not the only change waiting for our team. In the off-season the Zephyrs have left Chicago for Baltimore, and they've changed their name to the Bullets. I'm fine with the move; at least Baltimore isn't so cold, and we'll be farther from our rat-faced owner. No more freezing auditorium, no more overbearing stares, and no more berating tirades from an acrimonious coach who hates my guts. The season ahead seems to hold a lot in store for me.

I leave early for the long drive back across the country. Needless to say I don't stop in Illinois for a meal. In Baltimore I quickly find a place to live. It's nothing special: a little utilitarian one-bedroom, and rents are cheap in that town besides. There's no nightlife to speak of—I'm certainly sad to be without Tony Banks and the men (and women) of Flukie's—but it's okay. I'm not here to mess around. I'm here to get work done.

When preseason training camp opens in Ft. Meade, I have yet another reason to be excited: Walt Bellamy is nowhere to be found! I hope the team has traded him to give me the starting job, but it turns out I'm not that lucky. Rather, Bellamy's holding out—he's having a contract dispute with Trager (perhaps, I think, a tactic I should have considered), and until he gets signed for fair money, he says he won't play.

Good for him, I think. For one, I'm glad he's sticking it to Trager—someone has to. I wish I'd stuck to my guns. And two, as long as Bellamy isn't around, I have the starting job by default.

At last I have a chance to prove myself on the first string. And prove myself I do.

I'm bigger and stronger than I'd been during my rookie year, and with Bellamy gone I'm bigger and stronger than anyone else on the team, too. Everyone in camp that I go up against, I kill. Buckets pour in for me like droplets of rain down the spines of an umbrella, and Coach Leonard pulls me aside to say, "Billy, as great a shooter as you are, you should tear this league up this year." On the glass I'm rebounding with a new ferocity that I hadn't shown before, hadn't even known I had in me. It fills me with pride, and I play ever harder still, feeling like my old self for the first time in a long time.

As camp progresses I come to relish my new role of being the Bullets' starting center. With Bellamy missing and that demoralizing bastard McMahon gone as coach, I'm getting enough time to earn both my minutes and my position as the focus of the offense, just like I was at Utah. After a time I almost forget what it was like to be frustrated at all. I feel like the king of Baltimore and the whole mid-Atlantic.

Unfortunately, it doesn't take long for castles made of sand to crash into the sea.

It's in the middle of a passing drill at practice when I see him. Bent over and pulling up my kneepad, I catch a glimpse of a man, sports bag in hand, strolling past an open side door of the gym. It's Walt Bellamy.

He's signed. He's back. I'm screwed. Despite how well I've been playing, Bellamy's return automatically stuffs me back down onto the second string.

At the outset of our first scrimmage after his return, Bellamy greets me with a sneer. Though we acknowledge each other's ability, there's no personal respect or professional courtesy between us; we're damn near trying to kill each other over primacy and court time.

On the hardwood I'm playing in the same smooth zone I used to find with Lefty in LA. I D up on Bellamy as best I can and rebound like a man possessed. On offense I shoot my jump hooks with deadly accuracy, not easing up until I force Bellamy to concede that not in a million years will he be able to block my signature shot. Exhibition season opens, and though I'm not starting Coach Leonard does me a solid by at least giving me the opportunity to play. I do well, picking my shots and scoring bench points wherever I can, using every tool in my arsenal to show opposing centers why I led the nation in scoring at Utah. Playing for Coach Slick I find the fun again, the spark that turned me onto the game in the first place. Proving that I deserve playing time, everything's shaping up to look, at the very least, tolerable.

You'd think I would have learned by now never to get too settled. As always, just as I'm starting to get comfortable everything gets shaken up.

Right as the regular season starts Coach Leonard calls me into his office. "Billy," he says. "Sit down."

I don't know what he's about to say, but I imagine it's bad news. Mentally I review the no-cut clause in my contract, getting ready to defend myself by any means necessary.

"Billy," Coach Leonard says, "I won't beat around the bush. You've been traded. You're going to New York."

Now, for most players getting traded is bad. Getting swapped means, at some level, being told that you're not wanted anymore. And what's more, the New York Knicks are the only team in the NBA who are unquestionably worse than the Bullets are. Yet I couldn't be more excited.

Since the Knicks are so bad, that means they need help. They need talent. That means me. And that means more playing time.

Modestly, without betraying my joy, I thank Slick for breaking the news gently and shake his hand. It's not until I'm alone in my apartment that I let my true emotions show. With a smile on my face I pack my little clothes bag full, shove it into the Caddy, and hop on I-95 northbound. My second pro season is just two weeks old, and within hours of getting the news I'm happily heading straight for New York.

The Knicks

Though I'm in no way sad to leave the Bullets, it's with some trepidation that I make my way up to New York. First of all, I'm an unknown up there—sometimes even a mediocre reputation is better than none at all. Second, with a record of 21-59, the Knicks are the only team in the league who managed to finish worse than the Zephyrs last season. But the first man I meet when I arrive at the Knicks' camp eases all my worries.

"Billy," says coach Eddie Donovan, "this team needs strength. If you play well here you'll have all the chances you need."

Though I hardly know him I can't help but like the man. It's only been one season since I was still at Utah, but it seems like it's been an eternity since I played for a coach who cares about me and truly has the respect and admiration of all the players on the team. Donovan does. He's knowledgeable and fair, and the arena where his team plays—Madison Square Garden—is the greatest in the world. I'm excited to be a part of this squad already. Of course, there are two other centers already on the team who, I fear, may be less happy to see me.

The first is another new arrival, named Tom Hoover—"Hoov," they call him. He's fearless, he's big and strong, and under the boards he acts like he'll fight King Kong for the ball if he has to. The second is Gene Conley, another massive guy who, in contrast to Hoov's apishness, is actually a puppy dog. When I score on him with my jump hook in a scrimmage, he actually shakes his head and smiles.

"Nice form," he says, pointing at my arm, still hooked and frozen in the air. What a teammate! "But can you use that thing to hurl a fastball?"

Conley, as it happens, only plays basketball—professional basketball, under contract in the NBA—during what he calls "the off-season." "My real job," he tells me, "is pitching." Turns out he's a Major League ball-player for the Boston Red Sox, and he's pitched in three All-Star Games. He's also won a World Series with the Braves to go with his three NBA titles with the Boston Celtics.

Hoov, Conley, and I play each other hard, but unlike with Bellamy, there's no animosity between us. Hoov's quick to show that he'll fight *for* any of his teammates on the court, and I appreciate that. What's more, New York is not the Midwest: there's no overt racism in this city or on this squad, no cliques or factions or anger. Everyone here is here to play as a unit. Everyone's here to win.

In my first game as a Knick—a sweet one for me, a matchup against my old team, the Zephyrs-cum-Bullets—we knock out our opponents by nearly twenty points. As I watch us play—and I do a lot of watching at the outset, still working to earn my playing time—I realize that there're a lot of good players on our team. We've got Len Chappel, Art Heyman, "Jumping" Johnny Green, and a player I remember from the days of my youth: John Rudometkin.

Rudo doesn't get a lot of playing time, which strikes me as odd, since I remember how strong he was both in high school and college. I ask Rudo-metkin about it, but he just shrugs it off. That's when I notice he's look-ing a little thinner than I remember him being.

"You all right?" I ask. "You feeling okay?"

He says he's fine, but in my mind I can't help but wonder. I remember how in training camp the year before Andy Johnson had gotten on me about my kneepads, and once he'd even tried to yank them down in the middle of a practice as a joke, and I had swiftly covered up like an embarrassed woman at the beach who loses the top to her bikini. I never told Johnson why I was so protective about my kneepads; I didn't want to admit to my injury or discuss the problem. Maybe, I think, thin-looking John Rudometkin has something going on, too, that he doesn't want anyone to know about, so I decide not to pry. Besides, he certainly still has his swagger. The day after I ask him if he's all right, he approaches me with a challenge to a game of one-on-one.

"First to fifty points," he says. "Winner gets three hundred dollars."

I crane my neck down at him. One-on-one, and I've got seven inches in height advantage. Is he serious?

"Dead serious. Unless you're afraid?"

I'm not, and I beat him, of course. But the game's close. Very close. Maybe I've got no business discounting old Rudo after all.

Soon after that I do earn my starting spot on the team, and not long after *that*, on November 26, 1963, I prove that I'm worth it.

It's a Tuesday, two days after Jack Ruby killed the guy who killed President Kennedy and two days before a Thanksgiving that I'm sure to spend— yet again—alone. I wake up in my one-bedroom in the Bronx; it's nothing special, just a bed, kitchen, and a small sitting room. I still don't know New York too well—I've just been traded to this city, after all. But when you're the starting center for the New York Knicks the city knows you, even if you don't know it.

Looking out the window onto New York streets lightly covered with a cold mist that is almost, but just barely not, snow, I take it all in. The Bronx is how I imagine it's always been: a melting pot of faces, races, ages, and names. Here there certainly aren't diners that turn people away because of something so trivial as the color of their skin.

My landlord is Greek, and the neighbors across the hall are Italian. All over kids play stickball together, each one pretending to be Mickey Mantle—black kids, Hispanic kids, white kids, Christians, Jews; it doesn't matter. I can relate. When you're poor and you're young, you don't worry about those sorts of things. We didn't.

When evening comes I rush from my apartment to the car, trying to wave to the voices who cry, "Hey, Billy! Billy the Hill!" in the streets. But

I'm not trying to mug for fans; I'm trying to get my head in the zone. I'm trying to get myself ready for the Lakers.

"You ready, McGill?"

Indeed I am. I look up from the floor, eyes peering through the hanging part in the towel draped over my head. Coach Donovan is looking down at me, backlit by overhead lights.

When I was growing up the Lakers were in Minneapolis—that's how the team got its name, from the Land of 10,000 Lakes. But though they were good then, now that they're based out of my hometown, LA, they've really come into their own. They've won the Western Conference both of the last two years, losing to the Celtics in hotly contested finals each time. Their roster boasts the terrible twosome of Jerry West and Elgin Baylor, obvious future Hall-of-Famers who can be counted on to score twenty-plus points each game, and every time they've played us so far in this short season, they've had our number.

Our Knicks team, in contrast, is an unlikely bunch. About half the roster has, like me, just joined the team, and only two guys on our whole fresh-faced squad have played more than three or four years in the league. So it's with a healthy dose of reserve that the hometown fans applaud us as we take to the floor. It's a sell-out crowd—at least due as much to the Lakers as us, I think—but nobody really expects us to give the Lakers a run. But I know something no one else does: I'm about to tear it up tonight.

From the beginning of the game everything goes my way. The first time I get the ball on offense I take a pass in the low post, the spot right underneath the edge of the basket, and I immediately fake a shot. Now, Gene Wiley, the Lakers' center, prides himself as a great shot blocker, so when I fake going up for a shot Wiley, predictably, takes off. Too bad for him, I know it's coming, and as he launches I reign in my fake, step right around him, and stick the ball through the hoop unguarded.

I'm in Wiley's head from moment one, and from then on I'm on easy street. He's completely ineffective on D. I get the ball and fake; once he leaves his feet I finish with a jump shot. And when he plays off of me to leave himself a cushion of space to gain a chance to react, if offers me plenty of room to casually dribble across the lane and let loose with my patented jump hook.

Everything's easy. Len Chappel kicks me the ball inside, and I go up with a quick jumper. Johnny Green slides me a bounce pass, and I pop a jump hook. When I'm double-teamed after a Tom Gola inlet pass, I dish it to a wide-open Art Heyman, who lets loose an unguarded set shot for an easy two off my assist. During a time-out I look over at the Lakers' bench. The team is in a fit over me. Wiley's getting chewed out because he has no idea how to stop me; but then neither does Laker coach Fred Schaus. I'm playing the best game I've played to date at the pro level, and it feels absolutely glorious.

By the time halftime comes around I'm in the zone, knocking down shots like I'm playing on a four-foot Nerf hoop against toddlers. I crash every board, snatch rebounds even over Wiley, and keep on piling in the points. Of course the shot I go to again and again is my money ball: the jump hook.

Jerry West, the Lakers' big scorer, notices. He's a good player himself, a warrior like me, and he's not about to go down without a fight. Every point I score he matches; every time I hustle downcourt to take the ball under the basket, he comes back with a vengeance. It's like my battle with Lucas back in college. I may be stopping Wiley, but West knows I can't be in two places at once, and he guides his team to retake the lead.

The Garden crowd, both the home and away fans, grows more and more frantic as West and I put on an exhibition, leading our teams with skill and will and force. With every score the cheers come louder and louder. The energy catches on among my teammates, and we push hard to erase the deficit. We Knicks manage to get within three before the Lakers, led by West and Elgin Baylor, at last manage to pull away.

Though we lose by the score of 119–112, sports writers flood *our* locker room afterward, and they all want to talk about my jump hook. I guess that's what happens when you put on a scoring clinic against the LA Lakers at Madison Square Garden.

The next day the headline in the *New York Times* sports column mentions me by name. "McGill Leads Attack," the subheader continues, and my output quickly becomes news on both coasts. Another paper leads, "McGill Scores 41 Points with Kooky Hook Shot." Forty-one points. I didn't even know I had that many. Chick Hearn, the famous Los Angeles sports radio announcer, proclaims, "Billy McGill has come into his own! You don't lead a nation in scoring and be the number one draft pick in the country for nothing, folks, and the Hill's just shown us all out here how it's done." Even my mother, a woman who has never before shown interest in sports in her whole life, knows about what I've done. I call her the next day to gloat to her a little, but to my surprise it turns that out she has already heard.

"I'm so proud, Bilbo." That's all she can say—she's so proud. Because she's choked up. And I'm glad. I'm glad that my natural talents have at last come out to shine, and I'm glad that, for the first time I can think of in my whole life, my mother is proud of me.

I bet my father would be, too.

The Heights

Soon after the big showing against the Lakers, the five-time defending world champion Boston Celtics come to town. Playing the Celtics means two things: sell-out crowds and Bill Russell.

It's December, but there's Indian summer weather—clear and sunny, though the trees have long gone bare. On my way to the Garden the city feels vibrant and alive. As I get closer and closer to Madison Square, the packs of people seem to clump ever tighter together, pressed throngs of fans all anticipating a little bit of magic.

I get the starting assignment, and I'll be matched up against Russell. I already know Russell will win the jump balls over me—the man's as tall as I am, and he has two good legs that seem to be packed with wound springs—but when I get my first touch of the ball on offense, I know exactly what I'm going to do.

When I release the shot it's at the pinnacle of my leap, with my arm held high above my head and away from me. I'm doing just as I'd done years ago, just like the first time, but this time it's not Russell calling to me; it's the fans. And this time the shot needs not to wow Russell but to clear him, and the ball goes up, and up, and up . . .

I'm playing hard and hounding Russell like a man that he owes money, and my pressure is such that his teammates often have trouble getting him the ball. On offense I do my best to counteract his defensive prowess by stretching out my game, raining jump hooks from as far away as the free-throw line.

"Seventh grade," I tell myself. "It's just like seventh grade."

Russell has well-deserved pride in his defensive skills, but even he can't stop my jump hook. He's not taunting me like Bellamy used to, nor getting flustered like Wiley, but still he's clearly flummoxed that he's not blocking my shot. It's amazing but true: I've never once been blocked. I may be the only basketball player in the world who can say that, and I've played against Wilt and now Bill Russell.

The Celtics come into this game with a record of 23-3, having lost only to Big O's powerful Cincinnati Royals. On the strength of his play and his potent defense, Bill Russell has in fact led this Celtics team to a string of four straight NBA championships, with no end in sight. But tonight, against me and our baby-faced New York Knicks squad, he can't do it. It's another little miracle, made official by the last second finally ticking off the clock: our ragtag group of thrown-together journeymen topples the number one Celtics, 127–117.

Between my magic night against the Lakers and my early Christmas present against the Celtics, I find myself in an unenviable position: everybody, it seems, is suddenly gunning for me. This, I learn, is the problem with being King of the Hill—everyone wants to take your crown.

As I start to make a name for myself I develop the ungentlemanly habit of trash talking. Every center wants to be the first to block one of my shots, but as none do, I get to taunting my opponents after scoring on them. "Hey, man. If Russell and Wilt couldn't block my jump hook, how in the hell do you think you can?" It's obnoxious, but nobody ever has an answer. And so my ego begins to grow. By the time we head out to LA for a return match against the Lakers in January, I'm strutting like a peacock.

The return game is chippy the whole way and Wiley and I are all over each other, with him trying to prove that my forty-one points in the Garden was a fluke and me trying to prove that I own his ass. The game, also, is unusually close—unusual because, despite our growing team unity and pride, our Knicks are still at the bottom of the league standings. We're lowly enough that when we get spotted out at a comedy club, Lenny Bruce makes fun of us! The idea of us stealing a win during our California road trip makes our opponents furious, and the mighty Lakers are determined not to let us waltz into the Sports Arena and snatch away a win.

It all comes to a head on a loose ball late in the second half. I scramble for it and end up getting muscled up by Don Nelson, a former teammate of mine from when we both played on the Zephyrs. I body back against Don—ex-teammate or no, that's my ball—and when we get up, Don shoves me in response. I shove him right back, we ignore the ref blowing his whistle, and before anyone can get between us there are elbows and fists involved.

Every other fight I've been in my life, I've been cool and cerebral, remembering my father's boxing training. But this time it's pure emotion. We're furious at each other, and the both of us are swinging wildly—so wildly, in fact, that neither of us even hits the other. But once our teammates see the fists, they jump into the fray. Tom Hoover comes barreling onto the court from the sidelines, snarling like a rabid dog ready to attack (and if possible, decapitate), which leads to a brawl that clears both benches. Even though he and I started the whole damn thing, Nelson and I are quickly shoved to the sidelines by other Lakers and Knicks eager to take a piece out of one another—though not before, somewhere in the melee, I receive a hard shot to the thigh.

Hoov, Nelson, and myself all get ejected; the backup center on the Lakers who'd nominally been guarding me, Jim Krebs, does, too. Elgin Baylor, the Lakers' other big star alongside Jerry West, avoids both jabs and the refs' wrath by hiding the whole time under the scorers' table.

When time expires we lose by eight, but Coach Donovan isn't even mad—he's just glad to see we've still got signs of life!

"Well, boys," he says as we file back to the locker room, "you'll make the front page tomorrow," and I don't doubt Coach's words for a second— any sportswriter who saw that fracas would, I think, want to comment.

As it turns out they're not the only ones.

When I'm making my way out of the visitors' locker room to the team's chartered bus, a man stops me in the hallway. He's tall, but I can't see his face under the rumpled hat he wears; his overcoat hangs down to his dress shoes, which are scuffed but clean.

"Billy?" he says.

His voice is gravelly, like the sound of chickens pecking at rocks, but it's also oddly, tenderly, familiar. I'm already focused on the bus at the end of that cold, concrete hallway when I hear him; it's that voice that draws me to stop and turn and look.

"Billy," he repeats, and when I look into his eyes I recognize the voice and the man: it's Malone McGill.

The man standing before me in the Los Angeles Coliseum hallway is, after thirteen years of estrangement, my father.

A storm of emotion wraps itself across my body like a blanket of ice. I don't know what to do. Here he is, the man whom I longed for and missed for years and years of my life—the man who, for good or ill, I always figured would be the answer to all my problems. And now he's just standing here in front of me.

"Dad?"

I look at my father. The years appear to have treated him all right. He looks older, but he looks okay.

"Billy," he says, and there's a long chasm between us that neither of us knows how to cross. I want to ask him so much, but I can't seem to say anything. I want him to ask me, "How are you doing? How is your life?" I want him to ask me what I've done, where I'm living; what it was like to grow up without him all those years. What is it like to play ball?

"So," he offers. "Are you, ah . . . are you still going to church?"

Church? Church? It's the first time I've seen this man since I was eleven, and all he can ask me is whether or not I'm spending Sundays on my knees?

As a little kid, you can't make your parents be emotionally open. They either are or they aren't, and mine never were. Can my father even imagine what it was like for me to be ten, eleven, twelve years old, killing everybody on the court but consumed by this enormous emptiness inside me? Of course not. Just like my mom could never talk to me about her divorces, her cuckolding, or her drinking problem. They just can't expose themselves like that. So what does my dad ask me about, after almost a decade and a half of absence from my life? Something safe, something impersonal. Church.

I wish that we could say more, but I know that we won't. He won't offer any details; he won't tell me whether he's married again or where he's working. He won't offer a phone number, and we won't really catch up. Realizing this, I'm crushed under the surface of a thousand waves of sorrow all at once. "Yeah," I lie at last. "Yeah, I still go to church."

We stand here staring at each other in this cold cement hallway, desperate and unsteady as the moments tick by. A teammate passes and grabs me by the shoulder; he doesn't ask me a word about the rumpled man I'm talking to or worry that he's interrupting, he just says that it's time to get moving and directs me to follow him as he tramps off toward the team bus.

"Well," I say. "I guess I have a plane to catch."

"Okay, Billy," my father says. "Take care." I want to hug him, but I don't. I want him to hug me, but he doesn't. He just says, "So long," and I blink, and the next thing I know, he's gone.

I can't sleep at all on the flight home that night. I can't stop thinking about my mother and father. God, I wish it could have worked out between them. Or failing that, I wish my mom had at least tried to keep my natural father in my life. I wonder about the other players—what did their dads do to back them up? I made the NBA, sure, but how far could I have gone if I had two parents who cared, who were behind me? I've spent years killing everybody on the court, and I could do it because I had that pure talent. But how much of my potential got bottled up by growing up alone—how much more could I have accomplished with a father in my life? I feel tears trying to push their way out of my eyes, but I choke them back. I don't want a teammate to see me cry. Even though I've missed him all these years, I still carry the one lesson I learned living in my father's house: when you're hurt, never ever let it show. Just bury it down deep down inside you, inside a hole from which you hope it can never crawl out.

Thank You; Please Leave

The Knicks end the season with an abysmal record of twenty-two wins and fifty-eight losses, good enough for last place for the second year in a row. And yet I'm proud of us and of my play. I led my team again in scoring efficiency as well as in field-goal percentage. I'm also a minor basketball hero in New York now, which feels great. But just as my success and drive brought me on a collision course with trouble now and again on the court, more than once it does the same for me off.

For all my newfound fame, I still don't have the confidence to really talk to women. That means I never do enjoy a real, healthy relationship. Instead, I meet only groupies and hangers-on—and though that feels like fun, it's hollow.

One night I meet a beautiful black woman out at a club. She tells me that her name is Sheena and she's an executive in the record business. "I've got a wonderful apartment," she says. "The view is amazing. Do you want to see it?"

Ah, yes. Yes, I do.

We take a cab to her place uptown, a high rise on the east side near the East River. Her place is deluxe, with a doorman and everything, and when I see it, I'm just glad I didn't try to take her back to my dumpy little spot.

"Would you like a drink?" she offers, and I accept; as she pours it I make my way over to her couch. It's suede and accommodating. She approaches with a pouty smile and a pair of cocktails in her hands. This, as my teammates would say, is a slam dunk. But just as she's about to settle in next to me, there's all of a sudden a hard, heavy pounding on the door. It sounds like the entire Manhattan police force is on the other side preparing to bust in.

"What's that?" I ask, startled.

She visibly deflates, the sultry side whooshing out of her. "That," she sighs, "is probably my boyfriend."

Boyfriend? She hadn't said anything about a boyfriend. And right as the words are out of her mouth, the door swings open. Who's on the other side? Bobo Brazil, the feared, heavily muscled, intercontinental pro wrestling champion. And he's blind drunk.

I can't believe this. Forget about the problems Sheena has just made for herself; I've got to get out of here! But between me and the exit stands a raging 280 pounds of muscle—and he looks angry.

Somehow I manage to escape with my body intact—but what was that woman doing, setting me up like that? That's how a man can get himself killed. This probably ought to be another warning to me to stay focused on basketball and lay off the women. But once again I ignore the signs, and the very next week I'm out at Small's Paradise in Harlem making moves on a pretty girl named Jennifer.

Jennifer comes home with me, things go well, and I don't think much more of her after that. Until, that is, I get a letter in the mail three months later that begins, "Billy, I'm pregnant with your baby."

Uh-oh.

In the letter Jennifer goes on to ask for five thousand dollars to support the kid, money that after taxes, rent, sending money back to my folks each month, and the like I straight out don't have. Double uh-oh.

I decide to sit on this, hoping the answer will come, and it does. The good news is that Jennifer turns out to not actually be pregnant. That's a relief. The bad news is she's a scam artist, a groupie who likes to run with basketball players, then turn on them and extort them for cash. I may not have paid, but that doesn't change the fact that I'm now officially a target.

Jeez. It's like Woody warned me: this is a cutthroat league.

I report to Knicks camp at the start of my third season in the league ready to sign a new deal. It'll be a good one, I'm fairly certain—last year I was the number one scorer for the home team in the biggest city in America. There's no doubt in my mind that as a starter and a minor star, I'll get a raise, maybe even a bonus. That's why it's such a shock when I report to camp and receive a one-year offer at a salary of twelve thousand dollars. "It's what we think is only appropriate, given your clearly small contribution to the Knicks this past year."

"Small? I was the top shooter on the whole team!"

"We recognize that it's a pay cut from your rookie contract, but we think it's fair market value," says GM Fred Podesta.

It's the league minimum. I know that and I tell him as much.

"Billy," says Fred, "this is not a negotiation. It's take it or leave it." Where have I heard that before?

"Billy," he repeats, rising, "I hope that you accept and that we'll be seeing you out on the floor."

It's a slap in the face. Never mind that minor white players on the Knicks are getting paid more; never mind that I had such a strong season. It's take this money or take a walk; the Knicks know it and so do I. I'm fuming and frustrated, flooded with equal parts impotence and rage, but I sign. What else can I do? The ABL has folded; it's not like there are competing offers out there. What else am I cut out for besides basketball?

Training camp opens upstate. It's clear from the beginning that the Knicks are trying to revamp their roster and rebuild the team. A number of players from the previous season are no longer present, and there are plenty of new faces. One belongs to a tall, tough, scrappy youngster named Jim Barnes. Another belongs to an equally tall, equally tough player named Willis Reed.

Barnes is the number one draft pick, just like I was, selected first by the Knicks by virtue of finishing last the season before. Reed was the Knicks' second-rounder. In camp Barnes quickly establishes himself as the starting power forward, kicking Len Chappel down to the second string. That leaves Hoov, myself, and Willis Reed all lined up to fight for starting center.

Though all three of us do fine in preseason workouts, when exhibition season opens the writing on the wall begins to show. Reed's who they've drafted; Reed's who they're paying real money to. Reed's the guy the team wants. Coach Donovan gives Reed every start, too, which frustrates me to no end. He's a hell of a player, no question, but I'm coming off a good season and I want a fair chance to show what I can do. Yet I'm not getting it. Whenever Donovan does pull Willis out for a breather, he nearly always slots Hoov in right behind him. Hoov, who backed me up the year before, now seems to have leapfrogged me on the depth chart.

Just one day after the regular season opens—a four-point loss to the Lakers in which I never get a chance to see the floor—Coach Donovan pulls me into his office. "No ill will," he says, "but Billy, you've been traded to the Hawks."

"For whom?" I ask.

"It wasn't my choice," says Coach.

"Who'd I get traded for?" I demand.

He sighs. "A draft pick next season." I shake my head. "Billy, I'm sorry—the team's just trying to rebuild, and the word from the top is that we're aiming for new blood across the board. I'm sorry," he repeats.

Hoov, Barnes, Reed—these are all guys that the Knicks' front office handpicked themselves, and that personal investment means they're willing to ride those ponies as far as they can take them. Plus Reed, not me, is their newly appointed scorer; they want their backup center to play D when he's on the floor and let starters at other positions control the ball. Hoov can be a defense-first center, but that's never going to be me, and we all know it. Coach Donovan and I shake hands, and like that I'm on the highway headed for St. Louis.

As I drive my frustrations swirl and eddy in my mind. Was that the real reason the Knicks paid me such small-time money, to make it easier to unload me in a trade? And if so, couldn't they have told me earlier on, so I wouldn't have had to keep paying rent on my now-useless apartment in the Bronx all summer?

People don't realize the toll that moving teams takes. You have no friends, no allies. You don't know anybody, not even the coach. And what's more, whatever team you're headed to has already made all their strategic plans without you in the picture. Yes, last year I proved that if I actually get my time on the court, I can produce at the NBA level. But what if where I'm going I never get a real chance to play? What then?

33

All Good Things

When I get to St. Louis I don't know a soul. I ask the Hawks' front office where I ought to look to live, and they direct me to a downtown hotel near the Arch, where Hawks star Bob Pettit stays during the season.

A hotel. "Don't get settled," this tells me. My future looks less than bright.

Still, Pettit's the man in St. Louis; he's the king of their squad and their city, and if the front office wants to lump me in with him, maybe things aren't so bad. But there's a problem: Pettit plays forward and center. Backing him up is Zelmo Beatty, and Zelmo's good—he, like me, was selected to the '62 All-American first team. Is he better than I am? I don't know, but Zelmo's a fixture already—he's been here, and I have not. That makes me the third-stringer by default, just like I was shaping up to be in New York. It's the first time in my life I've ever been this far down on the depth chart, and now that I'm down here I have no idea how I'm gonna get back up.

Though it's nice to be back on a winner—playing for the Zephs and the Knicks marked the only times I was ever stuck on a team that didn't dominate—there are so many quality players on the Hawks that getting a chance to see the floor looks unlikely. Yes, we're gonna win a lot of games, but with all these stars what coach is gonna spread open court time for a new kid in town?

Trying to break in after the season's begun, I feel like the new kid at school, and just like in that situation, nobody reaches out to me. I'm not any better—I still kind of think of the Hawks as the team I played my first NBA exhibition game against, not as my friends. Not knowing anybody in St. Louis, once practice ends I generally slink back off to my hotel room. It's lonely being in a city where nobody knows your name, and though a few of the black bellhops at the hotel tell me I should go across the river and head to East St. Louis in Illinois, I'm often held back by the thought of that racism I encountered back on that side of the state line as I drove away from the Zephyrs not long ago.

As the season progresses my feeling of being a round peg in a square hole just grows. My relationship, such as it is, with Zelmo Beatty turns downright acrimonious, teammate or no. Frankly I think the guy's an asshole. He acts like he's God's gift to basketball, and I cannot stand it.

Even more than playing Beatty loves to talk trash. And he talks it to me. A lot. In practices he'll say, "Hey, no way you gonna score with that jump hook." Beatty's big, a raw-boned center, and I've never met a cockier player. But when I score on him and dish the trash right back out, he pouts like a baby. I'll pop a jump hook and say, "Looks like I got you again, Zelmo. Wilt and Russell never blocked me; how do you think that you're ever going to do it?" And then he gets angry.

When the snow starts to come down around Christmastime and I find I'm still riding the pine, I get to missing all the places I used to be. There's LA, where all my family is. There's Chicago, where at least I could have counted on Tony Banks to show me around. And then there's New York. No city in the world smells like winter in New York. The engine exhaust mingles with the piled-high snow along the street corners to make an aroma that almost has its own weight to it, that presses down on the chest. At nighttime the smells of roasting chestnuts and pretzels from street vendors combat for primacy, each one beckoning a man to open up his wallet and buy something to take along, each one something like a companion for a nickel or quarter a bite.

There's none of this to comfort me in St. Louis. In St. Louis I'm unquestionably all alone.

By midseason I've played a total of only ninety-six minutes with the Hawks. That's less than three full games worth of action. It's certainly not enough to make an impact, and I find myself starting to question why I'm even here.

After returning from yet another road trip without seeing much of the court, I find Bob Pettit eating dinner alone in the restaurant of our hotel, so I walk over to join him. With the possible exception of rookie Paul Silas, who did me the solid of taking me out once here for a night on the town, I don't imagine there's a single other player on this team who would give me the time of day, let alone break bread with me. Pettit and I may not be close, but company's company, and right now I could use it.

"How you feeling, Hill?" he asks.

Now, there are times in life when you should just keep your mouth shut. Sometimes putting on a happy face is the smartest thing to do. But sitting here one-on-one with the team captain, I find I just can't do it. I can't keep all these doubts bottled up inside anymore. So I tell him.

I tell Pettit that I'm worried about not getting any playing time, and I'm worried about why I'm here at all. I know that on most teams there's a player who's plugged in, who knows what's going on in the heads of the front office, and on this team Pettit is it. I know this might be one of those times when it would be better to hold my tongue, but I can't. So I ask him the question that's foremost on my mind.

"Bob," I say. "I gotta ask. How come I'm not getting any playing time?"

Bob Pettit eyes me, and he puts down his water glass. "Hill," he says, "I won't lie to you." He clears his throat. "Hill, you're about to be released."

My eyebrows burrow. "I'm what?"

Pettit glances around the room. Then he leans in toward me. "Billy," he says. "You're getting cut."

I don't feel myself getting up and going anywhere. But as Pettit talks on, it sounds as if he's speaking to me from down the end of a long, canted hallway.

He goes on to describe what the team needs out of a backup player, but he doesn't need to. I know what the problem is with me.

I can pop shots and score points all day long. But the Hawks already have scorers. All they want out of me—out of any backup player—is defense. They want someone who can hold the fort and shut down the other team's studs while our own are resting. And that's just not me.

I'm a scorer. I could always score. And I prove this every time we have practice. Hell, I even taught Pettit my jump hook, and he scored his twenty thousandth point with it. He's the first player ever to score twenty thousand points in the NBA, and he did it with my shot! Clearly I've got value!

But here's the thing. When you're playing a game—a real game—it's not A-line vs. B-line, it's your team vs. your opponent's; you only get five of your own guys on the court, not ten. That means your team only gets half as many possessions as you do in a scrimmage. Second-stringers rotate in and play a role, and the expectations of that role are to contain the opposition players as best they can and dish off the ball to the first-stringer scorers when they get it. They're not put in to be the locus of the offense, they're there so other starters can rest up long enough to come back in and effectively score.

What's needed from second-stringers is defense, pure and simple. And that's not me. So I'm gone.

I lurch through the next week or so of practices and travel like a sleepwalker until finally Coach Harry Gallatin calls me into his office to make the news official: I've been unconditionally released.

With nothing else to do and no reason to stay, I pack everything I own into the trunk of my car and pull out of my hotel. I start to drive, but almost immediately I pull over.

For the first time since I was a kid, I have no basketball team to play for and therefore no destination. So the question looms large in my mind: where do I go from here?

Can You Come Home Again?

Being forced out of the NBA leaves me feeling the lowest I've ever felt. Just two and a half years ago I was a bonus baby, riding high on the single best season a college center ever had. Just a year ago, I was scoring forty-one points against the Lakers in the Garden. Now here I am, twenty-five years old and washed up. It's a terrible feeling.

I feel almost like I'm drowning, or worse, watching everyone I've ever known and loved drown and not being able to save them. I feel like everyone's dreams—my mother's, Lefty's, Sweet Al's, Mr. Ward's, and mine—were all resting on me, and I failed them.

Luckily, there's T.B., a lifeboat in a storm.

From St. Louis I head to Chicago. I choose Chicago because I have friends there, real friends, and unlike in LA, I won't have to see anyone from my youth who I feel that I've let down. When I arrive Tony Banks sees how badly I'm getting down on myself, and though he doesn't sugar-coat it, he does his best to bring me right back up. Even though I'm not a star anymore, he helps keep me aloft, going out of his way to find me a job in Chicago's Parks and Recreation Department. There's no interview, just a handshake and a check.

My last position in this town was playing center for the Zephyrs in the NBA. Now I'll be working as a youth counselor, overseeing children who live in the most violent and crime-riddled neighborhood in the city. It's hardly a number one draft pick assignment. But at least it's a job.

My charge is to work the southwest basketball courts, helping oversee pickup games and running tutoring and mentoring sessions. "Courts" is maybe too grand a word for where I am; it's really just a raggedy old building to which I hold the key, and inside there's a half-sized basketball floor with one lone hoop.

The kids in my area are deemed at risk for being recruited into gangs—that is, if they don't belong to one already. One facet of my job is to try to steer them in the right direction. Ironically, part and parcel of this is trying to keep them in school. Do as I say, not as I do.

Occasionally I'll escort some of the younger ones home to talk with their mothers—not for disciplinary reasons or anything like that, 'cause that's not my job, but just to let the mothers know that their kids are out on the court and doing all right. When I do this the story is always the same. The moms are pleased that someone, anyone, is taking an interest in their sons; the boys' dads are nearly always gone, and that's something that I can relate to. Sometimes I get invited in for dinner, sometimes not; sometimes the moms know of me from my playing days, sometimes not. But still, they're always happy to see me, and that's rewarding. Yet the families' apartments are rarely any bigger than mine—and I live alone in a studio. It's tough for them in southwest Chicago, no question about that.

Because I live alone and because I've got plenty of time on my hands and because he wants to make sure I don't get too depressed about falling out of the league—T.B. and I start spending a lot of our nights going out to clubs again. It's on one of these nights out that I run into Willie "Bird" Jones.

Willie the Bird spent five years in the league, and he was still playing with the Pistons back when I started in the NBA. Despite that, I actually don't recognize him at first—it's not until he introduces himself and slaps me a soul five that I really notice him. But once he starts talking he has my full attention.

He cuts to the chase. "Are you still playing, Hill? You still in ball?"

The words cut like a twisting dagger under my skin. "Naw, man," I say coolly. "I'm out of the league." I neglect to mention how I began the season—how, just a few months ago, I'd driven to New York expecting to find my starting center position waiting for me just as I'd left it, only to be traded and then unceremoniously dumped, on my third city in half a year.

"Yeah, me, too," he admits, turning his head, as if it's a dirty secret we share that he doesn't want anyone else to know. In a way, I guess, it is.

"Got something else going, though," Bird says, looking up at me again. "Playing for a new team. The Grand Rapids Tackers."

Tackers? I've never heard of them.

"It's the NABL, a little midwestern league across the lake in Michigan. But still, you get paid. Just a little, but it's pro ball. You interested?"

My ears perk up. Am I interested? Is the pope Catholic? Last time I stepped on the court, it was to try to break up a fight between an oversized twelve-year-old and an unlucky runt who got between him and a rebound, and I tell Willie as much.

"I'll have to talk to the owner to set it up," he says, "but it should be all right. You're still fresh."

"Fresh?" Does he mean my knee? How would he know if I'm feeling good?

"Yeah," he says. "You're a fresh name. Fresh from the NBA."

Oh, Lord. I'm in my midtwenties and already I'm stuck trading on my legacy.

As it turns out the league *is* small. Very small. We have only one game per week, and we play it on the weekends. There are no organized practices. We just show up in little factory towns across the state of Michigan, slip on our uniforms, and play.

All the other players are guys whose names I recognize from college ball or the pros. We all still want to win just as much as we ever did. Only difference is, a few years back I'd been offered forty thousand dollars to play for Pat Boone. A few years back I'd been angry about getting only seventeen thousand and having to supplement my income with dice games. Now we're all out here playing for a hundred bucks a throw.

The season, such as it is—it's not even twenty games, but I guess when

you're playing but once a week there's only so much winter to go around—
is already half over by the time I join Willie on the Tackers. I go in not
expecting much, and that turns out to be a good thing. Yes, every game is
a sellout, but that's not hard when you're playing on a civic center court or
at a school gym. A part of me feels like I'm walking backward. What happened to the arenas? Am I, a grown man, back to playing at Jefferson High?

At least I do still love to play, and that's good. That keeps me coming
out week after week. There's also the fact that secretly—or not so secretly—
I, like everyone else out here, am playing with the hopes of using this little league as a stepping-stone to punching my ticket back to the big show.
And on February 4th, in the dead of winter, I get the news: it's worked.
I've been picked up on waivers, rescued from obscurity. The LA Lakers
have decided that they want me.

T.B. assures me that the Parks Department will make do with someone
else and the kids will be fine without me. I give him a hug, thank him and
the Bird for helping align the stars for me and, like a cadet being told to
hop to, pack up my things and drive straight to LA.

When I walk into the Memorial Sports Arena I'm struck by how much
has changed in just a year. Last season I strode in here a champion, the
starting center for the New York Knickerbockers and a man on a mission.
I'd just scored forty-one points; I came in ready to kill and I did nearly
that, starting a fistfight that got me ejected and led to a bench-clearing
brawl. I was the talk of the town; I made the cover of the sports page. I
was reunited with my dad. It was almost magical. And now here I am,
limping in from the cold, just months after having been told I didn't make
the cut as the backup to a backup in St. Louis.

I try not to think of any of that now, though. Now I have work to do.

Warming up alone before the other players arrive, I drive the lane and
throw down a dunk, listening to the *thwap* of the ball echo throughout
the empty seats and rafters of the arena. As the ball pitters across the hardwood underneath me, I hang on tightly to the rim, dangling.

I just hope I don't lose my grip.

When the other players arrive Jerry West makes it a point to approach me.

"Look for the ball whenever you get into the game," he says, "because I'm going to get it inside to you.

"I know that you're a great shooter," he continues. "I remember what you did to us at the Garden when you were with the Knicks."

That makes me feel good, being recognized like that. Unfortunately, West may be the only one who remembers—or cares. Elgin Baylor, the other stud player on the Lakers, doesn't say boo to me, and for all his concern I might as well not even exist. My on-again, off-again teammate Don Nelson? Forget about it. He harbors no love. And as for Gene Wiley, he still recalls how I blew up on him in the Garden. I want his job and he knows it, and I play in practices like there's nothing I'm willing to accept short of winning the role with my grit, fire, and jump hook. So he doesn't care for me.

Practices go well, all in all, and my knee holds up as well as it can, but I don't see floor time. At first I tell myself that's okay—they've got to get used to me first before they can slot me in during the playoff push. But as time passes, it becomes clear that isn't true.

In fact, my role with the Lakers becomes little more than that of a punching bag for Wiley to keep him sharp in between games. Despite my scoring prowess, I get next to no court time outside of practices. By the time the regular season ends I've only seen the floor in eight games, and then only for a combined total of thirty-seven minutes. That's even less court time than I got with the Hawks.

When the regular season ends and the playoffs begin it's more of the same: we win, but I don't get to play. We actually play the Hawks in the Western Conference finals—who've themselves just beaten the Bullets to get there—and we rout them. Still, that feels doubly good, bumping off both the teams who didn't want me. But I want to play. I feel like Carney Crisler all over again.

With the NBA championship on the horizon, I feel certain that if I can just get in the game I can contribute and have an impact. We'll be playing Bill Russell and the Boston Celtics for the world championship, and I'm itching to go out and show my worth, to prove to my coach, my teammates, my fans, family, and myself that I have what it takes. I'm not just a former number one NBA draft pick—I'm a player, and I can help us win.

Unfortunately I never get the chance. I sit on the bench for every minute of every game in the finals, and all along I'm forced to watch Boston dominate us.

It really frustrates me, to sit impotent like this. Our coach, Fred Schaus, is oblivious to my presence. In a few of the games we could really use some scoring from inside and Wiley's dead in the water, but it doesn't matter. Russell blocks Wiley every time he tries to come inside, but still I'm stuck riding the pine. Coach Schaus doesn't even think of giving me a chance and seeing what I can do. Such is the life of the player on the backup squad.

After Boston finishes mopping the floor with us and wins themselves the championship, Russell approaches me. "Sorry, Hill," he grins. "I'm sure glad Schaus didn't let you play, because you probably would have embarrassed me with that damn jump hook." He belts out that big laugh of his and then leaves to rejoin his team.

Sitting alone on the sidelines as the Celtics' fans celebrate, I wonder: was Russell trying to make me feel better? I don't know. But the more I think about it, the more I realize that what he said only makes me feel worse.

In and Out

All summer Russell's words echo through my head. Could I have helped my team? Could we have won if I'd taken the floor? There's no way I can know.

Next fall the Lakers' training camp opens at Loyola University, a school I recall from my days at Utah. The two-a-day workouts are grueling and take a toll on my knee, but I play through them. I have to. Along with me and Gene Wiley, Darrall Imhoff is at camp this year, and all three of us know that by the start of the 1965–66 season, one of us will be gone.

Fighting like my job is on the line—because it is—I kill myself in every intra-squad scrimmage. I play Imhoff as hard as I can to try to keep my place on the team. My rebounding is ferocious and, to the extent it can be, so is my defense. My plan is simply to do all I can to earn this spot and dare Fred Schaus to cut me.

My day of reckoning arrives in the form of an exhibition game: for the first time since last year's NBA playoffs, the Celtics come to town. Before the game begins Schaus approaches me and tells me to get ready—this is my shot.

Despite Coach Schaus's interdiction, the game starts with me on the bench. Though I'm sitting, I can feel the pressure begin to build. This is weird for me; I am usually so loose. But then I don't usually find myself desperate for a chance to prove my worth. I need to get out there and show that I'm as good as Wiley or Imhoff are, but the minutes keep ticking by, and still I don't see the court.

Finally, late in the third quarter, Coach Schaus calls my name. As I strip off my warm-ups and prepare to step onto the court, I know my prospects for the entire season will rest on how I play today against the Celtics and the single greatest defensive center in the history of the NBA: Bill Russell.

It's an odd feeling.

On my first possession on the floor I receive the ball off a bounce pass. I'm at the free-throw line, deep, but well within my range, and immediately I go straight up with my jump hook. Releasing it, I smile. The arc is perfect, and even Russell, as great as he is, has no chance of getting up high enough to block it. I watch as the ball traces its familiar path, heading straight for the hoop.

And then off it. The ball skips off the rim, skims up against the backboard, and falls into the hands of a waiting John Havlicek, who dishes the ball off and charges toward me on offense.

I missed. My signature shot, and I missed. From that moment on I know I'm in trouble. I'm just too tight! Each of the next four jump hooks I shoot on Russell rim in and then rim out. They say football's the game of inches, but for me, this day, it's basketball. After I miss five straight shots, none by more than a hand's breadth, I'm pulled. I don't see the court again.

Before I even unlace my sneakers, I already know my fate.

After the buzzer rings I return to the locker room. Slowly I shower and dress. On my way out, as I'm walking through the concrete tunnel, Coach Schaus pulls me aside and into his office. He leaves the door open. He doesn't offer me a chair.

"You know what I'm going to say to you," he says, and I breathlessly admit that I do.

"It's not what I want, you understand, but I've got no choice but to—"

"To cut me from the team," I interrupt.

He nods. "Yes. I'm sorry."

You're damn right you're sorry, I think, remembering how poorly he coached us in our NBA championship loss to the Celtics the previous spring. I intend to keep this thought to myself, but when I look up from the cement floor, he seems to almost be smirking at me, and that does it. I boil over.

"You're damn right; you are sorry!" I exclaim, and fueled by anger over being dropped, I start ripping into him. Schaus is shocked, dumbfounded even. That's not the kind of thing a player is supposed to say to his coach. But if I'm getting cut anyway, what's the difference?

I let loose in that office, wildly insisting that the Lakers are blowing it by letting me go. Once or twice Schaus even tries to defuse me by telling me what a great ballplayer I am. But I'm too far gone. I just shoot back, "Yeah, well, if I'm so great, why the hell are you cutting me?"

Actually, what I really say is peppered with far stronger words: f this and f that; I'm dropping f-bombs like it's f'ing World War III. Schaus just lets me swear myself out of steam, though, and when I'm done I pick up my clothes and leave, no looking back.

When I return to Chicago in the fall of 1965 after getting cut from the Lakers, little has changed. My apartment's the same, my job is the same, and my charges are more or less the same, too. The only difference is they're one year older.

One of the new faces of the local youth gang, the Blackstone Rangers, becomes friendly with me. He's vicious and violent, but for some reason he likes me, and I like him, too. When he plays he plays hard, fouling and shoving when necessary like Lefty used to do. When there's a loose ball he's as liable as not to start beating up one of his friends on the other team just trying to snatch it up. I take to calling him Mad Dog because of the way he plays, and frankly I think he likes it.

I pull Mad Dog aside one day and explain to him how I'm trying to do right by the young kids at the little basketball court and steer them straight. From that day on, even though they still hang around the court, none of the Rangers ever tries to recruit any of my kids outright; Mad Dog makes sure of it. Even when I venture into the projects to talk to the parents of one kid or another who's headed in the wrong direction—sapping the gang's potential membership, I suppose—they never once harass me at all.

But that doesn't stop me from buying a gun.

Why I do it I don't know. I certainly don't go hunting around for one. Just one day as I'm walking to work, a scraggly man with a knit wool cap and an overcoat comes up to me and beckons me over with a nod of his head.

"Hey," he says. "You wanna buy a piece?" And he flashes it to me: a black, six-chambered revolver with tape around the handle. "Thirty bucks."

I'm not sure why I say yes. Maybe it's the danger of the area I'm living in. Maybe it's being surrounded by gang youth every day. Maybe it's just the lingering memory of being cornered in my dorm room back in my college days. But for whatever reason, I buy the gun from this bum on the street, cash paid, no questions asked. It's a .22, and each chamber comes already loaded with bullets.

In addition to returning to my job with the Parks Department, I return to the NABL and my team, the Grand Rapids Tackers. All the Michigan press covering the league—what little there is, anyway—is agog that I've re-signed. Coming from the NBA, I'm less enthused. Still, I do my best to give the fans their money's worth. NBA or NABL, the basket's still ten feet in the air and thirteen feet, nine inches from the foul line.

No matter where I'm playing or who I'm playing against, it's still on me to score—and score I do. The opposing centers have no chance against me; I'm just better than they are. Really, it's not that different from old times. Save the fact that I get my payment in cash at the end of every game, and after each one's over I need to get ready to work another job on Monday.

The year passes by quietly in Chicago, and winter basketball gives way to spring thaw. By midsummer the NABL is quite far from my mind. Thus, I'm caught off guard when the phone rings on a steamy Sunday in July, and the caller wants to talk about basketball.

"Billy," says the man on the other end of the line. "I saw you had a good season with the Tackers."

"Yeah," I say, "I did." The Tackers won the NABL season title, and I made the All-League squad. So you could argue that I was the best player on the league's best team. Still, that doesn't feel like much to brag about—like being the fastest kid at a fat camp—so a caller lauding my play makes me suspicious. "Who's this?"

"Eddie Gottlieb."

The name means nothing to me. I tell him as much.

"I'm a front office man for the Warriors, how 'bout that? That name mean anything to you?"

The Warriors? The San Francisco Warriors?

"We want to make you a tryout offer."

I can't believe it. A tryout? It's been a year and a half since my last real game in the NBA, and I'm getting a tryout? I'm elated. I tell everybody. I call Willie the Bird; I call Tony B. I call my mother who, it turns out, is neither in church nor in bed. I can hardly wait until tomorrow to tell the Parks Department to put me on leave—but long leave this time, because I feel good, and this time I might not be back.

California is a long drive away, but I never get tired—now I can understand how Dave Costa felt. Fueled by determination, I crash through the cornfields of Iowa and Nebraska, and I zigzag up and down the mountain slopes of Wyoming and Utah. I'm so determined that even the dice in Reno offer no distraction, and I glide on westward toward the ocean and the cities on the Bay.

The worst thing any player on the bubble can do is appear out of shape. So when Warriors tryouts open and the new coach, Bill Sharman, sets us to running until we collapse, I don't say a word. The drills are hard on my knee, to put it mildly—Sharman, I think, must have conceived the majority of them in some kind of sadistic nightmare—and at the end I have trouble standing. But I keep that to myself, finding a doctor on my own. I'm putting my best foot forward.

As the lines shake out a clear picture emerges: the Warriors already have their starting center, but they're looking for another. Their starter, Nate "the Great" Thurmond, is one of the two stars of the team along with forward Rick Barry, and he's already guaranteed his spot. Thurmond's been an All-Star for the last two years, even playing one of those seasons under the shadow of Wilt the Stilt. The Warriors let Chamberlain go knowing they had Nate right behind him as their center for the future, which says a lot for Thurmond's talent. That leaves just one spot in reserve, and I'm determined to earn it.

I have two competitors for the role: Bud Olsen and Walter Dukes. Dukes is an old hand; at thirty-seven he's one of the oldest players in the camp. He broke into the NBA with the Knicks back when I was still at Jefferson, and though I'm sure I've got him beat physically, there's no discounting his knowledge and his tenacity. He's seven feet tall and a fearless rebounder, but he's old and just trying to hang on—a pig in the slaughterhouse trying to spare himself the ax.

Sharman comments repeatedly that he loves Dukes's fire. Well, his tenacity might be impressive, but my shooting damn sure is, too. When we scrimmage each other I lay in shot after shot, and it quickly becomes clear that the difference between Dukes and me is my jump hook. He fights hard, but I can score where he can't, and after a few days in camp I'm still there, but Dukes is gone. This leaves only Olsen to beat.

Bud Olsen is tougher to shake. After Wilt left the Warriors for the 76ers and his native Philadelphia last season, Olsen took over the backup center role. That means he's got inertia and team experience on his side. Yes, Bud Olsen's undersized for the position—he's shorter than I am and much lighter, and at center, that should give me an edge. But the thing is Coach Sharman seems to actually prefer Olsen's smaller size. Sharman made his name in the pros as a player by being little and quick; he is six feet one and tips only 175 pounds on the scale when he's been wearing his clothes in the shower. He looks at six-foot-eight, 220-pound Olsen and six-foot-eleven, 225-pound Thurmond and he sees what he wants: a slightly stretched-out version of himself. No wonder he let Wilt the Stilt get away.

There's a third hurdle beyond my newness and size, though, and this one is the toughest of all to clear: Olsen, the man I'm competing against for the backup job, has an in with the front office. The Warriors' owner, Franklin Mieuli, has taken to coming to practices, ostensibly to watch the players scrimmage. However, whenever I look over to him after nailing a shot or pulling down a particularly tough rebound, I find he's not watching me at all. Instead he's playing with a baby boy perched on his knee—a boy who, I learn, is Bud Olsen's kid.

Uh-oh.

This is Andy Johnson and the Zephyrs all over again, but in reverse: if a front-office guy has a problem with you you're sure to be out. But what if you've got an in with the owner? Well, you're more or less sure to be in, aren't you? And Olsen's wife and child sit in the stands with Frankie Mieuli *every day*. How am I supposed to beat the guy out for a spot when the team's owner is bouncing his baby on his knee?

As the close of camp looms, Nate Thurmond pulls me aside and confirms what I already know: regardless of how well I've been playing in scrimmages, I'm going to be cut from the team.

"Hill," he says, "they're not gonna keep two black centers." I watch Mieuli play with Olsen's kid, and I know Nate is right.

Suiting up for what I know is going to be my last scrimmage with the Warriors on the last day of training camp, disappointment, confusion, and anger swirl through me. I'm disappointed to see the abattoir waiting in the distance, to know that soon I'll be heading back to Chicago, my gangland apartment, and obscurity. I'm confused, too, as to why I was invited out in the first place. If Olsen was so in with Mieuli and Sharman liked his players small, why did they even bother? Finally, there's anger—my old companion anger. I'm angry at being let down once more, angry at being given half a chance, and above all angry at having to face being cut one last time. You'd think I'd be inured to it after these last few years, but I'm not. It consumes me.

The final scrimmage starts, and I channel all that emotion into dominating the boards and the paint. I'm swinging my elbows back and forth, oblivious to everything but getting the ball; I'm popping up skyhooks and jump hooks all over the place. I'm furious at what I know is coming, but the truth has set me free. I'm playing hard, and I'm playing great.

Late in the game our team turns it over on an upcourt pass, and Rick Barry fast-breaks toward our basket with the steal. I'm the only one left on D—it's one-on-one.

Barry's attacking, fast on the dribble; he jukes inside, then outside, and in a flash goes up toward the hoop.

It should be a meaningless bucket—two garbage points in an intra-squad game for a team that, in an hour, I won't even play for. But when Barry takes off time stands still. In that split second all the disappointments I've endured in my short career flash through my mind, all the coaches and owners that didn't give me a fair shake. The bum contract with the Zephyrs, getting dumped from the Hawks, and getting cut from the Lakers last year. Having to play in Michigan's minor leagues; knowing that this will be my last day with the Warriors because of the color of my skin and the cuteness of another guy's baby. And to top it all off, now a guy five inches shorter than I am is going to try to embarrass me on my way out the door by plowing straight through the lane and dunking on me. These disappointments, insults, and injuries avalanche in my mind, and all rational thought shuts down.

I don't even see the ball in his hand. All I can see is his head, and that I try to tear off his body.

Rick Barry jumps, and I foul him with such force that he does a one and a quarter flip in midair and lands squarely on the court on his back. The echo he makes when he hits the ground is tremendous. Everyone stops; in the aftermath the only noises in the cavernous gym come from the bounding ball and Barry, who, rolling, begins to squirm and squeal. I've hurt him badly, and I don't care.

"Practice is over!" Sharman shouts as he sprints onto the court. So is my tryout with the Warriors.

A Glimmer of Hope

After the Warriors debacle, little of import remains in my life save the list-lessness of waiting out Chicago summers and driving through midwestern snowstorms to play twenty-game stints in a second-rate Michigan basket-ball league. Though I'm named to the first-team NABL All-Star squad in each of the next two years, at the end of the 1967–68 season the NABL folds entirely. I try to tell myself it doesn't matter to me, but of course it does. Three years after my exit from the NBA, six years out from setting an all-time NCAA scoring record for centers, all I have to show for myself from a lifetime of basketball is a set of warm-ups from a team that no longer exists. Even mentoring kids has less of a draw for me than it once did: when I was out in San Francisco trying out for the Warriors, Mad Dog was shot, and he died. I wonder, am I cursed?

The cloud with the silver lining that convinces me I'm not is a phone call I receive from Bob Bass, head coach of the Denver Rockets of the newly formed ABA. The ABA is a new, black-friendly league full of personality—witness their basketballs—and Bass wants me to come try out for it.

Two years ago I got a call like this from the Warriors, but when I went to camp I didn't make the cut. This time I won't let that happen. It's another second chance. A third chance. This doesn't really happen to people. But it's happening to me.

I quit my Parks Department job to begin working out every day. This is my last shot, and I know it—this time I'm going all in. I'm either going to make it or go down trying.

Training camp opens outside Denver, and watching the floor during the first day of warm-ups I realize I recognize surprisingly few of the other faces on the court. Most of them look young enough not to be able to buy their own cigarettes. Am I that old? The one exception is a guy named Wayne "Spain" Hightower, who looks to be running the floor; I recognize him from the NBA back in the day. They call him Spain because he spent time in Europe living under Franco—what a big-ass black guy like that was doing over there I'll never know.

Coach Bass calls us in for our first running drills—what is it with coaches and starting off camp with conditioning? Though the practice is grueling, as day one comes to a close I'm glad that I spent my summer pounding the pavement in Chicago. My knee doesn't swell, and I'm able to run all morning and play all evening without breaking down or screaming in pain. I don't even have to get my knee drained—it's the first time that's happened at the start of the season since high school.

Byron Beck is the reigning starting center for the Rockets; he's six feet eight and a damn hard player. There's no question that Byron will be sticking around; even if I do manage to snag the top job, I won't win it in training camp. So my real competition is this huge, raw-boned white boy who wants the backup spot; I don't even bother to learn his name. He wants what's mine: my job. I hate him. In my head I call him Bud Olsen Jr.

I will crush this man.

All during training camp Bud Jr. and I go up against each other with such ferociousness that it's lucky neither one of us gets hurt. But that's not a consideration for me nor, I imagine, for him. We're in a battle for our professional lives, and we both know it. For once, at least, I don't feel like I've got the weak hand going in because of that old nagging factor: my race. Unlike at Utah, unlike in the NBA, here in the ABA they don't care about color. In fact, if anything, the league caters to a black audience, placing its teams in black cities and leading the way with black superstars, men not afraid to wear their funky styles on their sleeves and let their loud afros lead the way toward the hoops. We're in the black cities. We're in downtown Indianapolis, damn it; we're in Memphis. Every team's roster even gets featured in loud and proud *Jet Magazine*, pictorial spreads with all the white faces, for once, skipped out. So I'm on even footing, I figure, and while I've got failures in my past, I'm going to use them to my advantage this time.

My knee holds up well, and I play hard throughout the preseason, but as camp pushes toward its coda we're still waiting for a decision. Bud Jr. is playing hard, too, and he and I are still fighting for the spot. It's like a horse race with two steeds coming down the stretch nose to nose, neither giving the other even an inch.

As a precaution I get my knee drained the Friday before the last week of camp, when I know I'll have a whole weekend to let it rest. As I lie in bed that Saturday and Sunday, staring at the ceiling and playing out my mental game, I center my mind and try to will myself to victory. But it's difficult. Each morning during camp a list of players' names is taped on the bulletin board—the list is a notice of those cut from the team. I try to focus on visualizing my jump hooks swishing softly through the net, but each time I fall asleep, I dream about looking at the list and see, printed and repeated in block letters, "BILLY MCGILL. BILLY MCGILL. BILLY MCGILL."

The evening of our last practice we all suit up for an intra-squad scrimmage, and this one is open to the public. I'm on the line with Spain at forward, which is good—Spain is this team's Pettit, and he has a no-cut contract. Being on Spain's squad means it's the first string, which means I've got the inside track. Byron Beck's resting, so I'm up against my nemesis, Bud Jr. "This is it, Billy," I tell myself. "This is your time."

The jump ball goes up. I get the tip and knock it over to Spain. Like that, we're off. Spain pushes the ball upcourt and clocks me posting up high at the free-throw line; the ball comes to me and I go straight up with a jump hook that hits nothing but net. Applause greets my two points, and I bask in the cheering of the assembled fans.

I have to thank the second-string guards for aiding me in my quest to make the team. They're trying hard to make the team themselves; they pop deep, wild shots, trying to impress the coaches with three-pointers. I've been on the other side of this; this kind of guard play means Bud Jr.'s offense is nonexistent. And that's good for me.

During a time-out, Spain approaches me with a smile. "I'll be getting you the ball inside every chance I get," he says. Now, I've heard this before, and only half the time did it prove to be true. But as I think back on the guys who did make good on their word—guys like Ed Rowe, for instance—something dawns on me. It's a lesson I should have learned a long time ago, back with the Knicks, back with the Utes, even back with the Demos as a kid: the importance of working together. Yes, maybe the pros are cut-throat, and yes, maybe long careers are hard to come by. But basketball, like life, is a team game, and to come out on top, sometimes we need to rely on one another.

I decide to put my faith in Spain, and he proves true to his word. I get the ball plenty, and each time I do my shots slide easily through the bas-ket. It's like old times. My defender's bewildered, defeated, and beaten, and there's nothing he can do.

I steal a look at Coach Bass, and he's smiling at me. I don't need to be told what I already know: I'm in.

When the preseason ends I'm handed a contract for ten thousand dol-lars, the most I've made in a long, long while.

"Ten grand?" I say aloud, and the secretary in the Rockets' office eyes me with pity.

She expects me, I think, to raise a fuss over the figure. What she don't know. "But you've got a job in the off-season, if you want it," she hastily adds, "unloading shipments on the owner's trucking docks."

A roster spot and a job for the summer? I practically skip out of the office.

At the outset of the season Byron Beck and I trade off minutes at cen-ter, but as time progresses I begin to see more and more of the court. It's like the Knicks all over again. I'm playing for a good coach and earning my minutes the right way: by outplaying my competition.

Of course, it doesn't hurt to have a friend like Spain on my side. Wayne "Spain" Hightower is the best defensive player on our team, maybe the best in the entire league. He always guards the other team's highest scorers, and he nearly always shuts them down. Anytime I'm tired or start lagging because of my knee, Spain helps get me back on track. He's kind of like Sweet Al that way. Kind of like Lefty, too.

By the time the season ends I'm back on top. My jump hook's still not been blocked, though not for lack of other guys' trying—but of course, if Wilt and Russell couldn't block it, who could? I have such ease scoring, in fact, that I end the year with the best field-goal percentage in the league, .552.

I've proven that I've still got it, and that feels good. Still, there's no bonus, no trophy, nothing at the end of the season waiting to herald my achievement except a line in the newspaper. That and a job as a stevedore at a bay in an east Denver trucking dock.

Second Verse, Ain't Like the First

When the season ends I go to work on the docks loading and unloading the big trucks, with Byron Beck alongside me. The other guys on the docks—the lifers—know what Byron and I do the rest of the year, but they don't care. They don't ask for autographs or nothing; they just want to get their work done so they can get paid on Friday and get home to their families. Besides, it's a rough job—there's no time for fawning over someone when you're sweating your ass off every minute of every day, lifting hundred-pound boxes with your arms and hauling thousand-pound crates on a handcart. It'd be nice to have Spain out here with me, but he owns a small nightclub business that's doing well enough that he doesn't need a second job. As for me and Byron, we get close despite fighting for the starting spot; what bonds us is my car.

Now that I'm a pro player again, there's no reason not to travel in style, and I trade in my old car for a '69 Coupe de Ville convertible. The coupe is a light wisteria purple with darker purple leather seats. I have the dealer dye the white top purple, too, the same color as the rest of the chassis. It's a beautiful car, and I love it.

When I walk into camp come fall after a summer on the docks, it's with more than a little bit of swagger. Never mind that between the car, sending money home to my folks, and three years of a public service job I have nothing in the way of savings. For once I'm walking into camp feeling secure: I've got another one-year contract already, to say nothing of the reigning shooting champ title that sits in my back pocket. There's not a thing that can hold me back.

Do I realize that this is exactly how I felt when I walked into Knicks camp my third year in the NBA? Of course not.

When camp opens for the 1969–70 season Beck and I are surprised to find that the Rockets have signed a third center: a young kid by the name of Spencer Haywood. Haywood's barely twenty and a middle child out of a Mississippi family of twelve; he escaped college after just two years to rush into the pro ranks. He's got the ability, no doubt about it. He played for the U.S. squad at the Olympic Games in Mexico City and won a gold medal, and he scored 32.1 points per game—threatening my high-water mark—in the 1968–69 college season playing at Detroit. He's got hunger, too, both psychological and real; he needs this job to make sure his brothers and sisters eat. But what's he doing here? This is my town, isn't it?

It's a cutthroat game, basketball.

Spain and I, as the go-to court leaders from the previous year, decide to reach out to Haywood. The kid is big, talented, and cocky, and though we don't doubt his ability, he seems too brash—like he doesn't understand all the things a rookie needs to know. In practices he's too loud, and on the court he tries to do too much, not yet having learned the importance and value of team basketball. With our own histories on our minds, we decide it's best for us elder statesmen to head over to his pad and talk to him a little bit about what's in store, take him under our wings.

What a shock it is, then, when he invites us into his apartment and reaches under his couch to drag out a giant, olive green, army-issue duffel bag filled to the brim with marijuana.

I look at Spain and Spain looks at me—this is not our scene. We're up and out of there, telling Spence that we don't need this kind of trouble. As we split, though, Haywood seems confused, almost angry—I think he takes this refusal to smoke with him as a personal affront. From then on at practice, our relationship turns from friendly competitive to antagonistic. When he's matched up against Beck he plays well and plays to win, but against me he lets his ferocious and raw instincts bubble to the surface.

He grinds me down. When I try to play beneath the basket, he digs his palms into my back and starts shoving. "You can't come inside on me," he says. "You think you can shove inside on Spencer Haywood?" He fouls me deliberately, but he doesn't care. He does the same to Spain.

This physicality reaches the point where I get angry, and I start to rag on him and egg him on, adding fuel to the fire. "Whatever you're smoking," I say, "it don't matter; there's no way it can get you high enough to block my jump hook!" Sometimes I say, "That stuff's poking holes in your brain, making you think you can block my shot!" That pisses him off even more. We push back and forth on each other so much that eventually something has to give. And it does.

Coach Bass pulls me and Spain into the office to tell us that our contracts have been sold. I'm stunned.

"I'm sorry, boys," he says. "The team's just going in a different direction."

It takes time for me to fully digest what's happening. Here's this kid, big and skilled and aggressive enough that he clearly has the potential to lead the league in everything, even in his rookie year: games, points, minutes, rebounds, shots, whatever. But he'll be gone to the NBA within a season for sure—and for that the Rockets will jettison the reigning league shooting champ and their offensive floor leader and captain?

Apparently, yes, that is the decision the Rockets' front office makes. Even Spain, with his whole family and his business out here in Denver, gets shipped off—they have no need for the old floor leader now that the new model has hit town.

This is, indeed, a cutthroat game.

If I'm mad, Spain's straight-up angry. And to make things worse we've been sold to the last team I want to be joined up with: the LA Stars.

There's a reason I kept going back to Chicago instead of LA in my off seasons. My hometown is hardly a place full of good memories. What's worse, I don't even have before me the already trying task of building a new relationship with a coach. I've got to patch up an old one. The head coach of the LA Stars is Bill Sharman, the man who oversaw my final exit from the NBA. The man who I last saw when I was getting cut from the Warriors. The man who I effectively told to kiss my black ass as I kicked the walls of the training facility and stomped out the door.

He's my new coach.

Like they say, when it rains it pours.

When I show up in LA there's a message waiting for me at my mom's: my old buddy Tony Banks has gotten a job working for the publishers of *Jet Magazine*. As part of his duties as a correspondent, T.B.'s been sent to Los Angeles to cover the black nightlife scene in the city. Of course, the moment he hears I've been sold to the Stars—which, with his connections, doesn't take long—he's on the horn to me.

"Billy! I'm here, baby! Let's go out and celebrate."

Normally I'd be ecstatic to hang out with Tony again. But at the moment this is a problem. I'm in the swing of the start of the season, trying to hop onto a boat midstream that's captained by a man who has every right to hate my guts. I've got to impress him with my play and hard work and get him to change his mind about me . . . which is a doubly tall order if I also plan to hit the clubs and party.

Still, when T.B. calls we go out, not because I want to but because I've got to. It's my obligation: he took care of me when I was in Chicago, and now in LA I have to do him the same turn. We're out all night, though, and when I wake up the next day for a team scrimmage, my body feels as brittle as a tin scarecrow. Worse, there's no time to sleep it off. I've got to go out and play ball against a squad full of young bucks who are all gunning for my minutes.

I play like I feel, which is to say not great. This can't last.

I make a pledge to myself to get better rest the next night. But T.B. calls me again; he wants to go out, he wants to party, and it's all I can do to plead off and tell him I've got to wait until tomorrow.

Tomorrow he calls. What else can I do? I can't go with him, so I duck him.

I'm staying with my folks; whenever he rings I have my mom tell him I'm not around. I feel bad for skirting Tony like this—back in Chicago he took care of me in every way, getting me whatever I needed whenever I needed it, but I can't pay it back now. Not like he wants. Because if I go out and party, that's it for me. That's the end of my career.

My daily life descends into routine: I wake up, try to rub the swelling out of my knee, dress, and head to the courts. Then I practice, and when it's over I shower, ice my knee, come home, and try to tune out the pangs of my conscience when my mom tells me that T.B.'s left messages for me.

It works. I begin to earn my spot on the team, but barely. I have another season of professional basketball ahead of me. But when T.B. finally does get hold of me days later, he's pissed.

"Hello," I cringe into the telephone, full of timidity.

"So this is what I get, huh?" says T.B.'s voice on the other end of the line. "This is what it is."

There's anger in his voice; I can feel it. I want to explain it to him—I want to tell my friend that I'm sorry, that I didn't mean it. I want to say that I was just desperate to stick, that if I didn't make my spot with the Stars my career would be finished, this time probably for good. But I can't do it. The words stick in my throat. And before I can force them out, T.B. beats me to the punch.

"Hill," he says. "Listen close. If you ever come back to Chicago your name is mud." And as he places the phone in its receiver with a click that's far too gentle for the hurt behind it, I know our friendship has ended for good.

This is where the game has gotten me now.

The Last Waltz

I made the LA Stars' roster, and that's good. Unfortunately, time has not softened the animosity between Coach Sharman and me. I don't get to see the court much, and when I do it's just for a couple of minutes, after which he pulls me right out. I'm not his guy—the front office bought me, so Sharman's stuck having me around. That doesn't mean he has to work me into his plans for the team, though, and he doesn't. My shooting percentage rockets right to the top of the league again—.565, even better than the year before—but still Sharman won't let me play much.

Well, I figure, even if he doesn't give me full minutes. I'm doing too well to give the runaround to.

Yeah, right. Have I learned nothing all these years?

Just after New Year's, we fly to Dallas and play a double-overtime game against the Chaparrals. It's well after midnight when the game finally ends, and after showering and riding the team bus back to the airport, I'm elated to just fall into my seat and pass out on the flight home.

When I awaken and deplane, Coach Sharman is waiting by the gate.

"Billy," he says. "I just got word. Turn back around. You've been traded to the Chaparrals."

I take the news poorly, like a bumbling detective taking a slug to the chest. Sure, I want to get away from Sharman, but being traded again means I have another fight to earn a place for myself on another team midseason. Besides, couldn't they have told me that they'd traded me to the team we just played before I took an all-night flight?

The traveling secretary gives me a ticket for the morning flight back to Dallas and tells me to report back to the Moody Coliseum, the Chaparrals' home court, which I'd just left. I doze in the airport until boarding time then catch the first plane to Dallas/Fort Worth. But when I arrive at the Coliseum the next day a Dallas assistant does something I'd never have expected in a million years: he sends me right back home again.

"You're still a Star," he says.

Say what?

"The deal was never finished! It was nixed." He hands me yet another plane ticket. "You're still a Los Angeles Star. Head back to LA."

I take my third cross-country flight in twenty-four hours, return home, and pass out in my bed. Sleep is a very welcome visitor, but she's chased away when the phone rings some five hours later that evening.

Answering, I'm groggy and still a little angry at having been given the runaround and having been awoken, to boot. Of course, I'm not half as angry as I become when the voice on the other end of the line tells me that I've been traded.

"Again?" I ask.

"Yes."

"You sure this time?"

"Yes."

I sigh. "Back to Dallas?"

"No," says the voice on the other end of the line. "Pittsburgh."

I stare at the phone. I hang up then call back the Stars' front office immediately to double-check.

"No, no mix-ups this time," they laugh. "You've been traded to the Pittsburgh Pipers." I hang up and pack my bags. It's my fourth flight in twenty-four hours.

I'm welcomed warmly to the Pipers when I arrive, which is to say that as soon as I step off the plane and onto the tarmac, my jacket literally freezes solid in the Pittsburgh winter. Luckily I don't have to put up with the cold for long, because just a fortnight after I get to Pittsburgh I'm traded again.

It's true—I can hardly believe it, but less than a month after joining the Pipers, and while I still hold the top spot in the league in field-goal percentage, I'm traded again, this time for real, to the Dallas Chaparrals. Now that I'm on Dallas for real, it's my third team in just the first month of 1970.

When I get to Dallas for this third time in three weeks, I'm beat. I'm tired of learning new systems, I'm tired of integrating with new teammates—I'm just plain tired. What's more, all this moving has taken its toll, and my body finally starts to rebel.

It's not my knee this time—at least no more than it's always been. The problem now is the rest of me: my hand, my foot, my back. All at once the bits and pieces of my cobbled-together frame begin to corrode and fall apart. Some nights I can barely even drag myself up and down the court; my feet don't even feel right in my shoes. As the season winds down I go to a doctor who breaks to me the news that's I've always been dreading: I am done. For real this time.

"That tingling you feel in your hand, that numbness in your foot?" I nod. "That's nerve damage," he says, flipping pages on a sheaf of papers stacked on a metal clipboard.

"Nerve damage? What does that mean?"

"Do you ever feel like your hand, your foot, parts of your body don't really feel like your own?"

More than you know, Doc. More than you know. "Yeah. It started over the last few weeks—my foot; my hand, too, sometimes. It's like . . . it's like they feel kind of floppy sometimes. Like a flipper."

The doctor makes a note of this. "Mmhmm. Yes, that makes sense." He lowers his eyes from his chart and looks at me. "Also, from the X-rays I've taken, it seems you've broken your right hand, and it never completely healed."

Broken my hand? The insight comes to me in a flash: the fight with the Lakers. The bench-clearing brawl. That was the last time I ever saw my father, the boxer who taught me how to defend myself, the one who taught me how to hit. That was the day I broke my hand and didn't know it, and now that damage is coming home to roost.

"It's all related. Your knee, your foot, your hand, the numbness and tingling. It's common with your kind of a degenerative injury." He sees my quizzical look at the long word, and he takes pity on me and explains it. "That means it's something that's been in the making for a long time. That feeling of your foot being a big pancake inside your shoe—that's likely due to years and years of overstressing it. Perhaps there's an issue with your stride or your form, some reason why you've been overcompensating or favoring your right side and putting extra pressure on it for many years."

I don't need to dig through my memory banks on that score. Of course I've been favoring my right side. I've been doing it half my life, since I ran laps by myself around a track all summer when I was just seventeen.

"And as far as the recent problems you've mentioned you're having with your back, it seems like you wrenched it and pinched a few nerves, perhaps partially slipping a disc."

"But how could I have done that? I've played basketball all my life; I never had any back problems before."

"Well, you're a professional athlete. It's possible you've received an acute injury that you're not aware of, some jab or flying elbow underneath the backboards." I lie facedown on his examination table as he presses his hands onto my spine, and I wince as he prods. "Sustained heavy lifting can often cause it, too."

Sustained heavy lifting. The trucking docks.

The damn second job I needed to take because I never made enough money playing pro ball is the straw breaking this camel's back, pushing me out of the game? Who'd have thought?

By season's end I'm a wreck. When I get called onto the floor I can hardly move. I have to be subbed out almost immediately—it's the first time that has ever happened, and it's going to be the last. For the final few games of the season I do my best to look small, to hide all six feet nine of me on the end of the Dallas bench.

The moment the season ends (in a first-round playoff loss to—who else?—the LA Stars), I turn in my jersey.

An NCAA scoring record. The number one draft choice. Three years in the NBA, two years in the ABA, and at age thirty I have no choice but to retire.

The Fall

When the season ends I head straight back to LA. I'm not welcome in Texas or in Chicago, and they sold me out of Denver. I have nowhere else to go, so I limp home.

I have no job prospects for the summer, but what I do have is debt. Because I'd expected to latch on in Denver, I really overextended myself getting that new Caddy. Now I'm three thousand dollars behind on payments for it, and my summer's spent not dunking balls on the court but ducking calls from creditors. I begin to slide into a state of despair and depression, only leaving my bedroom at my parents' house to move the Caddy. To hide it. Turns out an all-purple Cadillac convertible is not exactly easy to camouflage in central Los Angeles, especially when you've just spent a year and a half showing it off to anyone with a pair of eyes.

Every now and again my mother knocks on my door to tell me there's a phone call for me, that some representative of one team or another wants to talk. The first time I get this news my heart leaps in my chest, and I all but bound to the phone. But there's something wrong with the call—something very wrong. The man's voice doesn't have that deep grizzle of a front office man, and when we talk ball he's all vague generalities. There's no mention of any specific games I've played or even my signature jump hook. When I ask about playing time he all but guarantees me the starting spot, something that no coach has ever done with me before. What's more, he invites me out to lunch here in LA, which makes no sense—wouldn't they want to fly me out and have me see their facilities?

"No," says the man on the phone, "I'm coming out to you. And you can even come over and meet me in that pretty new Cadillac of yours."

That's the giveaway—it's not a coach at all; it's my creditor or a repo man they've hired. And that's when I hang up the phone.

This goes on all summer. One after another, bank reps call me pretending to be GMs or coaches to try to trick me into turning up somewhere with my car so it can be repo'd. This stings, but it's not the money problems that wear me down the most. It's knowing that despite the bright spots I've had in my career, after the way I closed my last season—bounced around, riding the pine, having trouble even gathering the energy to play the game I used to love—not a single honest basketball man would still think of calling me. That's what kills me to the core. For the rest of the summer, when my mother tells me I've got a call from a coach or a vice president or a team's secretary, I don't come to the phone. I just have her tell them I'm not in, and then I roll back under my pillow and try not to break down and cry.

One day, when I'm moving my coupe again to hide it, I run into a guy I remember from my days at Jefferson, a sometime hanger-on named George. George doesn't seem to have done much with his life since high school. In fact, he seems downright shady—when I ask him what he's done since back in the day, he brushes off the question. But that doesn't keep him from starting to pester me to hang out with him at all hours of the day.

Deep inside I know I shouldn't run around with this guy. Still, I don't have anyone else in my life. Even though I can sense George is no good, I start spending more and more time with him. Most days we just cruise around the city in my coupe, talking to whomever we happen to run into. Every time he asks me to let him drive the car, and every time I turn him down. My career is falling apart and my bank account is empty; what's more, all the girls of my playing days are gone, and friends are nowhere to be found. The only thing I've got left, even if I don't own it, is this car. I don't even intend to let anyone else so much as touch it! But just like the ocean wears away stone if given enough time, after weeks and weeks of pleading and insisting, George defeats my resistance.

"Billy, please," he says, like he's said every day, "let me drive this big, pretty motherfucker."

An alarm goes off in my head, a big flashing light and bell that warn me, "Don't do it. Don't let him do it." But for whatever reason I ignore those signs, and the words slip out of my mouth as if against my will. "Sure. Go on ahead."

It's a sunny day, a beautiful morning, when I step out of the car and we swap spots. What could go wrong? George purrs as he slips in behind the wheel, and for a time everything is casual and quiet. But then, within minutes of George taking the wheel, we swerve hard to the right, as if the car is being pushed by a massive gust of wind. We hop the curb with a crunch, graze a tree, and then slam into a concrete embankment.

Stunned, I look at George. Has this really happened? He looks back at me, wide-eyed.

In an instant I'm out of the car and looking at the damage. The front wheels are flipped and flattened, completely bent under the forward end of the car. The chassis itself is crunched like an accordion. I'm not hurt, but I'm in shock. My car, the only thing I have in this world—the only thing I had—has been destroyed.

I look through the windshield and see George still sitting behind the wheel, stunned. It's like he's stuck by some mental glue. Well, I can unstick him. I spring around to the driver's side and pull him out by the neck. I'm going to choke him to death.

"What the fuck!" I scream. "What the fuck did you do to my car?"

"I don't know!" he gurgles, and that's all that he can say, because his windpipe is being blocked by my hands. His eyes begin to bulge from my grip around his neck.

"What did you do?" I'm screaming. People run out of their houses to see what's going on, but I can't control myself. "Were you sleepin'? Is that it? Well, wake up, you son of a bitch!" Then I lift him in the air and body-slam him into the concrete of the street.

He lands hard. I slap him in the back and take a handful of his shirt to pull him up again. Everybody's watching me. I don't care. I'm going to beat him within an inch of his life. George begins begging me to take it easy, everything will be okay. His insurance will take care of it, he pleads.

I crouch down and put my mouth right next to his ear. "It better," I whisper over the hissing smoke of the smashed engine. "Because if it don't, you're dead."

We wait for a tow truck to arrive. The driver puts chains on the car and seats us in his front cab; the three of us then drive together to a body shop just two blocks from my mother's. George is dead silent; the wrong word and I will kill his ass.

At the garage we wait in stiff chairs dumped next to an ancient water cooler. All the while I'm watching George out of the corner of my eye as if he's going to bolt. If he tries I'll murder him right here on this cheap carpet.

The mechanic inspecting my coupe enters after about half an hour. "Well," he says, "there's damage. It's bad." Obviously.

"How bad?" I ask, staring at George.

He hands me an estimate: over five thousand dollars. Combined with what I still owe to the bank, it might be more than what the car is worth.

"It's okay," George repeats, sensing my near-overflowing rage. "My insurance will cover it." He suggests we walk home to his place so we can call them. I follow right behind.

When we arrive his wife opens the door—right away she can see something is wrong. "I, uh," George begins, "I have to call our car insurance." She steps aside.

I stand right over him while he's on the phone. He dials the number on his agent's card, and I listen as he explains what has happened. "No," he says, "I was driving the car. A friend's car . . . no, he doesn't, but I was driving it . . ."

I somehow can almost hear the words before George can finish saying them. "My insurance doesn't cover someone else's car?" He tries to whisper, but before he even knows what he's just said, I throw a punch that lands squarely on his nose, breaking it. There's a crunch of cartilage and bone.

The phone hits the ground and George goes down with it. I can see blood furiously spurting out of his nose and mouth. George's wife screams, and I push her aside. I step over George like a gladiator about to deliver a killing strike.

"Nigga, if you don't come up with the money to get my car repaired, I'm going to kill you. You hear me?" His wife wails. "I said, did you hear me!" Whimpering, he nods.

I walk toward the front door and look back. "You'd better have the money by the end of this week." And for the second time in my life I slam a door behind me with such force that if it had been glass it would have shattered.

Friday morning comes. My hand, already battered, is still puffy and swollen. It's been four days, and I've not heard boo from George. So I call. His wife answers, hesitating. She says that he's not in.

"I know you're lying," I say, and I hang up, preparing to go over and find out for myself. But as I do, I remember that I have something that I ought to bring along with me. I turn around, go back to my bedroom, and dig through my small bag of belongings.

I don't leave until I find and tuck into my waistband my .22 caliber handgun.

When I get to George's his wife answers from behind a closed screen door. "Billy," she says. "George ain't home."

I smile. "Well, let me in so I can wait for him." She shakes her head no and tells me to get away from the door. Instead I kick it open and let myself in. Walking into the house, I feel like a vigilante.

Backing into her living room, George's wife loudly protests. But when I whip out my gun and brandish it before her, she falls mum and begins to cry and shake. I wave it in her general direction, and she collapses into a quivering heap on the sofa. I then take the liberty of walking all through their home, checking in every room, in all the closets and under the beds. When I find George—if he's here, which it doesn't look like he is, but *if* he is—I am going to empty this .22 right into him.

George's wife is cowering over in the corner like she thinks I'm going to empty it into her when I don't find her husband. Walking toward her, I catch sight of myself in the mirror, and it gives me pause. Is this really what I've become? A gun-toting thug? In an instant all the fight goes out of me, and I leave George's house and leave his wife with a message—a warning—to deliver to him.

As the door bangs shut behind me, I realize I have nowhere else to go and nothing else to do. I have no money. I have no job. I have nothing, so there's only one thing left *to* do: I walk, shamefully, to the unemployment office.

My knee throbs in pain and pulses full of fluid from the long hike across town—what a crazy juxtaposition, from cold-blooded would-be killer to prostrate beggar. With a shaking hand (and with my gun hidden away), I swallow my pride and enroll for relief; the desk clerk there tells me I'll receive my first check in two weeks.

On my way out I hear a voice say, "Billy! Billy the Hill!" I turn and look in the direction of the sound—it's an old ball player I used to practice with way back, back from my days at South Park. "What are you doing here?" he asks, like it's not obvious.

"The same thing you are," I say.

"I thought you were still playing pro ball," he says.

I just laugh. "Yeah, man. Yeah, I still play pro ball. I'm just here to get a little money on the extra." And then I walk out the door.

Bye-bye, Caddy, Bye-bye

When I return to my mother's place I'm physically and emotionally exhausted. For a few hours I sleep, and when I awaken the house is still empty. My mother and Daddy Lonnie are both at work, so I walk over to the body shop to check on my Caddy.

As I arrive I glance across the few cars in the lot. I don't see my purple beauty anywhere, but it's Friday afternoon; maybe they rolled it in for the weekend, I tell myself. Looking around the lot, I recognize the mechanic I talked to the day the coupe was towed in, and I wave him over.

"Hey," I say. "Where's my car?"

The mechanic shakes his head, pulls off his baseball cap, and mops his brow. "I hate to tell you this, but the guys from your bank came by and picked up what's left of it early this morning," he says. He puts his hat back on. "I'm sorry." And with a nod of apology, he steps back and walks away, not even acknowledging or cognizant of the fact that I've just lost my last relic of my playing days and my glory.

So that's it. My car is gone. What's worse: the fact that I've at last lost it for good, or the fact that, after years of having to move around at a moment's notice, my congas and all my best clothes were still tucked away in the trunk?

When I get home my parents are back, and they are arguing. Dazed, I duck past them and dip into my room, just like I did when I was little. The only difference is that now I'm a grown man—and now they're arguing about me.

Daddy Lonnie doesn't want me here—at least not now, since I'm not playing ball and sending money home like I used to. I'm no longer welcome. You'd think I hadn't lived with the guy and been calling him "Daddy" Lonnie since I was twelve.

My mom tries to defend me, but he tells her to shut her mouth. I want to hide my head under my pillow like I did as a kid, but I can't. I may have been hiding in this room from my creditors, but no one's going to talk to my mother like that.

"But Lonnie," my mom's pleading with him as I enter the living room. They don't see me walk in. They continue to fight.

"But nothing! He's a man; he should have a job and he should have his own place!"

"He needs our help," my mother begs. "Lonnie, we're talking about our son!"

"He's not my son!" Lonnie roars just a split second before I step on the squeaky spot in the floor. Daddy Lonnie and my mother turn to look at me, and in that moment, in the wake of that proclamation, there is only silence.

It's the shot in the gut that never came until now. But this—losing everything, being disowned, getting thrown away—takes all the breath, and all the life, straight out of me.

My mom sees it. Droplets of wetness begin to form across the irises of her eyes. Before she can burst into tears, I turn around and shut myself in my room. The next morning, while Lonnie—not Daddy Lonnie anymore, not ever again; from now on, just Lonnie—is at work, I move out. I can't afford anything nice—my only source of income is the public dole—so I move into a dilapidated boardinghouse on the east side, on a dirty residential street off of Jefferson Boulevard, my meager remaining belongings stuffed into a ratty little bag.

The boardinghouse is a mess, and my room is the smallest. It's the back cubby off a little hallway behind the common area, in the shadow of the stairs. Smelling of Four Roses whiskey, my fat landlord shows me in, drops the key into my palm, and walks out, leaving me alone in a musty, mildewed hole. As I close the door behind him I admit to the incontrovertible truth: this room, like its occupant, is miserable.

My room is ten feet by ten at most, with one chair and a lamp on a side table and a tiny little bed. Light streams in through a window covered by a ratty, yellowing shade; when I look out it I can see the decaying side of the vacant house behind me, with broken-out windows and a door hanging half off its hinges. When I settle into the chair, air wheezes out of the cushion and my lungs. From pro ball and packed houses to a home like this. The creeping despair, which started as a simple spore, blossoms over my whole being.

At night I dream that I'm a little kid peeking through a shattered glass pane of that abandoned building behind my room. Inside I see my father sitting alone on an unmade bed.

As days pass in this boardinghouse, the quotidian boredom of my life offers me no break from the mental prison I slowly build of earth and mud. I'm fighting trench warfare against my own sense of self-worth. How did I fall so far, so fast? Depression eddies around me, and as time progresses I lose the strength to even get up and go out anymore. Every couple of days I dress and make my way down the block to get a few groceries and a paper and immediately return. Every couple of weeks I take the long walk to my mother's house to pick up my unemployment check, hoping all the way that I won't be seen. My ideal day becomes one in which I don't have to talk to anyone at all.

My landlord sits on his easy chair on the front porch most days, drinking booze from a paper cup and staring at a nicer building down the street. With the smell of rot clinging to my nostrils and sunlight illuminating the dust particles dancing through the air, I sit at my tiny table with a rag, polishing the last thing that's mine: my gun. Unlike my car, my job, my money, my strength, my drums, my knee, my aunt, my mother, my father, and everything else I've ever had, this one possession has not been taken from me. What, I wonder, would it feel like to turn it on myself? I could do it; all the bullets are out of the revolving chamber and standing at attention, soldiers stacked in perfect formation atop the cheap wood of my scratched three-legged bench. All I would have to do is load the gun in my hand and squeeze the trigger. But I won't. As bad as this is, I tell myself I will never do that.

With the gun on the table I doze off. I'm so bored that I even dream of myself sitting up in my chair. I'm so out of it that I don't even notice the faint jingle in the keyhole. I only come to when my door slams open and two police officers burst into the bedroom with their guns drawn.

I wake up; I see them, and they see me. And then they see the ammo on my table and the revolver, chamber out, in my hand.

They jump into firing stance. "Drop the gun, motherfucker," screams one, "or we'll blow your goddamn head off!"

So this is how I'm going to die.

I lock eyes with the cop in front, and he's screaming at me; his gaze rapidly jumps from me to the bullets on the table and on to my .22 and the polishing rag in my hand. Is this it? Is this how I go out?

"Drop the gun, nigger!"

Nigger? I don't know what to say. This is no Chicagoland roadside shakedown. My lips feel glued shut, and my limbs feel almost pinned down. The chamber's not even locked into place; I want to say something—to tell them not to shoot, or at least to point out that the revolver is clearly not even loaded. But I can't. I can't say anything.

I shake one arm loose from its torpor, and as if moving through water, I carry the gun over to my uncovered bed and drop it. Almost instantly the second policeman flies across the length of my room and in a moment twists my arms behind me just above the base of my spine. My shoulders pop out of their sockets as my face is jammed forward.

My cheek slams into the wall, a resonating echo thrumming in the empty spot behind the wallboards. Out of the corner of my eye, past the stars that spot my vision, I can see the first cop's gun still trained on me. The other cop jams one fist into my spleen as he shoves a forearm into the back of my neck. All I feel is pain. Fear and pain.

"What the hell is going on?" I mumble.

"Shut the fuck up, nigger!" I feel hot breath on the nape of my neck. It's only at this moment that I at last realize that both these cops are white.

The cop behind us, the one with his gun trained on me, jibes, "Let's just blow this nigger away, partner. Let's just do it. We can call it self-defense." I hear a hammer cock. I feel the other cop's hands pull away from my body—and I wait.

Oh, shit. This is it. This is how it's all going to end.

In these drawn-out moments I realize that it's not death I fear. Dying, in and of itself, is not so scary. What frightens me most is not knowing if or when it will come.

Every second—tick, tick, tick—has the potential to be my last. Tick. If my bladder weren't empty, I might be peeing down my leg. Tick. Still no loud report. Tick. In the waiting, my fear and pain morph into rage. "Come on, assholes," I yell. "Go ahead and shoot me! I don't give a fuck no more!" And I don't. What do I have left to live for anyway? Would things be so much worse if these two cops just went ahead and put me out of my misery?

Tick. Here comes the hammer any second now, piggy. Tick. Tick. Tick.

Click. It is the sound of the hammer, but not pulling. It is the sound of a hammer sliding back into uncocked position. Outside my field of vision, I hear a gun slotted back into its leather holster.

"Come on, tough guy," barks a gravelly voice. "Let's go." I'm handcuffed, and though I'm wearing just pants, with neither shoes nor shirt on, the cops drag me out the door. As I'm thrust out of my tiny cage, a glint of light reflected from one of the bullets—still all in a row, as if standing at attention—seems to wink at me.

Central Booking

I'm taken to the police station in the back of a patrol car, and the whole way no one speaks to me. When we get there, I'm left in stir, sitting all alone in a barred jail cell for what feels like a whole afternoon until, at last, I'm thrown into an interrogation room. The noxious and pervasive odors of cleaning solution, barf, and stale coffee battle one another.

Two detectives step into the shoebox of a room, shutting the door behind them. "You know why you're here?"

I don't, and I say as much. They start to yell at me, but it has no effect. In my time I've been yelled at by the best professional yellers in the world: Jack McMahon and Dave Trager. No one else could hope to do worse.

One detective, angry at the lack of progress, spits right in my face. "Listen, tough guy. Start talking and we can make this much easier on you. Where'd you put the TV?"

"What TV?"

The other cop comes up to me like he's my friend. "Son," he says, "where'd you put it? Where is the TV that you took?"

"TV?" I say. "I don't know what you're talking about. I didn't steal no TV."

"Shut up, asshole," says one cop. "We know you did."

I shake my head again. Now I'm the one full of rage. "I didn't steal no TV!" There's nothing worse than being told you're a liar when you know you're speaking the truth.

They don't believe me. I'm apoplectic. "Are you serious? Have you seen my place? Where the hell would I have put a stolen television?"

One pounds the table with his fist. "You think you're smart? You're not. You're not shit."

"It ain't too hard to pin a six-foot-nine nigger stealing TVs," his partner says. "And your landlord already told us there aren't too many of 'em in your neighborhood."

My landlord. This is his fault? That son of a bitch.

Now, I didn't steal a television, and I know I didn't, but these cops don't want to listen. They want to threaten me; they want to cajole me; they want to talk over, under, and around me. I tell them the truth as loudly and as mightily as I can, but they still don't listen. They just keep repeating over and over, "We know it was you. Might as well fess up now, because we know you done it."

Finally the police switch tacks. "Your gun," a black cop says, "it's got a past. Want to tell us about that?"

"It's been used in a couple of robberies," jabs his partner. "So now you want to tell us what you've been up to?"

"The gun?" Oh, hell. What was I thinking having that gun? How stupid was it to buy a gun on the streets off a guy walking around with it in his trench coat? I tell the police that yes, the gun is mine.

"Oh, yeah. We know it is. And you've been pulling some jobs with this gun, haven't you?" says one of the cops.

"We can place it at the scene of a robbery two years ago in Gardena. We've got another one, too: three years ago, Torrance. So why don't you just go ahead and tell us what you've been up to"—he checks a manila folder in his hand that includes my information and mug shot—"Billy?"

Gardena? Torrance? The exurbs of LA? This gun wasn't involved in anything like that, and I know it. This is all a lie. If I was angry before at being cooped up like this, now I'm livid. "I've had that gun since '66," I intone, "when I bought it back in Illinois." That last word I speak out real slow, like I'm saying it to a toddler. "It wasn't used in no goddamn robberies, either—two years ago I was living in Denver, playing pro basketball." The two detectives exchange sudden, worried glances with one another. "What, your file not tell you that? You want to explain how I could have done some supposed robberies if I was traveling all over the country playing televised sports?"

They've been playing a game all along, and now we all know it. For a minute I thought this might have had something to do with George, but it didn't—it was just the cops trying to set me up at random so they could clear their case files. Silently the policemen leave the interrogation room, abandoning me in cuffs to stew in my rage. And I am mad. It's too bad I used up the phrase on those coaches who wouldn't give me a fair shot: more than anybody, it's the crooked cops of the world who ought to go ahead and kiss my black ass.

After another space of time, who knows how long, of waiting in solitude, the police at last open the door and tell me I'm free to go. "Finally," I huff. Of course just because I'm free to go doesn't mean that I can leave.

The cops pulled me out of my home with no clothes, shoes, or wallet. I have no money or ID, and I'm stuck at a police station surrounded by jackholes who, just hours ago, were hoping to pin some robberies on me. What am I supposed to do? Now that they've admitted that they know I'm innocent, they're not exactly champing at the bit to help get me back. And there aren't many people who'd be willing to give a ride to a giant, shirtless hitchhiker just released from the police station.

It's just as I accept that I'm going to have to walk all the way back to my boardinghouse barefoot that, miracle of miracles, one of the cops just coming on duty recognizes me.

"Hill?" he asks. "Billy the Hill?"

It's another cop, this one black but short—real short, like five feet six. He's smiling, grinning almost, and though I have no idea who he is, I reckon I'm glad to see him.

"You know this guy?" a tubby desk sergeant asks.

"Yeah," says the short cop. "This is Billy the Hill, man! Jefferson High! Two city titles, three all-city awards, two Player of the Years!" When the desk sergeant betrays no spark of recognition, my champion forges on. "Utah, scoring champ, number one draft pick!" He's rattling off my career like it was his résumé, and for a moment I almost blush.

"But now look at you," the cop goes on, still smiling. "You're a crook now? Jesus."

My pleasure fades.

"No shirt, no shoes—what did you do, knock over a liquor store? You look like shit."

I feel my fists clench into tight balls.

"Nah," intones the desk sergeant, who eyes me with some mixed measure of appraisal and contempt. "Mistaken identity."

The other considers this. "Okay," he says, appraising me. "Didn't do it. You want a ride back to wherever then?"

I swallow. The pressure in my knuckles abates. This kind of charity is a bitter pill. "Yeah," I say softly. "Yeah, I could use a ride."

As the cruiser drops me in front of my home I feel like I've reached a new low. I look up to find the landlord still sitting at the edge of the porch, staring over my shoulder at the nice place down the road like he didn't just serve me up to the police. He won't look me in the eye. Jesus, do I want to hit him. But if I did then I'd surely be headed to jail, and this time for real.

A few low-hanging leaves flutter before me as the police cruiser glides away down the road. I'm still not wearing a shirt. My neighbors are watching. The boardinghouse itself seems to stare at me like an evil jack-o'-lantern, with winking, crusted windows for eyes. I hate this place and I hate the man who owns it. But I've got no place else to go. Wordlessly I march to the drunk landlord on the porch and stick out my hand. He smells like the dregs of a whiskey bottle were just poured out into a urinal.

"You want something?" he asks.

"I need to be let into my bedroom," I say. "My key was still inside when you let the cops take me away."

He places a brass skeleton key into my palm. "I'll be needing that back," he says. I walk away.

Once I'm alone, safely secreted away from the harsh world, I fling myself down atop my bed. It hits me hard, like the mattress is itself made of steel and mounted to a cinderblock wall. This place, I realize, is really not too different from a cell. And in this place, with my face buried deep inside my lowly pillow, I begin to cry.

Indignation. Humiliation. Pain and hurt. A onetime star, now nothing, facedown on his bed and sobbing like it's his dying day. Is it possible to fall any lower than this?

It can't be, I think. It can't be.

Don't Call It a Comeback

Every two weeks I walk to my mother's place to pick up my unemployment check. In the span of just a few months I've fallen from bonus baby to a man carless, broke, and able to pay his rent only with the help of government assistance.

As summer rolls on toward its inevitable end I consider the fact that the 1970–71 season is right around the corner. Though I had considered my career over, and I doubt most teams would still want me, a miracle has happened: the Los Angeles Stars have relocated to Salt Lake City, Utah, a place where there're still plenty of folks who remember what I can do with a basketball. And what's more, there's a second miracle; the team has gotten rid of Bill Sharman and replaced him with a new head coach: Ladell Andersen.

Utah and Ladell Andersen combine to spell one thing in my mind: glory. In my mind's eye I can see myself as I was: the king of Utah, running the floor with my friends and mopping it with our opponents. Utah was the site of my greatest sports glory, and Utah once again represents to me a glimmering jewel of hope.

When I hear the news I pick up my mother's phone without an ounce of hesitation and dial the Utah Stars' front office. This call to my old freshman coach from the U, this is my first step in a road back to the top, I decide.

The phone rings once before a woman answers. "This is Billy McGill," I tell her, "and I'd like to speak to Coach Andersen."

All the stars in the universe are aligned and in my corner. "Just a moment, please," she says cheerfully, and without pause she patches me through.

My heart soars. This is it.

"This is Ladell."

I smile when I hear his old, gruff grunt from across state lines. "This is Billy McGill."

"Billy?" His pitch has grown strained with age, but it's still him. "How ya doing?"

How am I doing? "Not good," I confess to my old coach. Leaving out only those things that are absolutely necessary to omit—my bad body, my recent troubles with the law—I unveil all that's happened to me in the last two seasons. The tryouts. The shooting title. The trades. The shuffling. The hard knocks. The boardinghouse.

"Coach," I say, "I'm unemployed. I don't have no job." I empty the cup of my heart and soul before him in a way I've never done before.

"I'm still in good shape, though, and all I want is a shot," I say. "I'll get there on my own; you don't have to get me no plane ticket or per diem or anything. If I make it, I make it; if I don't, I don't. But just a shot to make the team. That's all I'm asking for."

This whole time Ladell hasn't said a word. There's a long pause on the line, and I hold my breath, fearful that he's on the cusp of saying no. But then, at last, Ladell speaks. "Okay, Billy," he says. "Give me your phone number and address."

Elation. That's what I feel. Pure and unadulterated joy. I give Coach my mother's contact info, and as I hang up I feel my heart swell with bliss. This is it; I'm sure of it. I'm going to get another chance to play pro ball in the city where I made my mark. After all I've been through I'm gonna make it back.

Walking home that day my legs are light and my knees are like a child's.

For the first time in weeks I don't even shy away from running into someone I might know. My troubles are washed away and I'm a man reborn. I start taking pride in my appearance again. I comb my hair. I iron my shirts. When I see a billboard for the Lakers I don't even seethe over how Bill Sharman has been named their new head coach. I'm just glad his departure has made way for Ladell to take over the helm. Ladell Andersen will be the new head coach of the Utah Stars, and I'm going to be their new center.

For the next fortnight I strut all through that fleabag flophouse that I call home, and for the first time since coming back to LA, I take to hitting the basketball courts to knock the rust out of my system. My body feels good, and my shots fly true. Yes, I've put on a little weight, but it will come off. I'm heading out of this dump.

My confidence is back. My body's stopped hurting. Whatever nerve damage had happened after the end of the season with the Chaparrals seems to have gone away, because I don't notice it. Ladell's going to give me my shot, and I'm going to be back where I belong.

Once two weeks have passed I go back over to my mom's house to pick up my check like I always do, but this time my head is held high. I'm still up the street a ways when she sees me loping down the road and bursts through the front door. "You got a letter, Billy," she calls, an envelope in her hand. "You got a letter from the Utah Stars!"

I knew it. I sprint the rest of the way to the house and into my mother's arms. If that phone call with Coach Andersen lightened my load, seeing that letter lifts it completely. All the disappointments, depression, and deep frustrations of the last few years breeze away in an instant. She hugs me and I hug her back; then my mother guides me inside.

"This is it," I tell my mom as she hands me the letter. "This is it." I'm going to head back to Utah. Maybe I'll rent a little place near campus so I can come back and help out at Ute practices now and again. Yes, that's exactly what I'll do, and I'll be fully focused, all the time.

I tear open the envelope. The letter is folded in three parts; it's typed on new Utah Stars letterhead. My hands are shaking as I hold the letter before me. I can see "Dear Billy" above the flap, and I open it up.

The note is short; just a few lines long. It reads:

Dear Billy,

I am sorry to inform you, but there is no way you can make the Utah Stars basketball team. I wish you the best of luck in the future.

Sincerely,

Ladell Andersen

I don't remember falling into a living room chair. All I know is that I feel like Ladell has reached into my chest and yanked all the lightness and passion from my body, along with my heart. I drop the letter on the floor. As it touches the ground I know I'm done. I will never play basketball again.

"Billy?" my mother says. "Billy, what's wrong?" Her words don't even register in my head; it's as if she's talking to a stranger. My mother picks up the letter and begins to read it. It only takes her a moment. She's crying before she's finished the second line.

"That's not right," she wails. "That just isn't right. After all you've done for the state of Utah and Ladell, that's not right. That's just not right."

My mom is stunned, and I'm broken. I wish she'd be quiet, but she won't. She's got her hand to her face, and it's almost like she needs comforting even more than me. But I can't give that comfort to her. What am I now? I'm nothing. I'm rusted iron, scrap. I stagger to the door. "I'll see you later, Mom," I say. And then I go.

As I step into the Los Angeles sunshine I feel the heat and light desiccate me, turning all my bones and sinews brittle. All my pain comes flooding back; the hatchling of self-esteem I'd nurtured this past two weeks disappears. I'm worse off than I'd ever been, for now even my dreams are dead.

I've nearly reached the sidewalk when my mother's voice reaches me. "Bilbo, Bilbo!" she calls, and I stop, turning back around. She pulls at the folds of her dress. I look at it, then look up at her. For a moment the tiny, furtive remnant of my self-worth peeks out from its hiding place. Perhaps this was all a cruel joke? Perhaps there's something left to live for after all?

"Is this—" I begin.

"This came for you, too; don't forget it," she says, handing me a second envelope. "It's your unemployment check." She gives it to me, and then she walks back inside.

Don't forget it, she says. Don't forget it.

I won't.

You Can't Go Home Again

I walk all the way back to the boardinghouse, the whole way wondering why Ladell didn't invite me to try out. Later on, I find out that the Utah Stars give the spot to Zelmo Beatty, and that just about does me in entirely.

The letter from the Stars—a team I'd played well for just one year prior—makes it clear that basketball is now fully, finally out of the picture. I try to apply for other jobs, hitchhiking to interviews when I have to. But I keep getting rejected, and there's only so much failure a man can take. When failures start to pile atop one another like grains of sand, I stop praying to God for help finding work and start asking for just the strength to be able to get out of bed and put one foot in front of the other.

Consumed now by depression, I wallow at the boardinghouse until my unemployment runs out. When the last check comes I gather up my few clothes without ceremony and take a final look around the tiny hovel that's been my home for the last half a year. As I do, I realize how much I've hated it here. If I'd had anywhere else to stay I would have left this dump far sooner.

And yet part of me still wishes I didn't have to go.

With my little bag slung over my shoulder I hoof it over to my mother's house. Mom is home when I get there and Lonnie isn't, which is good. If he were there I don't think he'd even let me through the door. My mother shepherds me back to my old room. I tell her that when Lonnie gets home I'm going to ask him if I can stay for a while. The look on her face tells me I'm on uncertain ground, but to my surprise, when he does get home he begrudgingly relents and tells me that—temporarily—I can sleep there.

I have about fifty-five dollars left from my last unemployment check, so the next morning I walk to the grocery store and spend two-thirds of it on groceries for us. To think: all that money I wired to my mother and Lonnie in my playing days, and now he has a beef letting me stay with them while I get back on my feet? Over the years I sent them thousands. It damn sure doesn't seem right that Lonnie is now begrudging me a bed.

There's nothing I can do about that now, though. Now it's on me to do right by myself.

Every day from then on I'm reading the classifieds and getting on buses, hustling to try to find myself a job. That's the thought, at least. But the problem is I'm like a busted sewer pipe: I'm not getting shit. Every interview I have goes more or less the same way.

"I see here on your résumé that under experience you have listed 'professional basketball player.'"

"Yes, that's right," I'll say. "I played eight seasons of pro ball," and for a brief moment they'll light up.

"Did you play in college?"

"University of Utah."

"Did you graduate?"

Here I'm forced to admit that no, I didn't, and at this point the interview is essentially over. Every time I'm told they want somebody with either a history of stuffing files—not stuffing basketballs—or a college degree. College scoring titles, ABA shooting titles—somehow a history of dedication and effort in athletics doesn't make an impression on the job market.

Bus fares eat up the last of my money real quick, and at the end of two weeks of job hunting I have nothing to show for it but a bunch of inkedup newspapers. I finally hit pay dirt, such as it is, at the Tishman Building at the intersection of Century and Airport Boulevard. The chief of the janitorial crew there tells me he'll take a chance on me; my job will be swinging a mop nights after the place closes down. I'm amazed to realize that I now look upon humping a rag mop across a tile floor on the midnight shift for a few bucks an hour as a lucky lotto ticket—or that anyone could think that this is enough of a job to have to "take a chance" on a person with, but still, it's work, and I'm glad to have it. For a short time anyway. Because on my third night on the job I get fired.

I've never been fired before—not from a normal job, anyway—and it happens so quickly, I almost can't get my head around it. My boss's supervisor—a woman I've only met once—sees me in the hallway, grabs my mop, and yells at me that I'm mopping wrong.

"Excuse me?" I say.

"You're mopping wrong!" she repeats. I don't get it. How could I be mopping wrong?

"Are you sassing me?" she challenges. And then she gets in my face—at least, as in my face as someone a foot and a half shorter than me can get. "What do you want? You want me to show you how to mop?" I'm on dangerous ground. The other janitors are pointedly looking away from me. But I don't notice the signs.

"Sure," I say. "I mean, you might not know how to dunk a basketball, but if you asked me I could show you." I pass her the handle. "If you don't like what I'm doing, why don't you show me how?"

Wrong move. She fires me on the spot. By the next day I'm back to hitchhiking after leads from help wanted ads.

Every day that I'm forced to stomp home from yet another rejection, I feel worthless. My stepdad begrudgingly takes my fifty-dollar check from my two and a half nights of work, but I can tell he'd rather have me out. He doesn't want me, no company wants me, and I can't seem to do anything to justify my existence save recalling the way I could once, a lifetime ago, toss up a jump hook. What am I going to do I wonder as I open the paper and dive once more into the brackish sea of classifieds. But then, just as I'm looking for answers, I come across a sign. I turn a broadsheet page in the *LA Times* to find a full-size spread for a show coming to town, open-ing the coming weekend at the Sports Arena: the Harlem Globetrotters.

THE HARLEM GLOBETROTTERS. I see the words in block type, and I think to myself, Maybe this is the chance that I've been waiting for. J. C. Gip-son did it; there's no reason I can't do it, too. Maybe this is a sign explain-ing why I haven't found a nine-to-five yet: I'm meant to be a Globetrotter.

With no money left for bus fare I hitchhike to the Sports Arena, and when I arrive I waltz right in. I'm surprised that no security guard stops me, and I have to fight to keep myself calm. There've been so many let-downs; I've got to keep from getting carried away.

I walk straight through the unlocked front doors and across the circular walkway ringing the stadium proper. Ducking into a tunnel, I emerge in a sea of folding chairs, and there before me on the parquet floor are the Harlem Globetrotters, practicing on the hardwood.

They're a sight to behold: a squadron of young, strong, black basketball players, all decked out in their shiny red-white-and-blue uniforms and running through snappy, crisp passing drills. Watching them, I feel myself being physically pulled to them, pulled to playing ball again.

It's not until I reach the very edge of the court that I realize I, too, am being watched. Turning my attention from the floor to the stands, I see sitting in the front row the captain of the team, the man who runs the show: Meadowlark Lemon.

"Hey, Meadowlark!"

Along with J. C. Gipson and the Grand Old Man of the squad, Goose Tatum, Meadowlark Lemon is considered one of the greatest Globetrot-ters of all time. He's a good player with skills, but more than that, he's a crowd pleaser. He's the one who calls the plays, the bits and gags that enthrall the paying customers: messing with the refs, hamming it up for the fans. Even though we've never met before I know immediately who he is. And he knows who I am, too.

"Billy McGill."

I have to admit I'm a little nervous standing in front of the Globetrot-ters while Meadowlark sizes me up, taking in my nappy hair, nappy clothes, and nappy shoes. I can feel his gaze scale my bulk and then retreat back down; I can feel him taking a mental inventory of me, and I wonder what he sees before him.

"What can I do for you?" he asks.

No point in beating around the bush.

"I was wondering," I say, pushing down my uncertainty. "What do you think my chances are of hooking up with the Globetrotters?"

He rolls the question around for just a moment. I watch the muscles on his face, and I feel my posture fall. I still have it; I know I do. But I know how I look, too.

"Well," he says, "you can talk to the owner." He throws a pointer finger over his shoulder to a group of men in suits sitting a few rows behind. "He's up right there. But you should know, we usually don't like to take on no has-beens . . ."

Has-beens. Is that—is he talking about me? He is. Has-been. I can feel the word penetrate my belly, rattling around like buckshot in the stomach of a dying cowboy.

Has-been. I shouldn't have come here. Before I felt bad; now I feel like a cowboy on the verge of bleeding out in the dirt.

You Really Can't Go Home Again

After these last opportunities are denied to me, things at home grow even worse. I have nothing left to contribute in terms of rent or groceries; I've even pawned everything I own to get a more few dollars for the buses I ride looking for work. Every day I do my best to hide away in my room, away from my folks' struggles. But I can't hide forever. Even worse than being yelled at is being yelled around. Finally the tension between the three of us reaches a breaking point.

It's a Saturday night, cold and pouring rain—unusual for LA. Once again my mother and Daddy Lonnie are fighting over me. My mother's telling him that I am doing everything under the sun to try to find a job and get my own place. But it's like he doesn't hear—or doesn't want to hear—a word she says.

"All I want," he keeps repeating, "is for him to get out of my house!" He screams it at her over and over at the top of his lungs, and it burrows deep inside me to my core. "Get him out of my house!" It breaks me down the middle.

I'm sitting quietly on my bed in my empty room, listening to my mother's husband threaten her and denigrate me. Though I've been quiet, though

I've tried to disappear, hearing the disgust and hate in the voice of my stepdad finally breaks me.

I throw open the door and bolt out of my room. I stride with purpose into the small living room where my mother and her husband are arguing. I can feel all the contents of my deep well of uncertainty and sadness bubble to the top. And that's when I launch into a tirade of my own.

"I'm trying!" I scream, right into Daddy Lonnie's face. It's the first time I've ever yelled at him. "I'm trying, don't you see that? I'm doing everything I can to find a job every goddamn day!"

Our angers clash like twin forks of lightning, and the two of us grow louder and louder.

"When I was playing pro ball and sending all those checks home each month, I know your black ass was enjoying that money. Now that I'm down on my ass begging for jobs, I can't even get a damn dollar from you for bus fare!"

I'm swearing at Daddy Lonnie now. He yells back, but I hardly hear him.

"You wanna kick me out, Daddy Lonnie? Fine. All those years I called you Daddy Lonnie—well, you ain't no damn daddy of mine. If you had been my daddy you would have looked out for me! But you never did."

My words fall off my tongue like a hissing snake's. "I don't have no damn daddy. I ain't your son? Well, you ain't my daddy. You ain't shit."

The two of us stare at each other, shaking in fury. For a solid minute, neither one of us gives an inch to the other. It's not until I hear her sob that I notice my mother is crying hysterically.

This breaks the fugue. It shocks me—the fact that doing what I've just done, saying what I always needed to say to a man who never loved me, hurts her. In a flood I realize how it must have killed her to hear Daddy Lonnie speaking so ill of me along. No matter how bad things got, she must have always assumed we'd work it out. She has never in her life heard me curse at anyone until now, and in her eyes I can see that she never wants to hear it again.

I stride back into my room and grab the one heavy coat I have left. I won't wait to find out if I've ruined everything—I'm leaving this house, this time for good. Sheets of cold rain confront me as I open the front door, and I don't have a dime in my pocket, but it doesn't matter. I have to go. With the wet tears of the sky splattering across my cheeks, I finally uncork the bottle of rage that's been sloshing around half full inside me all these years. I leave the house, screaming at the night until all the breath leaves my lungs in the cold night air.

As the rain pours down I crisscross the whole city, not seeing another human who'll look me in the eyes. My burning rage fuels me for a while, but over time I grow cold from walking so long in the rain. When I first notice this I find myself on Jefferson Boulevard, heading west toward the heart of LA. All I have on are my coat, a T-shirt, thin-soled shoes, and pants that have by now adhered themselves to my thighs. My hair is soaked through and sticking to my head like a wet Tishman Building mop.

Down the road I spot a lit neon sign for a twenty-four-hour laundromat. To escape the torrent I hurry toward it and duck inside.

Inside the air hangs heavy with the heat of the exhaust of dozens of spin cycles. I'm safe from the rain in here, and it's dry, and it's not until I sit down on a bench, grateful for the respite, that I realize just how tired I am.

I'm soaked through. My muscles ache. My feet hurt. Even my arms drag down. I'd be hungry if I weren't so thirsty; the chemical tinge of soap coats my throat, and I find myself desperate for a drink. I look at the clock; it's no wonder I feel so tired and downtrodden: it's 3:00 a.m. I must have been wandering the city for hours.

I lie down on the bench and close my eyes. When I open them again it's morning.

When I awaken I head straight for the laundromat bathroom. I wash my face and hands in the sink, and one glance in the mirror lets me know exactly what a frightening sight I present: a six-foot-nine black guy with a full, matted afro wearing a drooping coat that hangs loose over his huge frame. I'm like a black Frankenstein's monster.

I beg a few dimes from people doing their laundry, and with help from information and directory assistance, I begin calling everyone I know.

None are people I would call "friend," but at this point I'm hoping for a miracle. I don't just need a job anymore. I need a place to sleep.

First I call Chick Hearn, the old Lakers radio announcer. Then I ring Willie Davis, a beer distributor and ex–Green Bay Packer I knew from my days in Chicago, and I try Sam Gilbert, a UCLA alum who owns an Encino construction concern. Finally I call my old teammate Jerry West, who by now is in the Lakers' front office. Of everybody—or of their secretaries, if I can't raise them on the line in person—I ask that they keep their ears to the ground for me for a job, any job. "I'm homeless," I admit to varying degrees of shock. I even ring up old Wilt Chamberlain. I give each person the phone number here and the one at my mother's house, and I ask them to call if anything comes up. Chamberlain, to my great surprise, calls me back immediately. He's sympathetic, but he's not much help. "Billy," he tells me, "your money's in ball." Ball? Ball? No one anywhere wants me to play for them, and what team in their right mind is gonna hire on a homeless black man as coach? I thank Wilt for getting back to me, for taking the time to try, but what the hell has basketball got left to give to me—or me to it?

Finally, at last, I call my mother.

"Bilbo," she sobs when she picks up the phone. "Bilbo, where are you?" I refuse to tell her.

"Bilbo, come home. Please come home. Come back home," she says. But I won't.

"I'm fine," I tell her. "Don't worry about me."

"What are you doing for money?" I say nothing. "Even if you won't stay, will you come over to have something to eat?"

My stomach growls. I haven't eaten in twenty-odd hours. How did she know? But what if I do? Will Lonnie, formerly Daddy Lonnie, begrudge me another roast?

"I don't need anything," I tell her, and I hang up and buy a candy bar with some of my remaining change. I realize, however, as I return to what I now think of as my bed—the hard, wooden bench by the window of the twenty-four-hour laundry—and begin to drift off to sleep, that I'm going to need some kind of plan.

I'm awakened in the darkness of night by a sharp, jabbing prod to the ribs. I open my eyes and find two police officers standing over me with night-sticks in their hands. They menacingly, rhythmically slap their palms with the ends of their batons.

"Get up from there!"

Cops again. This spells trouble. I could get arrested, yeah, but that's nothing. A cop can beat up a black man without question. Hell, I almost got shot. And finding me sleeping in my clothes and loitering in a laundromat gives these men plenty of reason to do whatever they want.

I stand, and one of them whistles low and mean. "Damn," he says. "You are one tall-ass nigger."

I bristle. I remember what happened the last time I heard language like this from a thug behind a badge. I eye their guns holstered at their hips.

"What's your name?" one of them asks me. I don't answer. He pokes me in the ribs, and he asks, "Are you deaf?" and inside me something snaps again. I just can't take much more of this.

"If you're planning to hit me," I growl, "you're going to have to kill me, 'cause I'm not about to take no type of beating from you. Not tonight."

Their tapping continues. The one in front says, "Big mouth you got. Nigger, you should be playing with the Lakers, tall as you are." This cracks up his partner, and they both laugh. I stifle a roar rumbling low in my throat.

"How tall are you, anyhow?" he asks, and I don't say nothing. I just glower and ball my fists. If they're gonna hit me with their batons, they'll find they have a fight on their hands. If they're gonna shoot me down, so be it. But I will not go down easy.

The moment is as tense and tight for me as the last few ticks of the clock in any title game I've ever played in. For a long minute even the dryers seem to stand still at attention. Finally the tension breaks.

"Get out of here," the first cop says. "This isn't a place for you to sleep. Keep going." He points at the door.

I wasn't praying for death, but eviction I can handle.

I leave the laundromat and head eastbound down Jefferson under the streetlights. The rain's coming down in sheets again; rain two nights in a row in Southern California is something like a once-in-a-lifetime experience. Too bad it had to happen now.

Desperate for a dry place to hide, I turn off Jefferson and start wandering along the neighboring residential streets. This section of the east side is not the best part of town, so there are quite a few old, crumbling vacant houses that dot the area. I spot one—all its windows are broken out—and try the front door. It's unlocked. I walk in.

This place smells like it's been used as a toilet by man and animal alike. The only furniture in here is an old, beat-up wooden table that has only three legs of its original four. But at least inside, it's dry. I'm going to stay.

I clean the table off with the sleeve of my jacket and push it up against the wall. Then I cast myself atop the table, pulling atop myself a pile of old newspapers from the floor to keep me warm. Bone tired to the depths of my soul, I wait for sleep to take hold again. It's not long in coming.

I awaken to find water cascading in through the holes in the ceiling. It surrounds and outlines me, but none falls directly on my body—it's like the rain's outlining a crime-scene corpse, and I'm the body. When I find I can't go to sleep again, I wait until the rain slows and I can see daybreak through the holes in the roof. Then, once it's dry, I leave the house and return to the laundromat to clean up as best as I can, figuring the cops, if they're there, can do what they will.

No one stops me. I wash my hands and face in the bathroom, then I fish around in my pockets for another candy bar.

I eat it. It's all I'm going to have to go on for the foreseeable future.

45

To the Edge of the World . . .

This becomes my routine: sleep in the abandoned building, wash up in the laundromat, scrounge for change to buy whatever I can afford to eat, then walk back to the rat-crap hovel that I call home to repeat it all again. For the next several months I survive mainly through the grace of God. I do my best to try to find work—day labor jobs, mostly—and sometimes I'm able to get hired. I'll pass a man with a big four-by-four and tools on the bed of his pickup, and I'll ask him if he maybe needs a hand for the day. Sometimes I even get picked up to spend a few hours laying brick. But usually I get turned down. It's no great surprise why. I'm an unwashed man of scary proportions, begging people to pay me money. I'm exactly the kind of sight that parents warn their children to stay away from.

Every so often I'll check in at home, but hardly anyone ever calls my mother's house to leave a message for me. One day I hear word that Sam Gilbert—the basketball booster from UCLA with the construction company—has called, so I go to a pay phone and give him a ring. I explain to him my situation.

"Come on out to Encino," he tells me, "and we'll see what we can do."

It takes me four hours to hitchhike there, and when I arrive he seems none too excited to see me. What he expected I don't know. But one look at me and the state I'm in, and he hustles me out of his lush office real quick. One of the only things he says before giving me the bum's rush— how aptly named that is, I think—is, "Billy, there's no open spot on the crew right now, but we'll keep you in mind when a spot opens up."

Standing outside his office building not a half hour after I arrived, I stick my thumb out and wonder how I'm ever going to make it back to my little squat. I wonder what different he expected out of me. I told him I was homeless. Couldn't he just have turned me away over the phone?

As rough as that is, Gilbert's hasty "no" is the closest I come to a job for a long time, and I spend the better part of a year living in that abandoned house. How long exactly I can't say; it's like being in prison. I lose all track of time. The slog of everyday life begins to take on a dragging crush, a dark, unending, and steady tide of misery. Nights, I spend hours on my knees, trying to pray my way out of this hole. Days, I'm on my feet, hoofing all over the city to try to find a few dimes to rub together.

One day I run into that slick hang-around who crashed my car, George. He recognizes me immediately, and seeing the state I'm in fear overtakes him. I don't know if it's fear of physical violence or fear of what I've become, but either way he promptly gives me everything he has in his wallet.

It's only ten dollars. It hardly covers a totaled car. And yet, for me, now, it's a treasure.

I take the money and walk along Jefferson until I hit Western Avenue, where, hungry and exhausted, I sidle up to the counter at a Fatburger. Hot food has become the greatest luxury in my life, and I take pleasure in ordering myself fries, a soda, and a cheeseburger with onions, even if the other patrons are staring at me and wrinkling their noses.

When my order comes up I bring it to one of the outdoor tables, where I sit and eat very, very slowly.

As I eat I notice just how much pain I'm in—my feet, my back, my knee, and my heart. My feet are tired from crisscrossing the city, my back muscles have taken to continually seizing up from sleeping on that table all these months, and all this walking has led my bum knee to fill with fluid—it's enormous now; the swelling never goes down, and I can't afford to have it looked at. Even as I sit and eat I've got to keep the leg stretched out into the aisle because I can't pull it in.

As for my breaking heart, it's worst of all.

Once I finish—and I do eat slow—I can't bring myself to get up and leave. I have nowhere to go! Instead I just sit at my table watching cars and pedestrians roll by along the street. Finally, after hours of taking up space, I'm approached by a security guard—a young, black man in uniform—who tells me it's time to move on.

"You gotta get out of here," he says. "You got to get a move on, brother! You've been hanging around here all day." I don't say a word, though. I just nod, gather my bulk, and rise to make my way down the street. When he sees me at my full height, the guard starts. "Damn, look at you. A guy your height . . . have you ever played basketball?"

My heart leaps to my throat. I feel myself shake my head. The words cut me deeply as they leave my lips. "Nah," I reply. "I ain't never played the game."

From Fatburger I just start walking. I wander back and forth across the city, eventually finding myself right in the heart of LA.

Downtown LA was beautiful once. In the '20s and '30s, downtown LA was the center of the city's lush, ornate life. But the city's core, like me, has fallen on hard times. Like me, it has become just a shell of its former glory.

After passing under the 101 Freeway, I find myself walking north. I cross Pico Boulevard, then 12th, then 11th, then Olympic. It's as I keep walking, heading ever farther toward the heart of the city, that it dawns on me precisely where it is my feet are trying to lead me: 5th Street.

In Los Angeles, 5th Street is the place where nobody knows your name. Angelenos who want to disappear go to 5th Street to do just that. Downtown 5th Street is the home of lost souls: prostitutes, winos and alcoholics, drug addicts, the insane, and the irredeemably homeless; they all lay their heads down together on the 5th Street sidewalks. This street is the last circle of hell, and from 5th Street there is no return. You go there to vanish from the world.

As I get ever nearer—crossing 9th, then crossing 8th—I know that I can keep going if I want, but if I do there's no coming back. I can go to 5th and escape from all of this pain inside me, but once I go, I'm gone.

What do I do? It's a question that's confronted me so many times in my life, and rarely have I had someone I trust in my corner to provide me with an answer. I'm on 7th now; 5th Street is in sight. Do I go? Do I let myself extinguish all this anguish, and with it, everything else I know?

I stand at that curb for what feels like a very long time. I watch the light post. "WALK," it says. "DON'T WALK. WALK. DON'T WALK." The universe, like me, can't seem to decide what I should do. Should I go? What would I be turning my back on? I have no hope of employment, and I have neither friends nor, anymore, family. What is there really left to live for?

A car honks at me as I teeter over the edge of the crosswalk. It's time to make up my mind. I'm on the verge of choosing—though, in truth, I don't know what the choice will be—when suddenly I take pause. Or, more accurately, something pauses me.

Looking at the road that lies before me, I think about all the nights I've spent on my knees in my little hovel these last few months, praying for help. I never got an answer, or at least I never felt like I did. But right now, staring at 5th Street in front of me and preparing to step off the curb, I feel some kind of force like a hand in my chest, and it's pushing me back. What is this force? I don't know.

Is it God? I've tried to speak to him and I've said his name many times, but I don't know if I've ever felt his presence in my life before. And yet, right now, in this moment of my utmost need, I can feel something—and maybe it is indeed his hand—turning me right around.

As I walk back to the squalid, abandoned dump that I now think of as home, I don't wonder what this force that intervened was. I wonder why.

That night it rains again and the ceiling tiles right above the table begin to leak like a sieve. I'm tired, hungry, alone, and now I'm wet. Even getting down under the table is a no-go; the slanted floor has already corralled a growing puddle of water underneath my erstwhile bed. There's nowhere I can go to escape this sudden bath.

This is it. I can't take it anymore. This is the last straw. Reduced now to nothing by my emotions and the rain, I take to the floor and drop down to my knees. "Why?!" I demand of the air above me. Salty tears run down my cheeks and commingle with the heavenly baptism that drips brown and silted from the roof.

With not even an ounce of my old pride left to support me—with my body as rickety and precarious as the table on which I've slept these untold seasons—I cry. In this moment of weakness I call out to God with all my soul and beg him for love and succor. "I can't go any further," I beg, hoping that he's listening. And I remain suppliant, riding out the storm on my knees, praying for shelter from the world.

When at last, come morning, the rain stops, I trek back to what I've come to think of as *my* laundromat. I beg one of the women washing her clothes there for some change to call my mother, and she gives it to me.

"Billy!" my mother cries when she answers the phone. "I'm so glad to hear your voice." I'm glad to hear hers, too.

"Did anyone call for me?" I ask her. It's only the faint glimmer of hope that keeps me asking. I don't know why I always bother—no one ever calls.

Only today things are different. Today there is something.

"Bilbo, yes," she says. "Someone called for you."

This is an impossibility. Nobody calls for me. "Who?"

"Brad Pye Jr."

Brad Pye Jr.? For me?

I hang up and immediately ring the *Los Angeles Sentinel* for Mr. Pye. He answers, and the news he has in store almost overwhelms me. "Hughes Aircraft in El Segundo. I called in a few favors. It's just a clerk's job, certainly nothing so glamorous as the NBA. But it's honest work, Billy. And it's waiting for you."

"But, Mr. Pye—why?" I haven't seen Brad Pye Jr. since I was a high schooler. And it's not like we were ever close, either—I just played sports, and he wrote about them. But somehow, some way, he's found me and he's offered me help.

"Billy," he says, "once I heard about what you were going through, I knew I had to do something."

And just like that I have a job. It's all lined up, and when I call Hughes they tell me to report for my first day next week.

I don't know how to thank Mr. Pye, and I tell him as much—I'm reborn, and I owe my life to him. But he tells me no—it's my second chance and it's on me to make it on my own. The best thanks I can give him is to work hard and succeed.

I promise him I will.

And I will.

. . . and Back

I manage to stick at Hughes like I never have anywhere else. I work there for years, and though it's not all peaches and cream, it's a foundation for me. It provides me something to latch onto, something to wake up for, and that gives me something that I'd long since been missing in life: a purpose. And for that I'm grateful.

For the first time in a long time I draw a steady paycheck. Though I've got no collateral the Hughes Credit Union gives me a small loan so I can put a rental deposit down on a little one-bedroom apartment. Finally I'll be able once again to have and pay for a place all my own again. I'll be able to cook for myself. I'll be able to shower every day.

These routines, basic as they sound, have been a long while away from my life, and it takes some getting used to. It's difficult even to remember every morning when I leave for work to bring the key to my place with me. But I persevere. I mentally forgive George his debt to me, and I try to apologize to him and his wife for exploding at them in rage. I put the past behind me as best I can, and for the first time in a long time I look forward to each new day.

After this first miracle more and more come flooding toward me. One night I head out to a quiet little nightclub just down the road from my house. It's the first time in years I've had enough money in my pocket to go out, to be able to sit down and buy a drink and just talk to another person. I'm just relearning how to order from a waiter, the feeling of cash in my wallet, how to be comfortable in public—and that's when I see her.

Enjoying a ladies' night out, a beautiful woman bobs her head along to gentle music. She's gorgeous, and even in this dark club she casts a visible, beatific glow.

I don't know that I'd ever before believed in love at first sight, but now, at this moment, I can attest that it exists—it's happening to me. I stand up from my chair and begin walking over. I have no idea what I'm going to say, and when I reach her I just smile. She looks at me expectantly.

"Hi," I blurt out, extending my hand to shake. "I'm Billy!" Her friends laugh, but for the first time in my life when talking to a girl, I don't blush.

"Hi," she says. "I'm Gwendolyn."

It's my first conversation with a woman in years. We talk all night, and she gives me her number. This leads to my first date since before my homelessness, and it goes well.

This first date leads to my first real girlfriend in what I now think of as the first act of my real life, and after that she becomes my first love.

Finally, not long after, she becomes my wife.

One year after we meet I ask Gwendolyn Willie to become Gwendolyn McGill, and to my surprise and honor she says yes. In this shell of a person she sees a man. She sees a treasure. She sees a husband.

Gwendolyn has children from a previous marriage, and I love them right away. They love me, too, and I adopt them, promising I will be more than just a father—I will be a real daddy.

At long last I have a real family. And upon reflection I realize that that, in itself, is my greatest miracle of all.

As great as it is to settle into a stable home life, my new career remains just as rocky as my old one ever was.

At first everything looks great at Hughes. I do well at work, and I even have the opportunity to pay forward Brad Pye Jr.'s favor to me. One day my phone rings; I answer it to hear on the other end of the line Reynaldo Brown. Brown, like me, is an LA boy; though we've never met, his is a name I know well. He came from Compton and competed for the United States in the high jump in the '68 Olympics as a high schooler. When he returned to compete in track and field in college, he set NCAA records like I did, clearing seven feet four in the high jump. But after that he seemingly disappeared from the face of the earth. We've never met, yet here he is, ringing me from a pay phone.

"Billy," he says. "I'm standing outside a phone booth . . . with my family." He clears his throat, and in that gentle rustle I hear something I recognize all too well: desperation. He's homeless.

"I don't want to ask too much," he begins, "but I was wondering . . ." and I stop him right there. I don't need to ask about his destitution—I know. I have no idea how he's gotten the idea to get hold of me, but regardless, I can hear in him what I heard in myself just a few years ago, and I know what I have to do.

"Let me know how I can get back in touch with you," I tell him. "I'll take care of it."

I get Reynaldo's information and relay his story to the same manager Brad Pye Jr. convinced to hire me. I explain the drive of a man who's hungry, and I vouch that Reynaldo, whom I've still never met, will never let the company down.

By next week Reynaldo Brown has a job. Maybe this is a testament to my new place in life, I think, and soon the universe appears to reward me for my kindness.

In short order my phone rings again, and again, it's a call I could hardly have expected.

Apparently, some filmmakers started shooting a kung fu movie called *Game of Death*, but they never got to finish it because their star died partway through—a martial arts expert named Bruce Lee. They shelved the project but later decided to finish it using a stand-in for Lee's last scenes. Thing is, though, they can't seem to rehire the original actor who played the evil boss's henchman, so they're trying to hire me to be a body double.

At first I think there must be some mistake. "How'd you get my name?" A casting agent, they say.

"You know I'm a huge black guy, right?" They do. "Well what would I be doing in a kung fu movie to begin with? Who am I going to be a body double for?"

The man who originally played the lead henchman's bodyguard: Kareem Abdul-Jabbar.

The casting director offers to fly me to China and pay me for my time, and all I'll have to do is stand in the background in a couple of scenes while they reshoot.

It seems like a great offer to me, but when I approach my boss at Hughes about it—a man by the name of Jerry Hickman—he tells me flat out, "No. We can't have you leave for two weeks! What is the office gonna do?" Never mind that I have all the vacation time accrued. The man doesn't like me, and he just doesn't want to let me go. (Of course it may not be just me he doesn't like—I've seen how he acts toward other black members of the staff. Still, on that matter I, for once, hold my tongue.)

I'm about to give up on it altogether when Hickman's supervisor pops in. "What are you all talking about?" When I tell him his face lights up— and when I let it be known that I'm not going to be allowed to go, he shakes his head.

"I think we should make an exception here, Jerry, don't you?" he says. I beam. My boss tries to hide his scowl. "This could only be good publicity for the company. You have the vacation time saved up?" I nod. "Then I think you should do it!"

It's all I can do not to pump my fist in my boss's face as I skip out the door.

Within weeks I'm flying over the Pacific Ocean in a huge 747 heading for the Orient. I'm in the company of movie stars—Gig Young, Hugh O'Brian, Colleen Camp—and it is wonderful. For the whole first week I'm not even needed on set, so I just eat breakfast then spend the day exploring Hong Kong. One day Gig and his fiancée, Kim, even take me across the harbor to Macao. Raymond Chow throws a party at his unbelievable house built into the side of a mountain overlooking the Hong Kong harbor, and we all attend together.

With my life on the streets still fresh in my mind, it seems to me that I'm now guided by a lucky star.

Of course, that star soon comes crashing down to earth.

When I do start shooting my scenes call for me to pretend to be dead, which leaves me lying on the floor while stand-ins fight over my body. Filming lasts all night long, and it's cold on the cement! I end up contracting the flu due to exposure, and to make matters worse the Chinese doctors tell me I can't fly back to America—I have to be kept quarantined until the bug works its way out of my system. This leads to me coming home a few days later than I'd originally expected. Which, in turn, leads to me being terminated from Hughes Aircraft.

I can't believe it. I've just gotten home from what amounts to a promotional trip, and I've been fired? I call Jerry Hickman to try to find out what the hell is going on.

The glee in his voice is unmistakable. "You missed multiple days of work without cause," he says. "So you're fired."

"But I was sick," I protest. "I was in quarantine on the other side of the planet. Didn't they send a note?"

"I got a note," he says. "But you were authorized for two weeks of leave, not more. You didn't return, so we filled your position with somebody else. Good day."

The last thing I hear before the line goes dead is Hickman dropping the phone into the cradle. Just like that I've been kicked to the curb, and for what? Poor job performance? Or personal animosity? How can this have happened?

Once the shock wears off I contact the Equal Employment Opportunity Commission as well as the compliance officer at Hughes. They tell me they'll investigate, but I have no guarantee of ever getting my job back.

The worst part isn't even the loss of the paycheck, which I desperately need—it's coming home and having to look my wife in the eyes as I tell her the news.

I spend weeks and weeks hoping to hear back about my case and simultaneously trying to find a job. Unfortunately we're smack in the middle of the Carter recession, and there isn't any work to be had. I'm back on unemployment for nearly a year until at last I get a hearing.

Or, I should say, I get a hearing date.

The Friday of the week before my hearing date, I receive a phone call from one of the managing directors at Hughes. He asks me how I've been and whether I miss working at Hughes, and after we talk for a while he casually mentions that a position in my old department has opened up, and that if I want it he can slot me in.

I don't realize it, but he's hooking me. He's trying to get me to bite at a job so I don't proceed with the lawsuit. "You can keep your seniority—six years on the books," he says. I should know better than to cave and accept, but the thing is, I just want to be able to pay my bills again and take care of my wife the way she deserves, and this is an opportunity to do just that. I probably should be demanding a raise, or a better position, or back pay for my year spent on ice. But I don't. I'm just so glad for the prospect of going back to work that I accept on the spot. By Monday I'm back at work, and my EEOC case has been dropped without prejudice.

For the next decade and a half—for twenty-plus years at Hughes all told—I go to work day in and day out. I'm a marked man, though—the EEOC matter follows me, and for those next fifteen years, I never once get a promotion or a raise above a cost-of-living adjustment. Finally, in 1995, in the midst of the greatest economic expansion of modern American history, I'm laid off from Hughes Aircraft again, and this time it's for good.

So Much for a Hero's Welcome

After being let go by Hughes a second time, I'm fifty-six years old, I never finished college, and once again I find myself unemployed. I want to work, but who's going to hire me? After much consideration, I remember what Wilt Chamberlain had said to me all those years ago. "Billy," he said, "your money is in basketball." With that in mind, I reach out directly to the only contact I can think of—I call the NBA.

Surprise of all surprises, I end up talking to Rod Thorn. We'd briefly played together on the Baltimore Bullets together some thirty years back, and now he's the executive vice president of the NBA. You never know, huh?

When I ask if he can help me out, he directs me to Tom "Satch" Sanders, once a Boston Celtic and now director of the NBA Legends Foundation, an organization devoted to helping support old-time players. When I tell Satch my story—the whole story—and admit to him that my economic situation is getting tight, he promises that he'll figure out a way to find me something.

Within a week he calls me back with the offer of a job.

"A job?" I ask.

"A job with the Lakers!" he exclaims, and he gives me the name and phone number of a contact to call at the offices of the Forum in Inglewood, their new home after the closure of Sports Arena. I can't believe my good fortune.

The prospect of working for the Lakers gets me nervous and excited. It's been thirty years since I was last with that squad—I wonder, will anyone there remember me? Will I get to assist the younger players? What's it like at the Forum, which they didn't have in my day? I can't wait to call up my new contact and report for my first day of work.

All that excitement turns sour, though, when I do make the call and find out what this promised job is.

"Eight to twelve bucks an hour," intones the nasally voice on the other end of the line. "You'll be cleaning up the stadium after events and games. Yours is the midnight shift, 12:00 to 8:00 a.m."

So that's it. Twenty years of basketball experience and twenty-five more years working after that, and the best job they can offer is pushing a broom again? I'm not too happy about this. Isn't the Lakers' manager Jerry West, and didn't I play ball with him? Couldn't he help me get something better? Still, beggars can't be choosers, so I accept the job. But right before I'm slated to start a story about me turns up in the *LA Times*.

"This Climb All Uphill for McGill" reads the headline in Mike Downey's column. When talking about how I heard about the Lakers job, he writes, "McGill called, eagerly. And, sure enough, that NBA team offered Billy a job in its arena. Cleaning it." The closing lines read, "Will he take the job? He will if he has to. [But] he shouldn't have to."

I didn't think much of it when I gave Downey the interview. They asked me if I wanted to be a janitor for the Lakers, and I answered honestly: no. I wanted something better. But the story pisses off the Lakers' brass something fierce, and they yank away the job offer before I even start.

I get back on the phone again with Satch Sanders, and I explain what happened. "Listen, Billy," he says, "jobs don't exactly grow on trees." I tell him I'm aware of this. I hadn't intended to lose my janitorial job with the Lakers by talking to the press; it just happened. Satch is flustered, but he says he understands, and though he can't find me another full-time job he does have another idea.

In an attempt to prepare college draftees for life in the NBA—and after—the league has recently set up something they call the Rookie Transition Program. It aims to provide the kind of information that I had to learn the hard way, through Woody Sauldsberry, to every incoming draftee: that you can't play sports forever, and you have to prepare mentally and financially for a life after basketball.

The league certainly didn't have anything like this in my day. I wish they had.

On the morning the program opens I step into a conference room in Orlando, where I'll be giving a presentation to a number of young players. There I see a bunch of young, promising rookies, including Chris Webber, Jamal Mashburn, Bobby Hurley, Vin Baker, Allan Houston, Nick Van Exel, and Sam Cassell. There're also a number of much older players, many of whom I recognize from watching on TV but some of whom I've never even heard of. I get the message. The NBA has brought in a few of the successful and still rich ex-players and stars to speak to the rookies on how to stay on top after the NBA. Then, to pound that message home, they're planning to scare them with the sad-sack cases, the also-rans who fell out of the game without a pillow to cushion their landings.

Guys like me.

Though it's a bitter pill to swallow, I'm not too proud to tell these young players what my life has been like: it's been hard. My story is easy to recount—easy because it's my own story, it's fantastic, and it's true. I was on top of the world in college. I had plenty of promise when I was drafted. Then, for a number of reasons, I missed my shot, and when that happened I fell hard, far, and fast. I wouldn't wish the same on anyone.

I'm scheduled to speak once a day for three days to rotating groups of incoming NBA freshmen. It's my job to warn these rookies about how their lives could turn out if they're not careful. "Someday basketball will end for all of you, eventually," I tell them. "Hopefully not too soon. But the important thing is to make sure you're prepared for what comes after the game."

As my time ends one of these young bucks named Isaiah Rider asks me how much money I make. I admit that I certainly didn't see much when I was in the league, and these days I pull in little more than two hundred dollars a week after taxes. "There's not much more coming, either, because I don't have that college degree," I admit, and as it turns out neither does he.

"Two hundred dollars?" He guffaws. "You gotta be kidding, man. I can't relate to you. I ain't making no two hundred dollars a week!" He waves me away in dismissal, and I catch a glimpse of the gem-studded bracelet around Rider's wrist. Already I know he'll never hear a word I say, and it's a shame. It's a guy like that who needs this lesson most; guys like that usually fall the hardest. I think back to Andy Johnson and his high jinks in the Zephyrs' training camp, and how he got cut soon after. But Rider can't see that; all he can do is make fun of a sad case like me.

Another promising young player named Penny Hardaway takes a potshot at me, too. "Yeah," he tells me, "you had a tough break and all, but you had your time up in here. But now it's our time, you hear me?" He puffs his chest. "You had your day, and now it's our day in the sun!" And he, another degreeless black superstar athlete, walks off, sure he'll be the one exception to the rule.

It kills me how much some of these new boots lack compassion and understanding. They're in this most blessed position, and they don't know, don't want to know, or just don't care how players like me and others have sacrificed. They don't know about Hall-of-Famer George Mikan, who revolutionized the game but died nearly penniless; they don't know about the second jobs, the one-sided contracts, and the off-season toil. They don't know the discrimination that black players once faced, and they don't know what we forebears went through for them to enjoy the great spoils that they are now receiving in the NBA. And they also don't know that pride always comes before the fall.

Halfway through the conference I think about packing it in. Maybe coming back here was a mistake. Right as I'm on the cusp of heading home, though, one player changes my mind. Most unexpectedly, one of these young kids goes out of his way to boost my spirit, and that makes all the difference.

He says to me, "Mr. McGill, that was quite a story, and the rookies were really listening to your every word." He thanks me and shakes my hand,

and before he walks away he looks me right in the eye and lets me know that he has real compassion in his heart for me and what I went through.

The man who does this is Shawn Bradley, a tall, lanky, white Mormon. I'm flustered. Every one of the black youths I speak to stares right through me, and this upstanding white kid—from BYU, no less—goes out of his way to tell me that he admires my struggle. He's never faced racial discrimination, and he doesn't know what that was like. He didn't come from a fatherless home, either. But still, he goes out of his way to lift me up again when I'm feeling low—a rival BYU Cougar!—and that makes all the difference.

Dear Dad

Eventually I find another regular job, and while it isn't wonderful, it's okay. Every now and then some sportswriter or another approaches me to see what's become of my life. The *New York Times* does a "Where are they now?" article on athletes, and my name is mentioned along with former Super Bowl champion Ernie Holmes's. My disappearing act is also featured in *Sports Illustrated* and on ESPN, and when Keith Van Horn manages to just nip out my all-time scoring record at the University of Utah—a feat he pulls off in four years of varsity eligibility, when I was afforded only three—still more journalists swing by and ask for my read on him as a player.

I often find myself wondering about the stars of the modern day—not just about the Isaiah Riders and Penny Hardaways of the world and not just about the big salaries they receive, but about what it was like for them growing up. What was it like to live in their families? Were they encouraged and supported by their parents to play pro ball? Did they have fathers around? Did their dads back them up?

That more than anything becomes the great lament of my life. Yes, I wish I'd never had the knee trouble, and there's no doubt that my injuries kept me from really being able to consistently play to my full potential. But the root of my problem, I truly believe, has always been the crippling lack of a real relationship with my father. That, more than an NBA ring, more than fame or fortune, is what I've always wanted: to know and be known by—to love and be loved by—the man to whom I owe my very existence. My father.

What a surprise it is then when I get something like that chance.

One lazy weekend afternoon after I've done the rookie camp for the NBA, the phone rings and an unfamiliar voice on the other end of the line greets me. "Billy?"

Cautiously, I admit to my identity. "Who is this? Are you trying to sell something?"

"No," says the voice. "This is Myron. Myron McGill." There's a pause, and then he adds, "I'm your brother."

The world diminishes to the size of a pinhole. A tiny tunnel is all I can see, and it takes an eternity for life to flex back to size. "My brother?" Talk about a shock. I grew up my whole life as an only child unwanted in triplicate—sent off to Texas, raised at the YMCA, then reared under the roof of a man who would later toss me to the curb—and here on the phone is a man telling me that all along I've had a brother.

"Half brother," he says, and he tells me the story. It turns out that my father Malone remarried after he and my mother spilt. Malone stayed in LA, and Myron was the son he had with his second wife.

"I tracked you down," Myron tells me. "I was hoping we might meet."

We agree to have lunch, and when I walk into the restaurant I don't need to ask around to figure out which one is him—looking at Myron is like looking into a mirror of my own past. He's six feet six and broad, and I see in his face eyes that I remember from my youth. A face that, from the age of eleven on, was taken from me. When I reach out to shake his hand I damn near begin to cry.

"Listen," Myron says. "I ought to tell it to you straight off. I came because Dad—he's not doing so well."

Not doing so well?

"Yeah," he continues. "Dad's—he's got cancer."

Though I've not seen my father in years—though I didn't even know that he was still alive, let alone that he'd remarried and had another son after our family broke up—hearing this word, this curvy, mellifluous word of death, emerge from my half brother's lips strikes me like a fist in the solar plexus. I feel the breath leave me, and when I take it in again, it's in short, rasping bursts.

"He's alive," Myron says, filling in the space between us. "He's still fighting. He's at a nursing home."

There's a long break in the conversation. And then tears begin to well behind my eyes, and I admit to the truth I've been hanging onto my whole life, since I was a little kid peeking in through a clapboard house window.

"I want to see him."

Dad's nursing home is off Adams by USC—coincidentally, it's not far from the neighborhood where I squatted through all the time I was homeless. I don't know if I could have come here on my own, but Myron's here, and as my half brother ferries me up the street to see my father once again, I'm fraught with a combination of trepidation and elation, a heady blend of joy and outright fear.

When we enter the building I'm led by a uniformed orderly down a long, white hall smeared in strong, white light. It's the lighting, coupled with the smell of industrial cleaner that assaults my nostrils, that brings me face-to-face with the incontrovertible truth: my father is dying, and this reunion, the first time I've seen my father in years, will likely mark the last time I ever see him alive.

The male orderly ushers Myron and me into a drab, tiny, dark room, a sallow contrast to the hall from which we've just entered. The whole space is centered around a bed that's empty save a lump of dirty clothes stuffed underneath the blanket. It's not until that pile of laundry coughs and rolls over that I realize it's no inanimate sack; it's my father.

I pull the sheet down and, for the first time in thirty-plus years, I see my father's face. It's now old and weathered, but it's him. I see myself through that mask of years, and I smile. "Hey, Dad," I say, trying to sound jocular. "It's me, Billy. Your son."

I wait for a response. He says nothing.

Myron excuses himself to leave me a little time with my father—time, he says, for us to catch up.

"It's been a long time, Dad," I say. He doesn't respond—not a word, not a breath. Not even so much as a nod of recognition. But here I am. So I speak.

"I wondered about you," I say. "I've had a hard time of it since you've been gone." And then I tell him all about my life. I start with being eleven, with dunking, and then I tell him about living with Daddy Lonnie. I tell my father about my knee and rehabbing it alone all summer long, and how much I'd wished he'd been there to help me and to see me win the city championship.

I tell him about college, the good and the bad; I tell him about the ups and downs of my professional career as well as my life after. I tell him about my homelessness and about my jobs. I tell him about Gwennie. I tell him about my stepkids and my ever-growing family, which I love.

When I'm done my father's still not said a word. I sit with him a while, but still he says nothing. Finally, I get up to go, and I walk to the door. With my hand on the handle I turn and tell him what I've been holding inside my whole life. "I love you," I say, hoping for a response, but my words fade unanswered into the void like the gentle hiss of air seeping through the vents.

When I step outside I see Myron waiting for me; he nods and takes me back to his car.

"How'd it go?" he asks.

"Okay. Does he—can he still talk?"

"Yeah," Myron says. "He talks. Didn't he talk to you?"

I don't respond. I just let my newfound half brother pilot us back toward the freeway.

So he talks, this father of mine. Just not to me. I opened up my heart to him, but he didn't say "I love you" back. He never has.

Maybe he was still angry. Maybe he felt abandoned. Maybe he felt confused. Or maybe he was just so overcome with conflicting emotions that he couldn't speak.

I think about the day we met. Life—*both* our lives—was so full of promise and potential then. Was he thinking of that one time he wrapped his arms around me, his little Billy, and gave his son his first great hug?

I wonder.

For the rest of my life, I'll always wonder.

Epilogue

"Billy, did you hear? You're dead!"

The call came not too long ago, as I was hanging around the house with my wife Gwen. The TV was on, we had just finished supper, and I was getting ready to go upstairs and change into something comfortable to wear for the rest of the evening. I'm a senior citizen now, you know; just sitting on the sofa is hard work if I can't get comfortable. When my phone rang, though, I picked up. It was a friend from down the block who told me something that blew my mind: he heard I was dead.

"Dead?" I said. "What are you talking about?"

"I'm watching ESPN right now. Basketball. Bill Walton's commentating."

"Big fella. Love that guy."

"Right. Well, anyway, this kid just swished a jump hook and Walton said, 'Ah, a great jump hook. A shot first invented by the late, great Billy "the Hill" McGill.' The *late* Billy McGill, he said! So are you dead or what?"

I frowned. My being dead was news to me. I cupped my hand over the receiver. "Gwennie!" I called. "You hear anything about me having died?"

She gave me one of those looks like I'd asked her to buy me a Ferrari—married guys know what I'm talking about—and went back to washing the dishes.

Now, look, I may be a bit slower off the dribble than I once was—hell, I probably haven't touched a basketball in thirty years, except to sign one—but if a professional player, commentator, and NBA Hall-of-Famer like Bill Walton thinks I'm dead, that's not such a good thing. Sure, I may not be able to crash the boards anymore, but I'm still alive and breathing, thank you.

At least Walton remembers I invented the jump hook. Bill Russell does, too. Wilt Chamberlain would remember it as well, if he were still with us.

That jump hook took me quite a ways. It took me through high school and into college, where I set an NCAA record with my 38.8 points per game—still a mark never topped by any other center, before or since. It took me all the way to the pros, where I was a number one NBA draft pick and played against all the greats: Bill Russell, Oscar Robertson, Jerry West, Elgin Baylor and, of course, Wilt the Stilt. Very few people are lucky enough to say they were ever a number one NBA draft pick. Charles Barkley can't do it. Karl Malone can't do it. Neither can Kobe Bryant or Larry Bird. Even Michael Jordan, as great as he was, can't claim that he was the number one pick overall. I was blessed.

Not bad for a kid so poor he had to borrow his best friend's letterman jacket.

Unfortunately, that same gift that led me to the highest highs also dragged me down to the lowest lows. Can you imagine LeBron James being too ashamed to tell a security guard what he did for a living, or walking away from basketball only to have to scrounge for change to buy a candy bar?

How is it that the game—a game that was played for fun, made so many careers—chewed up and spit out so many promising souls, particularly among black youth? I'll never know.

Despite all the hardships and heartbreak I've seen, I've got to admit that it has been one heck of a ride—a journey from the peaks of the highest hills to the depths of the lowest valleys. And another thing I can say for certain is that no matter what has happened, by God's grace I'm still alive. At least for now. And while I remain blessed with that greatest of gifts, it seems like I damn sure ought to set the record straight. Because once the final buzzer sounds, there won't be any time left to do it.

And I have a damn good story to tell.

Over thirty-five years ago I began writing my life story while everything was still fresh in my mind. It was no overnight whim, or even a two- or three-month decision, to write this book. It took a long, long time for me to come to terms with everything I've been through, and I couldn't even get it all on the page without the extensive help of my very dedicated co-writer.

In the end I wrote this book because of the love I've had for basketball and the people that, through my life, believed in me, both inside the sport and out. Many times I felt I had let those people down—when I didn't live up to my potential or when I didn't turn the gifts I was blessed with into financial or extended professional success. But looking back, now I can see that it's not my height or my talent that's the greatest blessing that has ever been given to me: it's being here on God's green earth, with my beautiful wife of forty years still by my side. And that's something I've never taken for granted.

It's a hard thing for me to look back and say I wish this or that had or hadn't happened in my long journey through life. But with the benefit of hindsight upon all my years on this earth, I have come to one conclusion: the most important thing I ever hung onto—and what I hope others will take away from my story—is not my forgotten fame, nor is it the anger that I felt from my career being cut short or the sadness of my broken home. Rather, it is that nameless spirit that formed within me when I kneeled on the muddy, rain-soaked floor of that abandoned house. Whatever took hold of me that night when I looked up to the sky and decided to keep fighting for my life was worth more than millions of dollars or a storm of unstoppable jump hooks. The intangible spirit that lay dormant within me until I dropped to my knees and with tears rolling from my eyes asked God for help—that affected me more than anything else. That night my heart and soul were cleansed by the rain coming through that big hole in the roof, and in that water, which beat my face and mixed with my tears, I learned life's most valuable lessons.

I can clearly see now where I stood on top of hills and where I dragged myself through the bottom of valleys. I have to thank God for being there with me every step of the way, even through my darkest times. And you know what? He still is.

So be good to yourself, love yourself, and put your faith in the power above.

Billy

Where Are They Now?

With the exception of a few instances where I slightly shuffled the timing of events for the sake of clarity, everything presented in this book is a true and accurate representation of what I remember taking place. The childhood bus ride from Texas really happened. So did the phone call asking whether or not I was dead. And all the rest of the stuff in the middle that I will never forget.

There's plenty I could say to fill in what happened to all the people in my life as time went by. Here is some of it.

Billy McGill

Well, me first and foremost. These days I'm out of the public eye, but I'm not forgotten. I still get stopped in my hometown of LA with chants of "The Hill! The Hill!" And when I went back to the U for the fiftieth-anniversary celebration of our team's trip to the Final Four, plenty of Utah fans stopped me for my autograph or to take pictures with their kids. I appreciated that.

In addition to being inducted into the University of Utah Hall of Fame, I was recently named starting center to Los Angeles's all-time citywide dream team by the *LA Times*, which was quite an honor. I'm told I'm also now being considered for the NCAA College Basketball Hall of Fame. It would be nice if I did get in while I'm still alive to see it. Folks have run the numbers, and there are only seven players in history who've managed to score 2,300 points and grab at least 1,100 rebounds in just three years of varsity ball like I did: Elgin Baylor, Oscar Robertson, Jerry West, Elvin

Hayes, Kareem Abdul-Jabbar, Larry Bird, and me. Not bad company! All those other folks are in the Hall. Hopefully it'll soon be my turn, too.

No other center before or since has ever broken my collegiate record of 38.8 points per game, and at no point in my basketball career—high school, college, the pros—did I ever have one of my shots blocked. How many players can say that? Though my injuries and some bad breaks kept me from the kind of success in the pros that I had in college ball, I did manage to lead a pretty great life. And that's what I'm proudest of: my life. I have a large and loving family, and I'm still married to a wonderful lady: my Gwennie. Interestingly, our grandson, Ryan Watkins, is six feet eight, almost as tall as me, and he currently plays college basketball for the Boise State Broncos. You know what else? He can shoot the jump hook.

Malone McGill

My natural father died not long after I reconnected with him. I wish we'd had more of an opportunity to reconstruct a relationship. Not having him be an active part of my life remains one of my greatest regrets. Though I learned much and became stronger for them, I never doubted that I could have avoided so many of my hardships had I only had my father there to support me.

Dorothy McGill

My mom Dorothy is in her nineties and still kicking, alive and well. Though we never had what you might call an "open" relationship with one another, she did her best to raise me, and for that I am thankful.

Daddy Lonnie

Daddy Lonnie passed on. My mom was sad, and though he and I had a strained relationship, I was, too.

Willis "Lefty" Thomas

Sadly, Lefty passed on some years ago. He did eventually make it to pro ball, playing on the starting lineup for the first-ever Denver Rockets (now Denver Nuggets) squad to take uniform. Interestingly, joining him in that starting line were none other than my man Wayne "Spain" Hightower and Byron Beck. He only played that one year in the league, though, before getting pushed, for one reason or another, back down into the minor professional ranks. Still, Lefty's a member of the LA High School Sports Hall of Fame in memoriam, and he was one of the best men I ever had the honor of calling a friend. He is succeeded by his beautiful, loving family.

Sweet Al

Allen Holmes lives in Utah these days—he's had some kidney problems, but he's still well. I just saw him at our basketball team's anniversary celebration along with most of the other guys who are still alive. Rich Ruffel, Jim Rhead, Ed Rowe, Joe Aufderheide, and a number of other guys were all there. Everybody seemed to be looking good.

In 1998 Al's exploits on the court led him to be inducted to the Utah Sports Hall of Fame. His son became quite a ballplayer, too: Byron Scott (né Holmes) won three NBA championships as a player, helmed the Nets to two NBA finals as a coach, and served for a while as a basketball analyst for ESPN.

Carney Crisler

Carney Crisler taught and coached basketball at his old high school after graduation. We didn't get along, but he was a good man. I don't know if he ever forgave me for replacing him on the team at Utah.

Coach Gardner

The name Jack Gardner is still one of the most hallowed in all of Utah basketball history. He retired in 1971, having led the Utes to seven conference titles and an overall record of 339-154. He died at the age of ninety in 2000, and his name is enshrined in the Basketball Hall of Fame.

Dr. Olpin

I never knew this about Dr. Olpin when he was around Utah, but it turned out that back in the 1940s he'd worked on the Manhattan Project developing the first A-bomb. I knew he was smart, but I didn't know he was that smart.

The beloved president of my beloved University of Utah, Dr. Olpin died in the '80s. These days the student union's named after him—and no one minds if kids of mixed races hold each other's hands while hanging out there.

Jerry Lucas

Lucas had a great college career and a great pro career, too. I don't know if he ever got the same inspiration from me that I got from him—whether he knew it or not, he served as a huge source of my drive to keep improving and playing better. I always respected him, but I always strove to beat him, too. There's a story Joe Aufderheide likes to tell: one day senior year, both our teams were at a tournament, and we both had good games. Thing is, the next day all anyone could talk about was how well Lucas had played. I got so riled up that as soon as our Utes hit the floor, I swatted the first shot that an opposing player took right into the second deck of seats.

After basketball ended for Lucas, he settled down and became an educator in a small town in Ohio. He is enjoying his retirement outside of the public eye.

Woody Sauldsberry

Though he was a former Rookie of the Year, Woody ended up getting bounced all over the league just like I did, and he never lost the feeling that it was due to his race. He picked up with the Globetrotters after leaving the NBA, but when basketball ended he fell on hard times. When he resurfaced in the late '80s he was homeless and sick, and diabetes brought about by a hard life and neglect forced him to have his leg amputated. A few years later he passed on.

He was a good man, and his story could have easily been mine.

Walt Bellamy

Walt and I never saw eye to eye—something you can say about most of the people I competed against for spots on teams—but the guy could play ball. After a fifteen-year NBA career in which he scored over twenty thousand points, Walt was inducted into the Hall of Fame in 1993.

Don Nelson

Don and I came up together on the Zephyrs, and of course we got into that terrific fistfight when I was on the Knicks and he was with the Lakers.

Don eventually ended up catching on with the Celtics, winning five NBA championships there. He then coached for thirty-five years, amassing over a thousand wins.

Terry Dischinger

Dischinger had three great years at the beginning of his career and then sort of declined. I never did figure out why.

John Rudometkin

John was a great player in his time, but very early on he came down with non-Hodgkin's lymphoma, which sidelined him for good. He was able to beat the disease, but he quit sports shortly after our season on the Knicks, never physically able to return to pro ball. It's a damn shame—Rudometkin was a good man, and if medical technology then had been what it is now, he might have had a great professional career.

Then again, so might've I.

Willis Reed

Willis Reed had an explosive ten-year career with the Knickerbockers, leading the team to its first two championships. He was inducted to the Hall of Fame in '82, and his number was officially retired by the Knicks just two years after he left the pros.

Jerry West

West had a great NBA career, winning an NBA title with the Lakers and also gaining induction into the NBA Hall of Fame. He later became a coach and then a front office man, working as an executive for both the Lakers and the Memphis Grizzlies.

Elgin Baylor

Baylor, like West, made it into the Hall after a great Lakers career. In fact, he's credited with having saved the team; as the owner said in '71, "If he had turned me down then [and not signed with the Lakers], I would have been out of business. The club would have gone bankrupt." However, Elgin retired early and never won an NBA championship ring.

Oscar Robertson

Big O was a twelve-time All-Star in the NBA and the only man ever to average a triple-double for an entire NBA season. He was also instrumental in getting the U.S. courts to strike down the rules that bound players to one NBA team, the ones that forced guys like us to accept whatever low-ball salary offers management deigned to let us have. Though the team he broke into the league with, the Cincinnati Royals, is no longer (they're now the Sacramento Kings), Oscar still goes to University of Cincinnati games, and there's a giant statue of him outside their arena.

Bill Russell

Russell had a great career, and his rivalry with Wilt was friendly but never ending. They played against each other all their days, and when Wilt became the first player to ever get paid $100,000 in a season, Bill Russell demanded $100,001. He spent much of his career struggling against racism, even from his home-court fans in Boston, and I like to think he overcame it. These days he's living retired and happy in the loving arms of his family.

Wilt Chamberlain

Wilt the Stilt died before his time in his sixties due to congestive heart failure. However, he had one of the greatest sports careers ever, and in addition to his NBA and Globetrotter exploits—just one more black player who found sanctuary in that safe haven—he even managed to play his way into the Pro Volleyball Hall of Fame. What's amazing is I don't think he even picked up that sport until after his basketball retirement. Still, a guy that tall and athletic, you've got to figure he can do anything in the world of sports.

Anything, that is, except block my jump hook, which he never did. That, at least, is something of which I will always be proud.

Nate Thurmond

Nate the Great played for fourteen years in the NBA, mostly with the San Francisco Warriors; he, too, made the Hall of Fame. Between Bellamy, Willis Reed, and Nate the Great, I did not have the best of luck in finding guys to battle against for starting spots, did I?

The last I heard of Nate was that he owned a restaurant in San Francisco called Big Nate's B-B-Q.

Wayne "Spain" Hightower

Wayne had a solid ten-year career, playing for seven pro teams along the way—almost as many as me! He died, sadly, at the age of sixty-two, in his hometown of Philadelphia.

Byron Beck

Like Spain Beck played for ten years in the pros, but unlike Spain he stayed with one team the whole way. Though he never was a superstar, Beck spent his whole career with Denver, and when he walked away from the game he became the first player in that franchise's history to have his number retired.

Spencer Haywood

After his one year in the ABA, Spencer Haywood successfully sued to remove the NBA bar against players not finished with their schooling, thus opening the door for future stars like Moses Malone, LeBron James, and Kobe Bryant to enter the pro ranks right out of high school. Haywood was in the midst of an outstanding NBA career—a seeming lock for a future spot in the Hall of Fame—when in 1979 he was traded to the big city of LA and discovered cocaine, which ruined him like it did so many black athletes of the '80s.

Anfernee Hardaway

Anfernee "Penny" Hardaway was one of two promising rookies that I met at NBA transition camp who made me feel really bad about myself. Unfortunately, he learned not long after making his cutting comments just how tough life in the NBA can be.

Hardaway had four great years—really spectacular ones—before a knee injury, of all things, cut him down. Modern technology helped him bounce back—no doctors tried to insert an iron rod in him, that's for sure—but still, he was never really the same.

At his peak Hardaway was paid a salary of over fifteen million dollars per year. Too bad we didn't get that kind of cash back in my day. Still, I wonder if he's left thinking about his past. Does he wish he'd done it differently? Does he have anything he wants to say to the young bucks of today? Does he finally understand where I'm coming from?

Isaiah "J.R." Rider

Isaiah Rider, the other NBA rookie who seemingly went out of his way to cut me down, was, while he played, a dynamic scorer with unlimited potential. Unfortunately, he was also something of a hothead and an egoist, and his temper and selfishness brought him into constant trouble with the law and ended up ruining his life.

While averaging over eighteen points per game in his first seven seasons, Rider was arrested multiple times, including for assault and possession of stolen goods and drugs. He was also suspended multiple times, including for spitting at fans.

Eventually teams wouldn't take his shenanigans anymore, and he was forced into retirement when nobody would sign him. After he left the pro game his behavior just got worse: he was arrested for domestic violence, felony drug possession, theft, assault, kidnapping—the list goes on and on. He's fallen further than almost any can't-miss Hall-of-Famer ever has. Maybe he should have heeded my advice.

Shawn Bradley

After twelve inconsistent years in the NBA, Bradley retired and took a job at a school in Utah for at-risk youth, where he's an administrator, counselor, and coach. Though he may have never been an NBA All-Star, he's a father of six and unquestionably a good man.

Brad Pye Jr.

Brad Pye Jr. was one of the greatest positive influences in my life, and I'll never forget him. He served as sports editor for the *LA Sentinel* for thirty years, and he would later work for another twenty-plus years for LA County, getting the job done for the city that he loved. He retired happily in the spring of 2011. To this day I feel I owe him a debt that I can never repay.

5th Street, LA

5th Street is still, unfortunately, known throughout LA as Skid Row. It's the place where the homeless and lost congregate and disappear, eternally dissolving into the miasma of the masses. Nathaniel Ayers, the man who Jamie Foxx portrayed in *The Soloist*, did indeed live there, and the area was and still is just like that movie shows. I'm thankful to this day that I was somehow turned around and didn't fall into that pit. Plenty of fallen men from all walks of life have ended up there, and I could easily have faded away among them. I hope that any young people reading this book will be spared that fate.